# The Hip Hop Years

**Alex Ogg** was a consultant to the Channel 4 documentary series *The Hip Hop Years*. He is the author of the *Guinness Book of Rap* and the *Guinness Book of Dance*, and has contributed to many books and magazines on pop and rock music.

**David Upshal** is producer/director of the Channel Four TV series *The Hip Hop Years*. Formerly a print journalist, he wrote for the *Guardian*, *The Sunday Times* and the *New Statesman*. During nine years as a broadcaster at BBC Television he produced programmes for *The Late Show*, *Decisive Weapons* and *Reputations* and directed the award-winning BBC series *Windrush*.

# The Hip Hop Years

## A History of Rap

### alex ogg with david upshal

PARK LEARNING CENTRE
UNIVERSITY OF GLOUCESTERSHIRE
PO Box 220, The Park
Cheltenham GL50 2RH
Tel: 01242 714333

First published in 1999 by Channel 4 Books,
an imprint of Macmillan Publishers Ltd,
25 Eccleston Place, London, SW1W 9NF and Basingstoke

Associated companies throughout the world

ISBN 0 7522 1735 6

Copyright © Alex Ogg, 1999

The right of Alex Ogg to be identified as the author of this work has been
asserted by him in accordance with the Copyright, Designs and Patents Act 1988.

9 8 7 6 5 4

A CIP catalogue record for this book is available from the British Library

Typeset by SX Composing DTP, Rayleigh, Essex

Printed by Mackays of Chatham, PLC, Chatham, Kent

This book accompanies the television series The Hip Hop Years made by
RDF Television for Channel 4.

Producer/director: David Upshal
Consultant: Lawrence Yarwood

Picture credits: All photographs – Retna except Kool Herc, Afrika Bambaataa:
Graham Mcindoe; Grandmaster Flash, Sugarhill Gang – Vansilk; Fab Five Freddy –
Martha Cooper; Suge Knight – Press Association; Wu-Tang Clan – Loud/RCA;
Eminiem – Ed Miles, Interscope Records; Jurassic Five – Peter Stone.

# contents

# acknowledgements

Alex Ogg would like to thank first, last and always, Dawn Wrench.

I am indebted to everybody at RDF Television, especially Lawrence Yarwood, whose knowledge proved invaluable. My gratitude also to Charlie Carman and Jenny Olivier at Channel 4 Books for their ceaseless encouragement.

Others I would like to thank for helping in various capacities are: Bill and Marion, Sue Pipe, Alan Brown (as well as Andy Green & Andy T), Melanie at Millais Road, Viv, Mark and all at ITFC. Big love to the Huggies – Yo! Bully, Bum Rush The Show!

And thank you to Chris Taylor, Danni Violet and Jack Rabid, none of whom are hip hop fans, but whose love of music is a source of continuing inspiration.

David Upshal would like to thank the following people for their contribution:
Barbara Browne, Jo Crawley, David Frank, Ross Keith, Kamau Kordova, Maria Kubaskova, Stephen Lambert, John Middelkoop, Sean O'Neill, Joy Russell, Anna Schroder, Eliza Zazzera.

Also thanks to Ekwaeju Ohwoisi for constant encouragement and advice; Lawrence Yarwood for research and fact-finding; and Yasmin Anwar at Channel 4 for making it all possible by commissioning the TV series.

# introduction

*It's all about the beauty of hip hop. There are no constraints with this art form.*

Grandmaster Flash

*Hip hop is just black people's creativity, and we've always been creative people. So it's just a term for the last twenty-five years.*

Chuck D, Public Enemy

The latter half of the 20th century has often been defined as 'the rock 'n' roll years', an era when a new music swept Western culture and gave rise to the fast-changing attitudes of post-World War II society. In the mid-70s an equally radical and innovative musical form emerged in much the same manner as its rock 'n' roll predecessor. It too grew from impoverished black communities into a music with truly global appeal, acquiring the name hip hop as it flourished.

If one youth movement has been pre-eminent in the shaping of popular culture in the last twenty-five years, it is hip hop and the art forms and industries it has spawned. If the post-war music boom is often referred to as 'The Rock 'n' Roll Years', perhaps the century's final quarter may come to be seen as 'The Hip Hop Years'.

Despite industry reticence and often open hostility, hip hop is a commercial phenomenon. It accounts for eleven per cent of all US music sales – the biggest single sector of the American pop market. It outsells all competitors including country, R&B and even rock. And it continues to grow.

In January 1999, Garth Brooks was knocked off Billboard's number one album spot by DMX, the first artist in history to top that chart twice in a single calendar year. He was succeeded at the top by Def Jam labelmate Foxy Brown. That left hip hop occupying four of the top five album spots. As well as her record-breaking success in the Grammy Awards, Lauryn Hill became the first black American musician to appear on the cover of *Time* – the great American chronicler of trends.

A quick look at Billboard's charts at the time of writing (17 April 1999) reveals hip hop's incredible visibility. Clustered in the top thirty album charts are Eminem, Lauryn Hill, Everlast, Jay-Z, DMX (twice), Will Smith, Juvenile, 2Pac (two years dead) and Busta Rhymes. That's without counting heavily hip hop-influenced R&B act TLC. Of those albums, no less than four have been chart-toppers in their own right.

Where hip hop once attacked the mainstream, to all intents and purposes, it now *is* the mainstream. It has become the hub at the centre of America's cultural wheel. It is the vehicle which sells Coca-Cola, Sprite and clothing lines ranging from Hilfiger and Gap to Fubu and Phat Farm. It has been customised and redefined, not only in the ghettos, but throughout white suburbia and beyond, paying no heed to geographical or linguistic boundaries. The hip hop lexicon has seeped into the vocabulary of international youth, while its domination of fashion has been unprecedented. Even a young man as insulated against the wider world as Prince William, the future king of England, knows it's cooler to wear your baseball cap backwards.

*The Hip Hop Years* traces the history of this vibrant culture, from innocuous beginnings in the mid-70s as a soundtrack to block parties in New York, to its present status as the most volatile and innovative music of its age. From the chilly, derelict South Bronx of the early 70s to the glamour of Hollywood and beyond at century's end, it has been a rich and often contradictory rite of passage. *The Hip Hop Years* is compiled from interviews with those who played a pivotal role in that journey. We have adopted an anecdotal rather than observational tone, in keeping with the Channel 4 documentary series this book accompanies. Wherever possible, we allowed the MCs, DJs, graffiti artists and B-boys to tell us their story, in their words.

## ➤ *Terminology*

The terms rap and hip hop are often used interchangeably and with little differentiation between them. Strictly speaking, rap is a misnomer, as it constitutes merely one component of the music. The other element is DJing – the art of manipulating records on a turntable in a way that transforms a segment of a song, usually an instrumental portion (or breakbeat) to provide a hip hop rhythm. Rapping (or MCing as it was originally known) is the spoken word accompaniment for the music. While rapping/MCing has become pre-eminent in the 90s, it was actually the art of DJing which came first, forging the foundation for the music and creating a definitive basis for the culture of hip hop.

## ➤ *Transcriptions*

Where possible, interviews were transcribed in keeping with the speaker's delivery, rather than superimposing 'proper' English. This was not always possible, however, and some cosmetic surgery took place where it was necessary to clarify a speaker's meaning. Indefinite responses, pauses and half-thoughts were edited out to allow the quotes to run together more freely. Where a large section of text was omitted, this has been indicated with the use of ellipsis points.

## ➤ *Nomenclature*

In keeping with conventions established by the *Virgin Encyclopedia of Popular Music*, all words in song titles, including prepositions, have been capitalised to avoid confusion. Spellings of artists' names, wherever appropriate, have been taken from the relevant record or CD sleeves.

# block
# party days

# chapter one

# dancing in the streets

> ### *Play That Beat, Mr DJ – Enter Kool Herc*

Unsurprisingly, many have laid claim to roles as kings or kingmakers of the hip hop tradition. Most students, however, find one name cropping up time and again. To all intents and purposes, hip hop started the day Jamaican-born Clive Campbell, aka Kool Herc, first set foot in New York in 1967.

'At the age of thirteen I migrated to the States, early '67, to the Bronx. It was winter. It was cold.'

By 1969, Herc was partying regularly at local clubs, but noticed that the crowds he joined would frequently object to the city's distant, cocksure DJs.

'I used to hear the gripes from the audience on the dancefloor. Even myself, 'cos I used to be a breaker [breakdancer]. Why didn't the guy let the record play out? Or why cut it off there? So with that, me gathering all this information around me, I say: "I think I could do that." So I started playing from a dancefloor perspective. I always kept up the attitude that I'm not playing it for myself, I'm playing for the people out there.'

DJs needed to establish an identity or niche in this highly competitive market. Herc was determined to find records that no one else owned, to distinguish himself from the pack. As an example, he pressed his father into buying James Brown's *Sex Machine* LP in 1969.

'A lot of people wanted that record and couldn't really find it. So a lot of people used to come to the party to hear that.'

Herc did his research, checking out what was being played on local jukeboxes to test a song's popularity and picking up rarities at Downstairs Records on 42nd Street and the Rhythm Den.

'This is where your recognition, your rep comes from. You have a record nobody else got, or you're the first one to have it. You've got to be the first, can't be the second.'

While violence has become rap's defining characteristic in the 90s, hip hop actually started out as a means of ending black-on-black fighting two decades earlier. The Bronx citizen of the early 70s had much to live in fear of.

'The gangs came and terrorised the whole neighbourhood, the boroughs. Everybody just ran back into their house. There was no more clubs, everybody ran back into their house. If you did do a house party, it had to be: "I have to know you. Don't bring nobody who I don't know to my house." It lasted for a while until the parents started to come in early, and find a house full of kids, tearing up the new furniture that she just put some money down on. [The kids] were still seeking for a place to release this energy.'

Herc's sister asked him to help out by playing music in the recreation room of his family's housing block, 1520 Sedgewick Towers.

'OK, I throw my hand at it, and she rented the recreation room, I think for twenty-five dollars at the time. We could charge it at twenty-five cents for girls, fifty cents for fellas. It was like, "Kool Herc, man. He's giving a party, westside man. Just be cool, that's what I'm saying, come and have a good time. Just don't ditch the programme."'

Dodge High School, before it became co-educational, was an all girls establishment. Not least for that reason, it became, by reputation, the top venue for aspiring DJs, as Melle Mel recalls.

'If you got to do Dodge High School, you was the fuckin' man. And Herc used to do it every year.'

## ➤ Give Me A Break – The Origin Of The Breakbeat

Searching for further innovations for his sets, Herc patented the breakbeat, the climatic instrumental section of a record, partly through his existing knowledge of the dub plates or 'versions' prevalent in Jamaican reggae.

'I was using some of the breakdown parts. Every Jamaican record has a dub side to it. So I just tried to apply that. As the years went along I'm watching people, waiting for this particular break in it, the rhythm section. One night, I was waiting for the record to play out. Maybe they're [the dancers] waiting for this particular break. I could have a couple more records got the same break in it – I wonder, how would it be if I put them all together and I told them: "I'm going to try something new tonight. I'm going to call it a merry-go-round." The B-boys, as I call it, the energetic person, they're waiting just to release this energy when this break comes in.'

Herc saw a ready-made audience for his 'breakdowns'. The merry-go-round involved him mixing sections of James Brown's 'Give It Up Or Turn It Loose' into Michael Viner's 'Bongo Rock' and back out into Babe Ruth's 'The Mexican'. His audiences loved it.

The merry-go-round became the blueprint for hip hop.

## ➤ To The Beat Y'All – Breakdancing USA

The first to react to the innovations, naturally enough, were Herc's party-goers. Breakdancers, or B-boys, began to interpret Herc's idiosyncratic style with routines of their own. Some historians trace the development of breakdancing to the African martial arts form, *capoeta*, brought to America by slaves a century before. No one is entirely sure of the identity of the first New York breakdancer, but it was certainly popularised by members of the Zulu Nation. The discipline of breakdancing/B-boying was one of four separate styles that eventually converged through the late 70s. Up-rocking was a kind of non-contact mock martial art first seen in Brooklyn. Plus there were two imported West Coast styles – pop-locking (a mixture of strutting, robotics and moonwalking) and body-popping (developed on the west coast by Boogaloo Sam).

Richie Colon took the name Crazy Legs after being given the nickname by a high school cheerleader. Subsequently the most famous break-dancer of them all, he joined the Rock Steady Crew, a predominantly Latin team, in 1979. He did so by impressing founder members Jo-Jo and Jimmy Dee with a new version of the backspin which made the breaker resemble a spinning ball. He attributes the origin of the term B-boy, almost inevitably, to Kool Herc, who would encourage dancing by shouting out to his 'B-boys'. Breakdancers, according to Crazy Legs, were simply those partygoers who would wait on Herc's 'breaks' before going into action.

'A B-boy is a break boy or a break girl. There are people who call themselves B-boys and don't even know where the term comes from. That really comes from people being outside of the "foundation" when it started. By the time it hit Queens or Brooklyn, or something like that, they may have heard the term B-boy, but didn't know that it meant a break boy.'

He chanced on hip hop in the mid-70s and became an immediate convert.

'Say about 1977, I experienced my first jam, but prior to that hip hop music was just a combination of funk, soul and R&B. It wasn't considered hip hop music, because the culture itself wasn't labelled hip hop culture. The first time I ever heard someone on a mic, rocking a mic, it had to be in '77. I went to a jam in the South Bronx and the Cold Crush Brothers were there, Charlie Chase. My cousin Lenny Len brought me to a jam.'

In order to join the Rock Steady Crew, who had built an impressive reputation throughout the Bronx, Crazy Legs had to audition, or more accurately, duel.

'It wasn't about winning or losing, it was about how you maintained yourself within a battle. We lost the battle, but we proved that we'd developed our skills and that we were hungry. In 1979, you got to understand that was the first time the dance was dying out. So when I got into Rock Steady, breaking was already dying out. Thank God I ran into the people that I ran into throughout the early 80s within the Bronx and Manhattan and started re-establishing Rock Steady Crew again. Eventually the original leaders of Rock Steady saw what I was doing and they decided to give me the Crew and then I became president of the Rock Steady Crew in 1981.'

Respect, identity and competition were important factors for breakdancers, Crazy Legs states, but then so too was impressing the opposite sex.

'The high point at the jam [was] where everyone just starts battling each other, trying to do the dopest moves and get the most props. So that by the time you've finished you're either one of the dopest B-boys or you've got some honeys checking you out, now you have some girlies. A lot of B-boys did it for the girls. The competitiveness was important, but girls were very important as well.'

Kid Freeze, aka Clemente Moreno, another of breakdancing's most renowned exponents, recalls his introduction to the craft in the late 70s.

'I was walking down my block. I see these two kids with a boom box, and they had Kangols on. They had the music going and I seen them, they were hitting the floor, they were doing fancy footwork and I just stopped, amazed at what they were doing: "Oh, that's kind of cool." Next thing you know, my luck, my father is walking down the block from work and sees me looking at these guys. Any time I'd be hanging out with guys that have maybe fancy hats or nice sneakers that were expensive, he thought that either they were drug dealers or something about them wasn't right.'

After Freeze's family relocated from the Bronx to Queens in 1976, he had the opportunity to pursue his interest.

'You choose your weapon – either the microphone, the turntables, the spray can or the floor as a B-boy.'

He attained the name Kid Freeze during tryouts to join local crew the Dynamic Rockers at the Galaxy Disco in Queens. The dancing was as competitive as any gangland initiation ceremony.

'They had guys from Manhattan, they had guys from Brooklyn, guys from Queens, Staten Island. We were battling to get in the group. So I seen this kid who had on Kid Freeze [on his shirt] and I said: "Listen, do you want to battle for this name?" So he goes: "All right, if you win, I'll take off my shirt." And he was in the same group, Dynamic. So I battled him and second round I went down, I took him. He took off his shirt and said: "Here, you deserve it. You're really good and I can see you're really going far."'

Brooklyn native Nelson George, author of *The Death Of Rhythm and Blues* and *Hip Hop America*, got his first taste of the emergent new music at one of Herc's shows at Taft High School in the Bronx.

'The sun hadn't gone down yet, and kids were just hanging out, waiting for something to happen. Van pulls up, a bunch of guys come out with a table, crates of records. They unscrew the base of the light pole, take their equipment, attach it to that, get the electricity – Boom! We got a concert right here in the schoolyard and it's this guy Kool Herc. And he's just standing with the turntable, and guys were studying his hands. There are people dancing, but there's as many people standing, just watching what he's doing. That was my first introduction to in-the-street, hip hop DJing.'

Melle Mel remembers a physical frame which matched Herc's imposing audio set-up.

'This huge character, and he had a beard. He really was like fuckin' Hercules, he was built and shit. He was, just from my images of right now, just this really mythical character. Even before I was able to go to a Herc jam, I heard about him for about a year and a half.'

### ➤ *Junior Wants To Play – From Disco To Hip Hop*

Frederick Braithwaite started out as a graffiti artist working along the Lexington Avenue line with the Fab Five crew – hence his *nom de plume* Fab Five Freddy. Before working as a promoter, recording artist and later a TV presenter, he witnessed some of the earliest DJ parties.

'I was part of the disco era. This is disco before it became commercial disco, when it was underground. DJs giving parties in schools, at restaurants that they would take over at night and they would simulate "posh" clubs. That scene, those particular DJs that played what was then known as disco, those guys inspired the generation that became the pioneers of hip hop. So I was around as the transition took place in the mid-70s.'

That transition involved disenfranchised black youths reclaiming music from untouchable star musicians whom they could no longer readily identify with.

'Let's say a group like Earth Wind & Fire – that particular time, they were wearing elaborate, gaudy costumes. It was something that seemed very far away from what a ghetto kid on the street could realistically hope to attain, or be part of.'

Disco had left many urban black kids behind. Its celebrity-strewn mecca, Studio 54, could just as well have been on another continent. Impresario Michael Holman saw this desire for ownership of an indigenous music and the frustration with vacuous records produce a climate similar to the one which engendered punk. However, he emphasises the fact that peer group acceptance took several years.

'The people in the neighbourhood were into the artists who were coming out of California and from other places. Local groups and local rap artists who were rapping over turntables in the park were not quite that popular, especially with the older people from, say, mid-twenties up.'

Where punk had been a year zero explosion, hip hop was built block by block over several years, devouring its immediate past rather than ridiculing it. Disco was its most recent antecedent and provided a fertile gene pool. However, many other early hip hop jams and record releases employed rock signatures and percussion effects rather than dance music, because it was too 'soft' to freestyle over.

Before hip hop finalised its blueprint, disco kids in the Bronx were already hooked on the breakbeat sections the DJs would emphasise, as Fab Five Freddy recalls.

'When these particular records would come on, they would give a real interesting vibe to the party. The atmosphere, the energy would change. Kids that knew how to breakdance would start dropping to the floor doing these crazy moves. This is before things had names and titles so it wasn't breakdancing and it wasn't hip hop, it was just energy.'

Fab Five Freddy notes that the development of a cultural alternative to disco was at least partially inspired by working class blacks being excluded from the mainstream.

'When you would go to these disco parties, particularly when they were given in the cities, or at colleges. The crowd was primarily a college crowd. They would sometimes put on the flyers: "No sneakers". That would be a reference to what you could say was the hip hop kid, or the real urban foundation type of kid.'

## ➤ My Adidas – Hip Hop Fashion Statements

The sneaker (or trainer shoe) was becoming an item of almost mythical importance to breakdancers, according to Michael Holman. Woe betide anyone who stepped on the toes of the early B-boys.

'Back in the old days of hip hop, the sneaker of choice would be shoes that would be actually old school even then. They would have been ten-year-old styles, like the plastic shell toe, the shell-toed Adidas sneakers. These were kids who, what they owned was on their backs and on their feet. So when you talk about sneaker etiquette, or sneaker intrusion, you're talking about this idea of, God forbid, you were to step on someone's sneakers. I don't know how they did it, but you would keep your sneakers spotless. Absolutely clean. And you're going through the subway system, you are going through New York City – it's not one of the cleanest cities in the world. How they would keep them clean I have no idea. Stepping on someone's sneakers could easily be a death sentence.'

Some of the more interesting fashion statements were made by combining sneakers with exotic sportswear – sailing and skiing apparel – sporting activities that were way beyond the wearer's economic compass.

'That has always been part of black fashion, mocking them [affluent whites], mimicking it, taking that fashion and turning it into their own.'

Despite the confluence of areas like breakdancing, graffiti and music, the embracing of hip hop as an umbrella term was still some way down the line, according to Fab Five Freddy.

'There really was no comparison, there was no analogy. There was no four elements of hip hop at this point in time. Basically, you had graffiti going full steam, completely independent of what was going on in hip hop for the most part.'

## ➤ Watch The Closing Doors – The Graf Squad

Graffiti had decorated urban trains in New York since the early 70s. The origins of this DIY impressionism, or 'guerrilla art', are variously credited to Greek teenager TAKI 183 and Jean-Michel Basquiat, aka Samo, though territorial wall markings were a fixture of New York's urban environment in the previous decade. In the 70s they simply grew in size and ambition, often bedecking whole tenement walls as well as subway trains. This threw the authorities and graffiti artists into a headlong confrontation that is still smouldering today on several continents. Fab Five Freddy was one of graffiti's earliest adherents and advocates. According to his observations, its growth sprang from a quest for identity and recognition common to all hip hop's constituent forms.

'Graffiti artists come up with another name, another persona, paint it all over the city on the trains and everything and – "Hi! That's me! I'm just as big as an ad for Marlboro cigarettes or Coca-Cola or any other big product."'

Michael Holman first came to New York in 1978 to work on Wall Street as a credit analyst. But he immediately became infatuated with the subway graffiti that decorated his route to work.

'I would get in the subway, about to get on a train, and these trains would go by with these amazing burners, graffiti burners, multi-coloured name tags. They would take up the whole train and I would watch them go by and just think, my God, this is amazing. Other people on the platform – do you see this? And they were all sort of in their own world and not even noticing. I guess it was all old hat to them and just boring vandalism and I was just shocked. It was the first tug, the first pull into that subculture.'

Like Fab Five Freddy, Holman believes that the different strands of hip hop – graffiti, breakdancing, DJing and MCing – were only considered as a collective entity some time after the event.

'It never really plays out the way you think it would in a neat package that historians would like to see it. There wasn't at that time anybody saying, "OK, this is like a hip hop happening." No one was saying that, because it wasn't that yet.'

At this stage, the dominant persona in this new culture was the DJ.

'It really is important to note that the DJ was truly the important artist then. It wasn't the MC, it was the DJ who made the party happen. It was the DJ who was the producer, who was the one supplying the soundtrack for the breakdancers and for the B-boys.'

However, some loose movement was definitely stirring, signified as much as anything by a new dress code.

'It was slowly becoming apparent to everyone uptown and downtown that this was something like the rock 'n' roll of the 60s, which had its own look, style, fashion. This was a subculture that had its own fashion, dance, aesthetic, music, lexicon if you will.'

It wasn't subtle, but Big Bank Hank of the Sugarhill Gang credits Herc with creating a compelling distraction from the turmoil of inner-city life.

'You could hear his system, with no exaggeration, three blocks away. He had a countless number of speakers, bass bottoms, subs, mid-range, tweeters. And he'd hook up – they'd plug into the street lamps. Lights would go dark from how much power was being drawn and the parties that he would throw. Oh, man, it was like something you'd see at the Superbowl. It was people losing their mind and no violence, and that was the key – no violence. To have that many people together and nobody wanted to fight. Nobody wanted to shoot. Everybody going home safe.'

Afrika Bambaataa freely credits DJ Kool Herc with being the 'father' of hip hop, its founder and guardian, and also his chief inspiration.

'By 1969 he had that feeling of playing this style of music with break-beats, something like they were doing in Jamaica with the version type of music. They would take the instrumental style and a lot of the DJs would toast – as what you call rapping today – on the record.'

However, it is easy to overstate the importance of the Jamaican influence on New York hip hop. Herc, for example, was 'Americanised' very swiftly once he arrived in the country, playing basketball and involving himself in local graffiti activities. Despite the precedents set by U-Roy, I-Roy and other toasters, reggae records proved generally unpopular when he played them. It is debatable whether parallel developments in Kingston reggae and Bronx hip hop are any more than coincidental. DJ battles in New York did mirror the soundclashes of Jamaica, but would almost certainly still have arisen without the historical precedent. The simple connection between the two was competition.

And the competition was about to liven up.

# chapter two

# let battle commence

## ➤ *Bambaataa, Gangland Bronx and the Zulu Nation*

The Bronx of the late 70s was an area synonymous with poverty and hardship, a breeding ground for internecine warfare in which the American Dream was subservient to codes of survival. Though a uniquely vibrant environment, it was also a dangerous place to live. Afrika Bambaataa knew about those dangers better than anyone.

'The Bronx was declared one of the most destructive places in America. It was infested by a lot of drugs , a lot of street gang activity.'

Bambaataa first began DJing at the age of ten. By founding the Zulu Nation enclave – a loose community of street kids – 'Bam' helped transform New York's gang culture into something creative, empowering and, most importantly, inclusive. Crazy Legs, a Puerto Rican breakdancer, recalls that while Bambaataa's interest in African history and black legitimacy was deep-rooted, he felt equal kinship with all the urban poor of New York.

'Bambaataa taught me more about myself than I ever learned in school. Just about how to be a proud Latino.'

Bambaataa knew the destructive power of the gang culture. He himself had formerly run with the Black Spades and Seven Immortals.

Despite the dangers of the immediate environment, there were also positives. Black consciousness was sweeping the streets, with James Brown's 'Say It Loud, I'm Black And I'm Proud' serving as its rallying call. The civil rights movement had achieved much. The Black Panthers were on the march and The Nation Of Islam were beginning to organise in black communities, and magazines like *Ebony* were providing outlets for mainstream black culture. In defiance of the gang mentality and in response to these positives, Bambaataa established his own street army. Initially simply the Organization, it more famously became known as the Zulu Nation. The Nation was informed by its leader's research into his African origins and the discourses advanced by Malcolm X and Elijah Mohammed. The name, oddly, was inspired by the 1964 Michael Caine film *Zulu*, which had made a big impact on the young Bambaataa. His interest in Africa had been further piqued by a trip there with UNICEF in 1975, after he won an essay-writing contest.

'At that time we was into consciousness, being aware of our blackness and being aware of what was going around the city, as well as the United States with all the civil rights, human rights and all the black power movement and everything that was happening at the time.'

The Zulu Nation originally started out with the Zulu Kings, a five-member breakdance crew, in 1973. With gang affiliation dying down, lots of young people gravitated to the Kings, who were building a reputation for being the best dancers in the neighbourhood. Bambaataa describes their origins.

'I was part of the Black Spades, I used to be in the Seven Immortals also. I was a Savage Nomad, been in many other groups out there. I had a lot of power with a lot of the street organisations of the time. From speaking to the people from the Nation of Islam and other groups who came to our meetings to try to change our ways, and from my travels and seeing one of my best friends get killed by the police in the Bronx, seeing how a lot of the brothers and sisters was getting hurt, I decided to try to lead our organisation into another direction. And that's when we made the Zulu Nation and the Almighty Zulu Nation and we started getting people of different colours and races into our organisation. Then we became the Universal Zulu Nation and as we progressed on into the 80s and the 90s, that's when we started getting on "world thinking" and then "universe thinking".'

The following history of the organisation is taken from the Zulu Nation website.

'The Universal Zulu Nation is a music, community service and arts organization founded in the USA by Afrika Bambaataa. This organization has hundreds of chapters throughout the world, and all members believe in freedom, justice, equality, knowledge, wisdom and understanding. Our members come from many different races, cultures, nationalities, countries and religions. The Universal Zulu Nation members dislike divisions and want to see peace and unity with all races. The Universal Zulu Nation was founded in 1973 in the Bronx, New York. It was Afrika Bambaataa's idea to use music to spread the message of the UZN. He knew that music is universal and crosses all barriers. So with the birth of hip hop [which started in New York City, USA] Bambaataa and members of the Zulu Nation started to travel throughout the world to spread hip hop culture and uplift communities everywhere. Some of the community activities of the UZN include neighborhood clean-ups, block parties, talent showcases, seminars, conferences, canned food drives, tutoring and mentor programs.'

Bambaataa had first seen Herc play in 1973, with his MC, Coke Le Rock. He vowed to emulate the kingpin DJ once he had graduated. In the meantime, he set about his apprenticeship.

'The Bronx had a community centre, which was an area called the Old Center . . . We would bring down our house system, that your mother and father bought. And somebody else would bring down their house system and we would set up on different sides of the room and you would have a flashlight. That's when you had them old 45s and them discs that could hold six 45s. When it was dark you put on a certain record, you might put on "I Want You Back" by the Jackson 5, and when it's getting towards the end you would flash the light to the other side for the other DJ. He would put on the next record which might be James Brown's "Get on the Good Foot". It would keep switching back and forth.'

Bambaataa was soon recognised as one of the Bronx projects' 'music men'. Jazzy Jay, later a member of the Zulu Nation and a producer in his own right, would ride his bike past Bambaataa's window each day and be engrossed by the outlandish sounds bouncing off the walls. To Jay, it represented an alternative to the prevalent gang culture of the day.

'The gang aspect – that was always an evident prospect for anybody who wanted it. But for those who didn't want it, you got another alternative.'

➤ *Grandmaster Flash & The Wheels Of Steel*

Joseph Sadler, aka Grandmaster Flash, was the final member of the DJing triumvirate that bestrode early hip hop. Born in Barbados in 1958 but raised in the South Bronx, Sadler picked up some of the technical knowledge that distinguished him from his peers at Samuel Gompers Vocational Technical High School.

Renowned DJ Pete Jones was an early sponsor. Jones, like DJ Flowers, is a name rarely given the recognition afforded Herc, but both DJs were part of the 70s block party culture that moulded contemporary hip hop. Ultimately, they were too rooted in the past to be part of the future, though Flash learned much about blending records from Jones. He also watched carefully as Herc lured audiences away from the disco staples of the day, such as Donna Summers.

'The music that Herc was playing was more obscure. Or, the music that I enjoyed listening to. These songs were not hit songs, not hit radio songs, not hit commercial songs. The interesting thing about these songs to me was the climatic part, that particular passage. That's where my interest really became defined.'

Flash had grown up alongside a music loving father, paranoid that his son would damage his hallowed vinyl collection. Flash would not be deterred, however, even by the prospect of repeat thrashings.

'I would get in serious, serious beatings from my father for going in that collection. As much as he did it, as soon as he left the house for work, I would grab a chair, slide up in that closet, open that knob, get a record. Went over to that stereo with that little red light and turn it on. Kept doing that, kept doing that.'

The young Joseph Sadler didn't want to enter the fray until he could deliver something unique. On his birthday, in January 1974, his friend Joe Kid suggested he append Grandmaster to his existing nickname. He had long since been dubbed Flash because his close friend at school had the surname Gordon – hence Flash Gordon. His expanded billing compelled him to take his vocation seriously.

'I was experimenting. I was in search of something. Not sure what I was in search of. Watching my two heroes of the time, which was Kool Herc and Pete DJ Jones, both of them had their own styles. One was what I called the "slow blend" style, which is Pete DJ Jones, and then "hit or miss" is what I kind of tagged for Kool Herc. I think what I wanted to do was come up with something that would take these obscure records with these breaks that were so short and manually extend them. Wasn't sure how I was gonna do it.'

Flash sat in his bedroom improvising and cooking up new sounds, destroying his old Pioneer turntable in his pursuit of the perfect breakdown. That process required two copies of the same record to be played along-side each other. More importantly, the DJ needed to be able to listen to one of the duplicates while spinning the other.

'I've tried all types but the turntable of choice, which was the turntable that everybody bought after I picked it, was the Technics. And the Technics that I used was the SL-1200 [the world's first "direct drive, strobe-monitored turntable"]. It was kind of an ugly looking thing. It looked something like a Sherman tank, almost. Once I figured out the turntable my next obstacle was – how do I take these duplicate copies of records and, with the one sound source, continue hearing it over and over again? So I'd come up with some sort of device and that was called a mixer. But the mixer that I had, which was an MX8 at the time, was a microphone mixer, so I had to convert it somewhat. I had to do some electrical conversions to make it from a mic mixer to a turntable mixer. Once I figured that out, I then had to figure out how to pre-hear the mixer, hear the cut before the people hear the cut. That's when I came up with the thing called a peek-a-boo system. Later it was called cueing. I don't take no props for inventing it, but all I know is that I had to invent something so that I can hear the turntable before I mix it out to the people.'

Flash devised a new arsenal of techniques, which his peek-a-boo innovations now made possible, and set about revolutionising the DJ's art.

'I called it the quick mix theory. It consisted of techniques like back-spinning, cutting, which was later called scratching, double-backing – that was like a ping-pong effect where you take two duplicate copies of the same record then push one slightly upbeat ahead of the other. Coming up with these techniques is what intrigued me and it's basically my con-tribution.'

Promoter Cool Lady Blue remembers seeing Flash in action for the first time at Disco Fever, the Bronx nightspot which opened in 1978.

'I saw Flash in the Fever. He was doing different things, he wasn't doing what Bam was doing, he was actually doing turntable acrobatics. He was cutting records and doing his quick mix theory. He was doing things beyond my comprehension. I remember going up to the Fever and going up to the turntables. There's a booth there and you can sort of peek over the turntables to the DJ. I was just watching him and thinking, "God, what is he doing?!" I was just awe-struck.'

## ➤ Cut And Mix – Theodore Comes Of Age

Grandwizard Theodore is often cited as Flash's first student, though he also taught his teacher a trick or two. Bitten by the block party bug, he branched off with two siblings to form the L Brothers in an effort to stamp out his own identity.

'I always wanted to be different from all other DJs. When I would go in the park and see a DJ play music, or go to a party, most everybody was pretty much playing these breakbeats pretty much the same way. I just basically did research every day. I'd just play music and just try to be different in everything that I was doing.'

This process led to the development of scratching, although the discovery could be attributed as much to accident as design.

'A lot of DJs, when they're playing music, [they] have one record playing and they're holding the other record with their hand. But the people that's dancing don't really hear it. In the earphones they're rubbing the record back and forth in order to keep the groove. Only thing that I did was move the mixer over so that the people can hear it, and make a little rhythm to it. I was playing music one day and my mom came banging on the door. "If you don't turn that music down, you're going to turn it off." Anyway, she was in the doorway and she was talking to me. I was moving the record still, moving the record back and forth. Then when she left the room, I was like, "Wow!" I never realised what I was doing until she left the room. I just kept experimenting with it and figuring out new ways to do it with different records. It became a "scratch".'

The technique, also adopted by Grandmaster Flash, drew an immediate reaction, and became the staple of the hip hop DJ's repertoire in later years. Another of the DJs who came up through the Bronx party scene, Grandmaster Caz (Curtis Brown), shared with Flash a reputation as a graffiti artist as well as his aggrandising prefix. He first encountered hip hop, like so many before him, when he wandered into the Hevalo club and saw Kool Herc spinning the discs.

'I had never seen it at that level. I was fourteen years old and that very day, when I saw his sound system and how loud it was. The records that he played would just change the way the party was going, and that's what I wanted to do, for life. That night, that's it, that's what I want to be.'

## ➤ Come To The Hip Hop Jam

Prior to 1975, Bambaataa, in consort with friends Cool DJ D and Disco King Mario, was still trying to make something out of the 'Hustle' disco craze (after the hugely successful single by Van McCoy). That soon changed. He began to play records like 'Give It Up Or Turn It Loose' by James Brown, which had been popularised by Herc. But he also brought his own, eclectic choices to the mix.

Bambaataa's sets were the most esoteric and daring. Alongside funk staples such as Sly & The Family Stone, James Brown and Funkadelic/ Parliament, he would spin rock standards by Pink Floyd, Led Zeppelin and the Rolling Stones, 60s pop from the Beatles and Monkees, dashes of calypso and salsa, plus obscurities such as 'The Chant' by the Mohawks and various cuts from Filipino group Please. There were even Hare Krishna records, which offered interesting rhythm breaks and instrumentation. He also introduced audiences to Fela Kuti. The late Nigerian highlife singer was a powerful anti-authoritarian figure and a spokesman for African unity, whom Bambaataa met on the UNICEF trip in 1975. Towards the end of the 70s, he began introducing electronic music from Gary Numan and Kraftwerk to the 'wheels of steel'.

His popularity, along with that of Flash, mushroomed and spread beyond the Bronx. It was at this point that the term hip hop fell into common usage, inspired by MC Lovebug Starsksi's use of the term from 1974 onwards, as Bambaataa narrates.

'On our flyers we used to say, "Come to the hip hop jam this, or the be bop jam that". When we went to Yonkers and other places in the tri-state area, we started naming different areas. Yonkers might be Jitterbug City, so "Come to the hip hop jam in Jitterbug City," stuff like that. More MCs was picking it up, talking about: "the hip hop, you don't stop," and that cliché just started catching on.'

Michael Holman, however, remembers the term originally also carried negative connotations.

'The audience, in a disparaging way, would say: "Oh, I don't want to go to that hip, the hippy, hippy hop". Everyone picked it up from [Grandmaster Flash MC] Cowboy – "the hip, a hippy, a hippy hop, you don't stop". So the term hip hop as a tag to the subculture actually acquired that name in a disparaging way, funnily enough.'

## ➤ Apache – The Ultimate Break

It's possible, even profitable, to pontificate on hip hop's ancestry in everything from African ritual to jive-talk. Yet the truth is that neither the Last Poets nor Gil Scott-Heron were the evolutionary missing link. Records like 'Apache', popularised by 60s stalwarts and Cliff Richard sidekicks the Shadows, were. The day Herc discovered the breakbeat was the day hip hop was born and the most definitive breakbeat record of them all was 'Apache', discovered by Herc in 1975.

Later a staple of the parties thrown by Herc, Bambaataa and Flash, "Apache" was a version of the Jerry Lordan song popularised by the Shadows. It was commonly known as 'The Rock', from the title of the 1973 LP it appeared on, *Bongo Rock* by Michael Viner's Incredible Bongo Band. Despite the song's fame in England, 'Apache' – like the Shadows – was unknown in Bronx DJ circles. It has remained a dominant record in break-beat culture into the 90s, with Fatboy Slim recently recording a version. For Grandmaster Flash, it was a record that helped unify the early movement.

'We were playing obscure records but we really didn't have an obscure record that stood out. And 'Apache' just stood out. It was just monster to the beat, just incredible. It had depth. All it was, was just bass drum, snare drum and bongos. Herc had me and Bam [Afrika Bambaataa] going when he played that song, we was trying to look at the label. He kept that quiet for a long time until eventually I found out what it was. A monster record, very important.'

Grandmaster Caz was another who span 'Apache', often building other songs around it in his set lists.

'It was one of the longest breaks. A lot of times you had to get two records out of a break because it was short and you wanted to keep it going. So you got another one and you cut it before the music comes in. 'Apache' – all you had to do was [put it on] and the B-boys go crazy.'

Jazzy Jay, head of Afrika Bambaataa's Jazzy Five, concurs.

'You could play it for a new-born baby. That's just the way that record moves you, it's that tribal rhythm.'

To the old school Bronx hip hop fraternity, 'Apache' will always be hip hop's 'national anthem'.

The innovations in music were matched by breakdancers, as teams like the Dynamic Rockers took on the Rock Steady Crew or the Floor Masters, as Kid Freeze recalls.

'You [always] needed a fresh style. I started learning the back spin to the freezes. From there, one day I was practising with [fellow Dynamic Rocker] Nelson, and I kicked up and spun on my head and I landed it. And he was like: "Oh! Do that again! That was hot." I was like: "Get out of here!" Back then no one had head spins, so I decided to go on and people started doing the one-shot head spin.'

Bambaataa was among the first to develop the habit of scratching out record labels so other DJs couldn't work out what he was spinning. He remembers the rivalries were friendly, but keen.

'We had spies in each other's camps that used to go around trying to peek – "What's that record Bambaataa's playing?" And there's a lot might hear something [Grandmaster] Flash was playing that was kicking. So you'd try to find out what's that record Flash is playing, what's that record that Herc is playing.'

Bambaataa trained himself to recognise the colours used by different labels. That way, even a disfigured record could give a clue as to the artist who originated the break or tune.

## ➤ Enter The Arena

The DJ originators, though all based in the Bronx, had long since cut out their own territory, in an area still defined by its gang affiliations. Their confrontations were dubbed 'battles' or 'throwdowns', but violence was rarely involved. DJs would set up at different ends of a park or hall, and the one who could attract the largest share of the audience would be victorious. In the beginning, the combats were usually won by the DJ with the most powerful system. But from there the battles evolved into something a little more sophisticated. Bambaataa recounts one such engagement with the enemy.

'We had a big super battle where [Disco King] Mario was going against Grandmaster Flash, and Flash brought this wall of speakers that was stretching from far yonder. Mario didn't have all his speakers at the time. He called out for help, so I went and got my speakers and I had another DJ by the name of Tex get his speakers, and we made a big super crazy wall against Flash's speakers and then it was on.'

Flash remembers the stand-off.

'Actually, we rented extra speakers, just to be the "bomb". See, Bam's thing was, couldn't nobody mess with them when it came to records for selection. He was quite incredible with that. So I was gonna try to get him with sound. It was ridiculous. I couldn't even get everything working that night. There were so many problems trying to get the darn thing working. I think Theodore played, Bam played. It was like me against all of them – not even against them, it was like when they turned off I turned on. It was all good.'

Jazzy Jay remembers the Disco Twins, a DJ crew who took the noise to Spinal Tap proportions.

'The Disco Twins, they were phenomenal for blowing people away. They used to have a speaker that was so big, they used to have to come, set it up, and actually put it together at the party. They'd come in with these screw guns and drills. It was ridiculous.'

The Disco Twins had established a niche at the Hotel Diplomat after making their name on the Queens disco circuit (they looked alike rather than being actual twins). Though it was only in the early 80s that they began to spin anything other than mainstream dance records, they did play a part in formulating hip hop's growth in Queens.

'Our home was in the Hotel Diplomat, when they had Rush Productions downstairs, which was Russell Simmons. We was in a grand ballroom where Eddie Cheeba and DJ Hollywood used to perform. We used to go outside and battle some other DJs. People used to come down from all over to see what we were doing, because we had a very good system. We had MCs called DJ Smalls and Sesame and Kory Dee, and we used to perform together. We used to do a few tricks but we were mostly known for our sound system and the little stunts we used to do.'

Battling wasn't just a contest between DJs, as breakdancer Kid Freeze remembers.

'They started having parties in parks where people used to go. These guys are pretty smart. They used to get juice off the lamp posts. They used to get a screwdriver to open it up and attach the juice there and then they plugged it in and rode it all the way to the park. Then they hook up the wire to the turntables and they used to give out flyers and people used to come to the park. They used to have a lot of battles back then, as in who's the best MC. So at the same time as who's the better MC, they had DJs, they had B-boys. So the whole segment of hip hop started nurturing.'

Melle Mel, Grandmaster Flash's principal MC, saw the battling as a direct route out of gang violence.

'It was coming out of the era of drugs and stuff like that. Everything evolved into the music, so the competition was still there for your area. You represented your area. Even if we went to a Kool Herc party, we was dancers, we would battle Herc's dancers.'

As Melle suggests, that competitive element also extended to the breakdancing teams. Crazy Legs recalls how seriously the build-up to a given jam could become.

'Battling is always important. You practise all week and you get a dance studio which would be a hallway in a tenement. So when you're prac- tising for that whole week, your goal is to hit the jam and battle. And when you do your thing you have to come out with something fresh and new, and something that sets you aside as an individual. Even if you bit [copied] someone's move from the week before, you took that move and you made it your own move.'

The unprepared breakdancer, MC or DJ risked derision, especially if they were judged to be trading on someone else's style, as old school B-boy Jorge 'Fabel' Pabón recalls.

'That's the number one issue in hip hop, originality. Without that you're nothing. Back in the days you could get booed out of a circle or laughed out of a circle if you looked too much like the next man. They'll tell you right off you're a biter [copyist] and you're wack. We used to battle a lot back then, so we knew that if I did a move one day, I definitely better go think of three other moves, because someone else is gonna try to use my move against me. So you had to be on top of the game.'

Big Bank Hank of the Sugarhill Gang saw the clashes as a non-violent way for young men to compete without physically tearing strips off each other.

'It was all about system. It was all about who we are, what we're about and my system's going to crush yours. But it was all good, it was all in fun. But it was all for pride. It was like two race drivers, just going at each other to the tape – win, lose or draw, I'm going to give it my best.'

Grandmaster Caz, often outgunned by DJs who could afford bigger sound systems, still relished the contests.

'It's just like sports – you playing me, I'm playing you. I'm taking you out. My man, we're going to have a beer afterwards but during this game, I'm taking you out.'

He remembers one particularly ignoble defeat at the hands of Afrika Bambaataa.

'I played that record by Queen ["We Will Rock You"]. I came on as Casanova Fly [Caz's MCing alter ego]. I came on to my little intro – "Honey you're a . . ." I'm making a statement, you hear me. Mr Biggs [Afrika Bambaataa MC], he got on the mic. He said: "Casanova Fly, we can't hear you!" – BOOM BOOM BA, BOOM BOOM BA – Oh, he just blew me out. They never even gave me a shot because if your system can't hold up, they're going to drown you out. Nobody will get a chance to hear it, 'cos they're going to drown your ass out.'

Fab Five Freddy credits Afrika Bambaataa more than anyone for distilling the energy of the Bronx while minimising the potential for violence.

'Flash and Theodore and them, they had the techniques on the wheels, with the manipulation of the turntables and the cross-faders etc. But your Afrika Bambaataa – first of all, his stature was legendary, because he was the head of the Zulu Nation. You really have to understand that the Zulu Nation had originally been the Black Spades. They were the biggest, most feared gang in the Bronx. They'd wear these denim jackets with the cut-off sleeves and fur around the collars and Black Spades written across the back. This was before gangs had a lot of guns, so it was all about getting beat down with sticks and with knives. It was brutal. And Bambaataa had the inspiration to stop this gangbanging nonsense, stop killing each other and let's get creative. So he turned one of the most violent street gangs into one of the most influential cultural organisations.'

Crazy Legs has a slightly different perspective, believing that few genuinely criminal gang members were ever attracted to hip hop. However, he does concede that there were some redemptive aspects.

'Actually the best thing about hip hop was that if you were a criminal back then and you enjoyed hip hop, in order to become good at what you want to do, you had to develop your craft. So that meant less time bull-shitting. It's that simple.'

Fellow breaker Kid Freeze contrasts the competitive but peaceful vibe at block parties with modern hip hop's affinity for violence.

'Now it is all about cars and girls. Back then, it was all about respect, looking fresh, getting your name out there. Like graffiti – who could get the most back them days. Between then and now things change. Even rap music had kind of changed because it has got a lot of violence in it. Back then it was all about love, how could you express your skills and how far could you take it when you were in the presence of a lot of people and you are exploring your skills. It wasn't about a record deal.'

Grandwizard Theodore emphasises that money, at this stage, was not a motivating factor.

'We didn't really do it for the money. We did it because we loved it. The average old school MC or DJ or whatever, they got into it because they loved it. The money came eventually, but we got into it because we loved it.'

At times DJs would bet their 'systems' on the outcome of a duel, but this was rare. It should be noted, also, that not every DJ relished the battles. Kool Herc, for one, was always keen to suggest that different systems took turns to play rather than operate in direct competition. Despite regular park summits, each of the big draws had their own territory, recalls Bambaataa.

'Kool Herc was doing a lot of his parties on the west side of the Bronx where the hip hop culture started. In the summertime they would play Sedgewick Park, what they call Cedar Park he would play in. Grandmaster Flash coming up right behind us playing in the Back Door over in the south Bronx, so we all had our different territories. I had a big community centre [The Bronx River Center].'

The Flash, Bambaataa and Herc sets, which often lasted between five and eight hours, were self-promoted and organised, adopting a spirit of independence and a DIY ethic that mirrored the development of punk in the UK. With the exception of Herc, most of the pioneers were still in their late-teens.

'We were all young entrepreneurs at the time 'cos we had to learn how to rent the places, or get an adult to get certain things. If we couldn't get to rent the spot we could get an adult to go in there and rent the spot for us.'

## ➤ Diggin' In The Crates – Vinyl One-Upmanship

Although it was only much later that hip hop became a lucrative business, each DJ expected a dividend from their parties, to cover the costs of audio technology and the distribution of flyers. More importantly, they had to buy the freshest breakbeat records. The need for a constant turnover of new records meant that the DJ, often otherwise unemployed, had to make his parties pay. This was about survival of the fittest, or in hip hop terms, survival of the phattest beats.

It was Grandmaster Flash's thirst for musical knowledge that gave Grandwizard Theodore his opening in hip hop.

'I became the record boy 'cos they [Flash and Theodore's brother Mean Gene] were doing parties every weekend, I was responsible for going downtown and looking for records, to this place called Downstairs Records. The guy would sit there and play little 45s all day long and if you liked the 45 you buy it. Basically I used to just hang around there all day long and just buy 45s.'

Author Nelson George describes the strange ritual.

'People were buying these cut-outs [discounted records] for $1.99, $2.99, really obscure records. And they're looking for certain cuts or certain bits of congos, bongos, Latin percussion, cowbells. And the buyers who were working the store were mystified but getting a lot of business out of these DJs.'

Tom Silverman, later manager of Tommy Boy Records, was another who learned about hip hop through visiting record shops. By the time he arrived, however, the vendors had wised up to the value of their deleted vinyl.

'Downstairs Records was in the subway on 6th Avenue and 42nd Street. They had a room that was called the Breakbeat Room. These little twelve-year-old kids would come in together in a group of four and they'd pool their money to buy two records, two albums. And they'd buy the weirdest things. They'd buy the Eagles' *The Long Run* album, which was a cut-out record now it had been over-pressed. It was probably being bought for twenty-five cents and they were selling it for ten dollars – which for an album in those days was an extraordinary amount of money – as a rare record, a breakbeat record. And they'd have [Dennis Coffey's] "Scorpio" and records like that. They were all selling at high prices and there was a line out the door. Kids were trying to come in and buy these records and they were all very specific. They'd play "Mary Mary" by the Monkees. Do they play the whole song? No, they just play three seconds, and they take a beat from three seconds, use two records and make it last for five minutes. "Mary Mary" from the Monkees had just a kick snare, with a sort of hip hop feel to it. They'd just loop it. They did it live so they had to have two of those. Billy Squire, there was a twelve-inch promo of a song called "The Big Beat", you'd hear the same kind of thing.'

Bambaataa's eclecticism influenced many other DJs, including Grandmaster Flash. Flash, in turn, unearthed some of the era's most important records.

'I would play anything, like Yellow Magic Orchestra, they were Japanese, so what? "Trans-Europe Express" was probably the record that I brought out, my discovery. Music didn't have any colour. Didn't matter, if it was funky, I played it.'

'Trans-Europe Express' was an example of what Nelson George terms hip hop's selective vision. Like the most virulent scavengers, hip-hoppers took what they wanted, stealing the kernel of the music, but leaving the husk behind.

'They never played the entire record, but they played certain sections of "Trans-Europe Express", so it was a very selective kind of vision that evolved partly out of a rejection of disco, partly out of a sense of finding a new kind of percussive sensibility.'

He attributes the appetite for invention to the monopoly that sub-urban disco music held over New York's airwaves.

'There was a certain kind of vacuum for a gutsier kind of funk, a gutsier sound of black music which you weren't really hearing in New York any more.'

## ➤ Bad Days – Kool Herc Bows Out

Sadly, Kool Herc would never reap the fruit of his efforts, as his influence began to wane. One night at the Executive Playhouse he was stabbed three times, once across his hands, when he intervened as three youths attempted to push past his house security. But Grandmaster Caz believed he had also been superseded by up-and-coming DJs.

'Herc never really went that route, he never tried to get nice on the turntables. He let the younger guys do that.'

Others, like Melle Mel, felt that his inability to recognise the MC as the new focus of hip hop ensured he would be left behind.

'What made [Grandmaster] Flash popular was he had rappers and he could cut. Herc never evolved to that level. He would never submit to the fact that he needed somebody's help. I guess it was pride or ego, thinking that he could keep up with everybody. But he never went to that level.'

That new generation of DJs, most of whom were ex-breakdancers, and all of whom were Herc fans, took up the mantle. Herc, for his part, was impressed by the vitality that they brought to the scene, especially Afrika Bambaataa.

'He's playing a lot of stuff that was music to my ears at that time. I go to somebody's party, they're playing a lot of my stuff, so I'm not impressed with that. And although he plays some strange stuff, it was still music to my ears because it was strange, but it was him being himself.'

# chapter three

# rapper's delight

## ➤ *From MCing To Rapping*

Contemporary rapping, as various authors have noted, can trace its origins in African *griots* (priest-poets) through to the political tracts issued by the Last Poets ('Niggers Are Scared Of Revolution') and Gil Scott-Heron ('The Revolution Will Not Be Televised') in the late 60s and early 70s. The trajectory takes in bebop singers such as Cab Calloway, early rock 'n' roller Bo Diddley, 'soul' rapper/preacher Johnnie Taylor, American jive-talking radio jocks and the Jamaican toasters such as U-Roy they influenced. Muhammad Ali's ringside boasting has a place in hip hop's lineage, and so too the insult battles or 'dozens' that took place in Harlem in the 60s. The linguistics of signifying, testifying, schoolyard and jailhouse rhyming all play a role in the aesthetics of urban verbal exchanges, upon which rap draws so heavily. One of the common threads is the idea of competitive bragging or *braggadocio*, which characterised the spirit of early hip hop and the first rap records.

These antecedents and influences are undeniably important. However, while hip hop openly borrowed from previous traditions, its development was ultimately organic and self-sustained. As its pioneers confirm, rap music is a collision of accident with design, of forethought with spontaneity. It is not a tributary of rock 'n' roll, reggae, disco or anything else, but a rich and individual standalone musical style.

Like so much else in hip hop, the development of MCing can be traced back to Kool Herc. To improve his sound, Herc had invested in an echo box for his microphone – ensuring his voice would boom out over his record selections. DJs speaking between records had long been accepted practice. What Herc said, and how he said it, was not.

'I used to call people's names and say: "Yo, Wallace D, D-D-D." Or: "This is the Joint-Joint-Joint, you never heard it like this before."'

Eventually, these introductions expanded.

Ya rock and ya don't stop

And this is the sounds of DJ Kool Herc and the Sound System

And you're listening to the sounds of what we call the Herculoids

He was born in an orphanage

He fought like a slave

Fuckin' up faggots all the Herculoids played

When it come to push, come to shove

The Herculoids won't budge

The bass is so low you can't get under it

The high is so high you can't get over it

So in other words be with it.

Coke Le Rock, Herc's partner and friend, began to extemporise the vocal introductions to records.

'Coke Le Rock, my partner, he used to have the poetry and he used to come on, say a couple of lines. Used to tell me things to say. The time we played the Dodge High School for my sister's high school dance, he came up with the phrase: "You rock, and you don't stop, keep on, and don't stop." And he did that over "Bongo Rock".'

MCs like Busy Bee Starski began to recite improvised rhymes over records. There had been disco DJs on the radio, like Hal Jackson on WLIB and Gary Bird on WWRL, who would improvise words in time with the music they were playing. But now the format was becoming conceptualised. Bambaataa:

'It was really with the hip hop culture, from Herc, myself and Flash, that the MC was really developing into the rhyming, or saying a lot of clichés or certain words that was catching on.'

Pretty soon rapping, as it was now being termed, became an art form in itself. Some attributed its development to the pioneering rhyming style of DJ Hollywood – it is said that the Fatback Band decided to use their party MC, King Tim III, after hearing Hollywood at the 371 Club. Bambaataa, however, believes that Hollywood and others, notably Eddie Cheeba, were part of the radio jive-talk tradition and nothing to do with hip hop.

'I got to give most credit to Grandmaster Melle Mel and the Furious Five, 'cos they was getting into the rhyming cliché, and then also with the fast style of rapping from Soul Sonic Force.'

DJ Bobbito Garcia notes that allusions to historical precedents can be misleading.

'People talk about Gil Scott-Heron and the Last Poets as being hip hop pioneers – I don't think so. I think they were instructive and definitely seminal artists of the 70s in terms of black music and political expression through music, but by no means were MCs influenced by these people. No one had ever been on a mic and rhymed to a beat in the manner that MCs had done.'

Others, like Grandmaster Caz, saw the accent switching to rapping as retrograde, an erosion of the importance of hip hop as a cultural package.

'We're MCs, we rhyme. We're masters of ceremony, we're mic controllers. We're MCs, not rappers. I just have a problem with the term, OK? MCing evolved from the DJ having a microphone to make announcements, to announce when the next party was going to be, where the next party was going to be, who was going to be at the party, to acknowledge members of the group. Then people started to embellish on how they said things. Instead of saying: "There's a party next week and we want you all to come," you say: "Yeah, next week at the PAL, we want to see your face in the place, we're going to party hearty with everybody." People would try and put a little flare to it to make you want to come to the thing. Then every DJ did that himself or he had somebody that would make the announcements for him. They started to embellish, and they would say things till they grew into sentences and to paragraphs.'

## ➤ Mix Tapes: A Bronx Cottage Industry

Although the embryonic hip hop movement shunned the mainstream record industry, another way to make money was to record their shows and DJ battles. The mix tapes that resulted became a vital source of revenue, as well as one of the main ways in which the music gravitated downtown and through suburbia, as Fab Five Freddy recalls.

'The parties in the Bronx that Flash and Theodore and Bambaataa and those guys were playing in the mid-70s, they luckily had the foresight to record almost all the gigs. Those tapes would then become circulated. They were spreading all through the city. The word was getting out that there's a guy named Flash, a guy named Theodore, a group called the Funky Four, there's a group called the Treacherous Three, there's a guy called Busy Bee Starski.'

Mix tapes were the reason many, like Darryl McDaniels of Run-D.M.C., got into the hip hop game.

'It was all about tapes back then. In my neighbourhood, tapes used to filter in from all the shows that were happening in the Bronx and all the Harlem World tapes. They used to filter into Queens. A lot of people don't think that Queens had a scene, [but] we had a lot of DJs, DJing in the parks and at the local clubs in our neighbourhood. So rap was in our neighbourhood, but on the stardom level, the celebrity level, you used to have to go see Grandmaster Flash and artists like Grandwizard Theodore. Their tapes were coming to our neighbourhood, people would go tape these shows, come back to Queens and sell them.'

He was particularly impressed by one mix tape featuring a performance from the Cold Crush Brothers.

'There was a promoter, who at the time all the rivalries in the Bronx and Manhattan was going on, heard about these rappers out of Staten Island. He brought the Force MDs into Manhattan to battle the Cold Crush Brothers and to battle the Funky Four (Plus One). That was the level that I was on. I wasn't really rhyming off the records, I was rhyming off the tapes. To me, the tapes were more of the real thing that I was accustomed to hearing in my neighbourhood, even though the party MC was a big part of everything. But the rivalries were the thing that really generated your interest. So that's what really made hip hop interesting to me. I used to see groups like the Cold Crush Brothers giving out flyers about their shows and stuff like that. I bought my first Cold Crush tape, paid fifteen dollars for it.'

According to McDaniels, you can see that heritage of mix tapes, of block parties and jams, throughout their work.

'If you listen to Run-D.M.C. records, it's exactly what the Cold Crush do. Because that was the rawest thing, the reason why nobody wants to go on after us, the reason why everybody says: "Run-D.M.C. got the best show". The reason why we lasted sixteen years in hip hop. We haven't had a record out in six years, but the reason why we can still tour, do shows and all of that. We're not about the industry, we're about that thing that began before these big corporations and industries tried to direct what's hip and what's not. That Cold Crush tape in 1982 was the defining moment in hip hop, because if that would have never happened, I don't think Run-D.M.C. would have ever came out and did what they did.'

## ➤ *Hip Hop Reaches Vinyl – Rapper's Delight*

As vital as these mix tapes were, especially for a movement as street-orientated and organic as hip hop, every musical phenomenon salutes its first recorded release, even if the finished product isn't entirely representative of the genre. Hip hop on vinyl arrived officially on 13 October 1979 with the release of 'Rapper's Delight'. Over a studio recreation of Chic's disco smash of earlier in the year, 'Good Times', three MCs rapped personally about themselves and their music and set in motion the wheels of the multi-billion dollar modern rap industry.

Having grown up between 166th street and Boston Road, Big Bank Hank (Henry Jackson), one of the trio of rappers who comprised the Sugarhill Gang, had first encountered Kool Herc at a Mitchell Gym party, four or five years previously.

'The crowd just lost their mind and I lost mine right along with it.'

Herc's first MC, Coke Le Rock, attended the same high school as Hank. Coke could have been hip hop's first star MC, had he not opted for an alternative career. He certainly helped inspire Hank, who realised the potential of the music.

'It was an escape for the younger generation to get out of the bad scene for a moment and take them into something that was a little bit positive. Instead of people fighting and using guns, if they wanted to battle, instead of having the gang wars, they would grab the microphone, challenge somebody in the court. They'd only lose on the MC mic. They wouldn't lose their life.'

When spotted by Sylvia Robinson, owner of Sugarhill Records, he was working in a pizza parlour in Inglewood, New Jersey, practising his rapping to pass the time. He was also manager of Grandmaster Caz, booking his shows and distributing his tapes. He'd taken the pizza job to pay off a loan from his parents, funds he'd diverted to purchase a bigger sound system for Caz.

'Sylvia Robinson came into the pizza shop along with her son, Joey Robinson Jnr. They had heard about me, and they asked me: "Did I want to make a record?" Picture this – I'm in a pizza shop, full of dough, flour all over me, and I'm going to audition to make a record! So I go into the back of her son's ninety-eight and they have a cassette in the car and I'm rapping along with the track and she really enjoyed it. She said, "OK, I'm going to use you on the record." At that exact time, as I get out the car, Guy O'Brien happened to be walking down the block. He was a member of a group called Phase Two and he had heard about what Miss Robinson was doing and he said: "Miss Robinson, I can rap also." So we started kicking verses back and forth together. Miss Robinson said: "Mmm, this is pretty good. Maybe I'll use both of you." Now also during this time, across the street – this is for real – Wonder Mike, which is Michael Wright, was across the street. He had heard all the commotion and came over across the street and said: "Miss Robinson, I can rap too.'"

Husband and wife team Joe and Sylvia Robinson had previously over-seen a number of record labels, including All Platinum, Turbo and Stang, before Sugarhill, which had bland, utilitarian offices in Englewood, New Jersey. They had tasted success with acts including the Moments, Whatnauts and Shirley & Co in the R&B field, before problems with distribution scuppered their efforts. Sylvia was also well-known for her 1973 hit, 'Pillow Talk'. Alerted to the power of hip hop through Bronx mix tapes her son had been devouring, she was the first major figure in the music industry to see the music's potential.

Despite being a whopping seventeen minutes long, Hank confirms that 'Rapper's Delight' was totally improvised after the first few words and recorded in a single take.

'One take, no mistakes, didn't stop or stutter. A seventeen-minute record done in seventeen minutes and fifty seconds. When you're hungry, you want to do something right.'

When the Sugarhill Gang reformed and performed 'Rapper's Delight' for a show on 18 August 1994 for *Vibe* magazine's first anniversary party, an online report castigated them for being opportunists, particularly Big Bank Hank's verse -

'Check it out, I'm the C-A-S-An-The-O-V-A

And the rest is F-L-Y'

The enunciation of C-A-S-A-N-O-V-A had been lifted from a routine by Grandmaster Caz, who was less than thrilled at its appropriation.

'He didn't even change it to Big Bank Hank, he just said the rhyme the way it was in the book [which Caz had loaned him], except for maybe there might have been a curse in there and he changed it to something else. The rhyme about Superman and Lois Lane, that's my rhyme too.'

The handclaps were insipid while some of the words, close to 3,000 of them in total, lacked the ingenuity and guile demonstrated by the Sugarhill Gang's peers. 'Rapper's Delight' was a poor man's imitation of Bronx hip hop. The song was merely repetitive and topical where much of the competition was inventive and incisive. Yet, as *Vibe*'s article was forced to concede:

'Flawed as it is and controversial as the circumstances of its birth may have been "Rapper's Delight", of all the hip hop records that have ever been released (and there have been many, many great and greater ones) is unique for one simple reason. It's the only record after which, no matter who you were or what you did in hip hop, everything was different. It changed the rules of the game. Its wide release made hip hop instantly inter-national. Its commercial success renegotiated the scope of what was imaginable, possible, probable, do-able.'

Within a week the record had become a mainstay of New York's airwaves. It went on to sell an estimated fourteen million copies. Hank found himself with a serious outbreak of celebrity to deal with.

'Everyone knows what happened after that. We couldn't walk the streets any more. That big.'

Bambaataa and other pioneering DJs worried that the success of 'Rapper's Delight' might 'mess up the parties'. Bambaataa also advances 'King Tim III (Personality Jock)', the 1979 b-side to 'Candy Sweet' by the Fatback Band, as the first true hip hop record. In terms of both form and content he has a point, but the Sugarhill Gang's effort was the one every-body accredited with the status of first rap record.

Grandwizard Theodore relates the feeling that 'Rapper's Delight' engendered among some of hip hop's pioneers.

'Big Bank Hank used to be the bouncer at the door for the venue that we used to play all the time called the Sparkle. And for this guy to all of a sudden, overnight, make a rap record, it was really incredible. It just goes, one day you can be a bouncer at a party, and the next day you can be travelling round the world.'

Kool Herc, too, was less than overjoyed.

'I wasn't too pleased. Hank is a homeboy that wanted to be with the fellas and had a lot of mouth. He was a football player. This was his way of getting into the business. That's fine, I didn't know you had that in you. I didn't know you wanted to be in with the music . . . It hurt, man.'

He was not surprised, however, that hip hop had taken off as a global phenomenon.

'Hip hop 'bin around since 1970. It got exposed in 1979. So once it's exposed, this is it. Just like crack. Crack 'bin around, till Richard Pryor got burnt up, then it went: whoosh! So I wasn't surprised. People in the Bronx weren't surprised.'

Grandmaster Flash sums up best the feelings of the originators:

'They weren't the most talented that I would have seen on a record if I had a choice, but it served its purpose.'

One of the biggest detractors was Hank's former friend and client, Grandmaster Caz.

'It lowered the standard drastically of what an MC was, and what you had to be to make a rap record. If you never saw nobody play basket-ball in your life and some knucklehead just played it in front of you – he played terrible but that's what you saw – that's the way you'd think you have to play basketball.'

Grandmaster Caz was also embittered about the use of his 'C-A-S-An-The-O-V-A' routine appearing in the song.

'People knew me for my rhymes. People said: "I heard you on the radio." That ain't me. "No, but I heard your rhymes." I know, it's not me though. "Well, I know you're getting paid." Yeah, well . . . It's fucked me up ever since.'

Hank, for his part, was reconciled with the fact that:

'There's always going to be envy in groups. Because you did it first, they didn't. Or, they may have been in business a little longer than you. But, overall, we got nothing but love.'

Melle Mel, conversely, had nothing but contempt for rap's first super-stars.

'When "Rapper's Delight" first came out, every traditional rapper was fuckin' mortified. It was like: "What the fuck are they doing with our art form?" It's like they axe-murdered the shit.'

Yet as Melle's colleague Flash conceded, the Sugarhill Gang had upped the ante.

'Once you heard that record – it was definitely a consideration to wanting to become an artist, as opposed to just performing. Definitely, it enlightened all hip-hoppers.'

## ➤ *Grandmaster Flash Responds On Enjoy*

Grandmaster Flash looked to exploit hip hip's new-found popularity on record. His original retinue of MCs (Melle Mel, Cowboy, Kid Creole – nothing to do with August Darnell of Kid Creole & The Coconuts) had long since expanded to become the Furious Five, who debuted on 6 September 1976, with the addition of Rahiem (formerly of the Funky Four) and Scorpio.

Melle Mel, aka Melvin Glover, grew up in the Bronx ghetto before becoming a breakdancer with the D-Squad, then a DJ, with his brother Kid Creole. Grover was christened Melle Mel by Flash in 1976.

'He was just a regular DJ, a neighbourhood DJ. I used to breakdance on my own. One time we danced against Flash and his old partner [Mean] Gene. They used to play music in a centre. That's where I first met him. They was older, thinking that they could really do their thing or whatever. And they got spanked a little bit. Genie did his thing, but Flash wasn't much of a dancer. He was a DJ, but everybody used to dance back then. So that's how I first actually met him. He was just a neighbourhood DJ.'

From there, it was a short step up to becoming Flash's MC.

'When Flash played the music, he didn't have a good speaking voice, so he needed somebody to rap for him. He wasn't a good talker. He wasn't very witty. So he needed somebody to rap for him and then that's when we started. He just left a mic there and anybody would just get on the mic. That's how it started.'

Melle's main influence, however, was Kool Herc. In fact, he had offered his services at one point.

'Me and my brother Kid Creole, we wanted to rap for Kool Herc. But he was so huge back then, he didn't think that he needed to bring in other people or needed to take on other areas. He just thought that him being Kool Herc would last and nobody would be able to overtake him.'

Flash secured a contract with Enjoy Records after proprietor Bobby Robinson, an industry veteran since the 50s, saw Flash & the Furious Five play with the Funky Four (Plus One) in the Bronx. Robinson recalls:

'They were both very good. The crowds were having a field day. So I got to the groups and decided to record both of them.'

Most of Enjoy's productions were overseen by gifted multi-instrumentalist Pumpkin. In common with Sugarhill's early catalogue, they were predominantly speculative, opportunistic efforts. Melle Mel, while bearing Robinson no malice, notes that:

'He was the local guy that just scooped up all the local talent. Then he cut records on everybody. None of the records were major hits, but it did give everybody a shot to be heard. None actually got played on the radio but they played them in clubs and then they gave Sugarhill a chance to hear all the other talents.'

Aware of hip hop's burgeoning commercial prospects (his nephew, Spoonie Gee, was an aspiring rapper) and keen to make sure no one else hit on his artists before him, Robinson rush-recorded and released records by both groups on the same day. The Furious Five issued 'Super Rappin'', while the Funky Four debuted with the lengthy 'Rappin' And Rocking The House'. Rodney C, the 'Plus One More' adjunct to the Funky Four, recalls:

'It was the longest rap record ever created at that point. One side was sixteen minutes, the other side was fourteen minutes. Thirty minutes of non-stop rap.'

Flash was also responsible for two further releases, under the pseudonyms Younger Generation and Flash And the Five. Then Joe Robinson Jr (no relation) bought out their contract with Enjoy and took them to Sugarhill Records. Bobby Robinson never gained the commercial rewards his nose for talent entitled him to. By 1984, he had given up on hip hop.

'I figured rap was about had it. I never dreamed it would last twenty years. So I sold off three or four of my groups and whatnot and got out of it.'

The success of the Sugarhill Gang spurred numerous others into action, as a deluge of rap twelve-inches hit the streets. As well as providing extended length, the format was popular partly because it made handling records easier for DJs than conventional seven-inch singles. Among some substandard non-descript fare came worthy efforts by Spoonie Gee, the nephew of Enjoy's Bobby Robinson, who cut 'Spoonin' Rap' for Peter Brown's Sounds of New York USA label, and the Nice And Nasty Three's 'The Ultimate Rap'. Kurtis Blow also took a bow with the gimmicky 'Christmas Rapping', which reached number thirty in the UK while failing to chart domestically.

## ➤ Kurtis Blow Slams On The Breaks

Born Kurt Walker in Harlem in 1959, Blow studied vocal performance at the High School of Music and Art at the City College of New York, then worked the Harlem club circuit as Kool DJ Kurt. His friend, Russell Simmons, remembers persuading him to adopt the name Kurtis Blow:
'I started promoting parties. I had a company called Rush. That company promoted Eddie Cheeba and Kurtis Blow and DJ Hollywood and Grandmaster Flash. So those guys were pioneers, we promoted parties with them at the Hotel Dukeman on 43rd Street or in Queens, Brooklyn, the Bronx or Harlem. Just those five boroughs. But that was a big deal moving them from one borough to another. Bringing Grandmaster Flash downtown to Manhattan was, at that time, an unheard of event. And it was a big event for us, so that's what I did. That's how I got involved with them, by promoting their parties. The next obvious step was to manage them when they made records and that's what I did.'

Blow became the first rapper signed to a major label and scored his breakthrough hit in September 1980 with 'The Breaks', a co-production with DJ Davy D, which reached number eighty-seven in the US charts. However, its impact was more correctly gauged by a number four showing in the R&B charts, selling half a million twelve-inch singles in the process. For Simmons, this was a vindication of Harlem's role in hip hop.

'In Harlem and in some places in other boroughs there were kids experimenting with their own music. They were all using old James Brown beats or old rock 'n' roll beats and they were rapping over those beats and those kids became popular in the street. Their tapes were popular because the records that were out weren't popular. Donna Summer wasn't a star in the community, community stars were DJ Hollywood, Eddie Cheeba, Kurtis Blow. Those were the guys who were developing that new sound and it was obvious that it was for us and by us and about our real lives and we could relate to it. That's where it grew. It grew from an organic, honest spring-board, as opposed to the industry sold it to us, which is what disco seemed to have, that kind of quality.'

Hip hop was becoming steadily more visible. In 1980 members of the High Times Crew were arrested for breakdancing at a subway in Washington Heights. Photos of the incident appeared in the New York Post. Mr Magic's Rap Attack, the most influential New York radio show, also began its run on WHBI on Saturday nights.

# chapter four

# hip hop goes global

## ➤ *The Rapture Tops The Charts*

As hip hop spread beyond the Bronx, the connection it made with more affluent areas came about initially through graffiti. Fab Five Freddy and Jean-Michel Basquiat both exported their art from the subways to Manhattan galleries. Through Glenn O'Brien, editor of Andy Warhol's *Interview* magazine, Freddy was introduced to approachable new wave bands Talking Heads and the internationally successful Blondie, then riding high in the charts with hits like 'Heart Of Glass' and 'Sunday Girl'. Debbie Harry and Chris Stein became Freddy's patrons, purchasing a number of his graffiti pieces and encouraging him to exhibit them and become a gallery star.

'I would basically hang out with them a lot. They would invite me up to their apartment In the upper westside of Manhattan. This was at the point when Blondie was literally the biggest pop group in the world. I'm still living at home with my parents. I'd hop on the A-train, come into Manhattan, go up there and hang out with them.'

Debbie and Chris promised they'd use Freddy's name on a record at some point. Freddy thought it was the weed talking. Yet one day, after recording in England, they invited him up to Manhattan to play him some of the tracks from their new album.

'Then they put on this one record which started off – I said: "Oh, this here has a really good beat." Then they break into this rap, or Debbie breaks into this rap.'

Fab Five Freddy told me everybody's fly
DJ spinning I said 'My, My'
Flash is fast, Flash is cool

'I'm like: "Wait a minute!" So I thought: "Oh, this is a complete joke." I thought they'd made a version of this record just as a joke to me.'

What Blondie had done was pay homage to the Bronx hip hop fraternity, expanding international interest in the phenomenon and securing a global chart-topper in the process. The record also paraphrased a rap about 'A Man From Mars' that Freddy had been tinkering with ('And out comes the man from Mars/And you try to run but he's got a gun/And he shoots you dead and he eats your head'). Grandmaster Flash was as delighted as anyone at his recognition in song.

'Freddy, who used to come to my parties all the time, was a good friend of Blondie. He had always told me that he would bring her to the Bronx, because she was interested in rap and, like: "Yeah, right." At the time she had "Call Me", big songs, gigantic superstar, you know. He said he was going to bring her, and one time he did and I got a chance to meet her. It was so cool. He kept his word. She was very nice. Next thing I know I heard this crazy rap record by her with my name in it. It was cool. Definitely. Of course, it opened the door to the pop audience. So it was all good.'

Released in January 1981, 'Rapture' became a US number one single on 28 March 1981, holding John Lennon's 'Woman' off the top spot. Fab Five Freddy returned the compliment by featuring 'Rapture' in his film *Wild Style*, which would shortly enter production, and for which Chris Stein would help provide music.

## ➤ Wild Style – *Hip Hop's Blackboard Jungle*

Charlie Ahearn's film *Wild Style* finally surfaced on cinema screens in 1983 although production began in 1981. A white film-maker, Ahearn was integrated into the hip hop culture by Fab Five Freddy, the real star of the movie.

'I told him the ideas that I had about this culture going on and how I was moving from graffiti into the art galleries, and how there was DJs and breakdancing. And he was like – "Really? Where?" So we decided to come together and started collaborating on the making of the film. I'm taking Charlie Ahearn deep into the Bronx, Upper Manhattan. He literally is the whitest face in the room and every time we go, I'm expecting, "Jesus Christ, Charlie's going to get murdered. I'm going to get murdered along with him."'

An attempt to chronicle the Bronx scene, *Wild Style* remains the best starting point for any student of old school hip hop, as Grandwizard Theodore recalls:

'I don't think nobody in the movie was acting. Everything was real, which was pretty cool. I think that's the only movie that you could look at and tell that, hey, this is real. Nobody's doing no acting once they say action.'

Flash, the 'guest star' of the film, remembers with fondness Ahearn's organic approach, which was accentuated by budget constraints.

'It was a small, low-budget film, first of its kind. He wanted to show the world what this was in its rawest form possible. No smoking mirrors, no tricks, no flash of brilliance, just see it in the raw. That film was important because that was the blueprint to what was real, although it was low budget. If you see anything else you can always refer back to this and see how Hollywood-ised everything might have been after the fact.'

One of the biggest production headaches was how to source music for the film without paying exorbitant fees. Fab Five Freddy happened upon a solution that made a virtue out of necessity.

'The idea of sampling was not on the face of the map yet, so we wanted to create the feel and the vibe of these particular records. Charlie was, rightly, very scared about just using this music because we had no money. "It's simple, I'll get some musicians together and we'll create little short snippets of music. Then we'll make up a small amount of these records and we'll give them to the DJs that we're going to feature in the film and these DJs will then create their own little mixes with our own original music." We basically went out and made these records that we would use in the film.'

Fab Five Freddy sees *Wild Style* as the point at which hip hop achieved some form of definition, its component elements registering an identity that was at once secular but interdependent.

'Graffiti art, breakdancing, rapping and DJing – it was revealed to everybody that these things are very similar in that they all come pretty much from the same place, meaning the same people, meaning urban heads in different parts of the city who tried to magnify their identities.'

Later Michael Holman took the *Wild Style* concept and turned it into a cable TV show, *Graffiti Rock*. An instant success, it eventually foundered on the resistance of corporate America.

'We got it on the air in eighty-eight markets. Kids loved it, it got incredible fan mail. But when we went to the National Association of Producers for Television Entertainment, this place where you go to sell your programme, two years in a row they refused to buy into this show. Their reasoning was that this was a passing fad, it was going to be dead in a year or two. Of course, they were wrong, but what are you gonna do?'

## ➤ Hip Hop Moves Downtown

Helped by impresarios like Fab Five Freddy and Michael Holman, as well as the mix tapes that were now circulating throughout New York, hip hop slowly began to move 'downtown'. One of the earliest ventures was a gathering at New York's trendy Mudd Club hosted by Fab Five Freddy.

'The Mudd Club was the mecca for the coolest heads. They allowed me to curate this exhibition. Alongside the exhibition, I put together a group of some of the dopest heads from the Bronx that were making it happen – Bambaataa, Cold Crush [Brothers], Fantastic [Four], Jazzy Jay, the Five MCs – and the crowd loved it. It was an overwhelming response to new records, new energy.'

Around this time Michael Holman was introduced to Malcolm McLaren, the legendary Sex Pistols manager, who was in America promoting his latest big idea, Bow Wow Wow. McLaren asked Holman to help him find out more about this new Bronx-based music. McLaren received a crash-course education not only in hip hop, but also urban New York life.

'There was going to be a big throwdown in the Bronx River Community Center up in West Bronx, thrown by Bambaataa, Jazzy Jay and a few other people. So I said, "Malcolm, I'm gonna show you something really amazing. You are going to get to see a new subculture emerging." Bambaataa had set up a turntable and he is playing his records. DJ Jazzy Jay, who was his right hand man at the time was scratching and spinning records. It was a big dance but it wasn't a big B-boy breakdancing scene. It was mainly the DJing and the music and kids partying. But true to the Bronx it was an incredible melee of insanity. People were having fights here and fights there. Glass bottles were being thrown out of windows. It was chaos, and I'd got Malcolm, this lily-white guy, behind the ropes to be with Bambaataa to experience this whole thing with the scratching, DJing and whatnot. He was petrified, looking round at this incredible chaos of urban insanity. It really was quite frightening. I was telling Malcolm [to] take a look at what the DJ is doing, and Malcolm was like: "Michael, we have got to get out of here." I was saying: "Malcolm, there is no way we are going to get out of here in one piece without their escort, so let's just chill. Watch what this guy Jazzy Jay is doing." Bambaataa wasn't a special effects DJ, Jazzy Jay was. Bambaataa would take really interesting soundtracks and whatnot and create these amazing things from TV shows and Kraftwerk. Jazzy Jay was a special mix DJ. And when Malcolm saw Jazzy Jay quick-cutting, and I believe there might have been a few breakdancers at the time doing something there, he was like: "Oh, my God! What is this?" We eventually got out of there [escorted by] Zulu Nation security guards. They got us out in one piece and put us in a cab and Malcolm was so jazzed by the whole thing — he was really, really turned on to it.'

As a result, McLaren asked Holman to arrange for Bambaataa to support Bow Wow Wow at their upcoming Ritz show. Holman finalised a 'Bronx revue' line-up featuring Bambaataa, Jazzy Jay and the Rock Steady Crew. He also screened a short film he'd produced, *Catch A Beat*, which predated *Wild Style* as first celluloid tribute to breakdancing.

## ➤ *Club Nights – From The Negril To The Roxy*

Working for McLaren at that time was one Ruza Blue, aka Cool Lady Blue, who subsequently occupied a pivotal role as a sponsor and advocate of old school New York hip hop, despite being an ex-pat white English punk. She immediately spotted the potential of this new movement with its extravagant sounds and visual flair.

'They did like a ten-minute skit before Bow Wow Wow. I saw them and that was my first taste of it. When I saw it I was just blown away. I just wanted to dig deeper and find out what else was behind whatever this was that I was seeing. Just what Bambaataa was playing as a DJ completely threw me off because he was mixing Aerosmith with Queen and James Brown and Bob Marley and doing all these crazy mixes with the records. Then seeing the breakdancers do all this crazy acrobatics and all these weird rhythmic dances was just mind-blowing.'

Cool Lady Blue was introduced to Afrika Bambaataa by Holman.

'This guy that looked like an African king, he has such an incredible presence, standing there with these turntables and just playing all this mind-boggling music. I just thought whatever it is that this guy is doing, I want to meet him. I want to know what all this is all about and I have to get involved. It was just a gut thing.'

'Bam' befriended her and took her to parties in the Bronx at venues like the Fever and Bronx River. There she met the other main players, including Grandmixer D.ST, Mister Magic and Fab Five Freddy — who christened her Cool Lady Blue. For the first time, she saw the hip hop culture working together in full flow — music, graffiti and breakdancing. Amazed, she announced she wanted to take the sound 'downtown'. Some artists, especially Grandmaster Flash, were initially cynical about their music's export value. Until they learned that she actually intended to pay them for their efforts.

Cool Lady Blue established her own club night at the Negril, a reggae venue on Second Avenue. As well as imported punk personalities from England like Kosmo Vinyl of the Clash, she booked several hip hop acts, employing old school B-boy and graffiti artist Phase Two to create flyers. Michael Holman cites the Negril, hip hop's first downtown venue, as an important staging post in its expansion.

'Not only was Negril possibly the first hip hop venue ever, but it was certainly the first time that this subculture was put before the downtown scene. You could dance all night. There would be Bambaataa and Jazzy Jay mixing records and bugging out watching these downtown kids with their green hair and orange hair, and there was this incredible clash of uptown and downtown kids. But it was instant love.'

As well as musical acts, the Negril became home to both the New York City Breakers and Floor Masters, both of whom battled against the Rock Steady Crew – led by Crazy Legs. However, the Negril was closed down after a few months because of fire restrictions. After running the club temporarily at (noted new wave venue) Danceteria, Cool Lady Blue happened on the Roxy, which became hip hop's new home.

'One night Freddy and I were just wandering around on the westside and he said: "Have you ever been to the Roxy?" And I was like: "No, what's the Roxy?" He took me there and I just bugged out! It was so cool, it was such a great space. It wasn't a dance club at that time, it was a skating rink. It took me about six months to convince the owner to give up the space to turn it into a dance club.'

Fab Five Freddy remembers the club's early growth.

'In the first few weeks at the Roxy, it was fun. The experiment was off, but it wasn't really successful yet. Blue had the idea of showing [Sex Pistols film] *The Great Rock 'n' Roll Swindle*, which a lot of the hip downtown heads had heard about but hadn't seen. So the cream of the downtown scene came out to see *The Great Rock 'n' Roll Swindle*. She's scheduled that a little bit earlier than the typical Roxy crowd would come, around 10pm or 11pm. So she showed the movie about 8pm. What happened was, after the movie, which was very interesting, a lot of the English and the downtown white folks didn't leave. And I knew in a minute all the uptown heads from the Bronx and Upper Manhattan were coming. Up until that point there hadn't been much of a mix of that type of scene. I think it was a treat for both groups of people, they were checking out a completely "other" cultural group, and that was really interesting. It was like two groups of people at a zoo looking at each other.'

From initial Friday night attendances of between 200 and 300 people, the crowds grew to ten times those numbers. New York celebrities flocked to the venue, including Madonna. Fab Five Freddy believes La Ciccone's initial look owed a lot to hip hop fashion.

'With the whole boy toy [look], with the belt buckle, all this was a blend of everything that was going on at the Roxy. You had like the Latin thing, you had the punk rock English thing, and you had a street thing. So she was a blend of that, culturally.'

While Bronx's Disco Fever incubated hip hop after opening its doors in 1978, it was never the type of venue which could attract a downtown crowd. The same was true of the Back Door (later the Dixie Club), another Flash haunt. Eventually the fame of Cool Lady Blue's club night, dubbed the Wheels Of Steel, spread beyond America, with journalists from Europe and Japan showing up to document New York's latest musical fashion. Throughout, Cool Lady Blue tried to stay true to hip hop's eclectic nature.

'The entertainment was also varied. I wouldn't just keep it to the hip hop culture. I would mix it, introduce dance elements. Madonna would perform. I had American Indians there one night performing, which was sort of interesting!'

### ➤ Bambaataa Throws Down Planet Rock

As other hip hop originals reached vinyl, there was movement from Bambaataa's corner. He had been dissatisfied with earlier, feeble attempts at recording, including two mix tapes for veteran R&B producer/breakbeat compiler Paul Winley. According to Fab Five Freddy, he was trying to 'time-capsule' the spirit of the Roxy.

'From that experience of him being in a room, dominated by young white new wave heads, people with weird haircuts, who were just super cool beyond belief — that inspired him to go and make a record called "Planet Rock", which kinda changed the whole state of the game.'

Bambaataa hooked up with Tom Silverman, a dance music journalist who would eventually found Tommy Boy Records. Through Silverman, Bambaataa met DJ Arthur Baker. He impressed on both his wish to record some 'black electronic' music, having become a huge fan of the Yellow Magic Orchestra and Kraftwerk.

'Me and Tom started going up to his father's house in White Plains and trying to create this new record that we was getting ready to call

"Planet Rock", giving him certain fills and grooves. Me and Tom was working on it, getting the groove, then I met this synthesizer player [John Robie]. I asked the guy: "Can you play like Kraftwerk?" He said: "Oh, I whip the butt off of those guys!" That's good enough for me, so I introduced him to Arthur Baker and Tom Silverman and the rest is history.'

'Planet Rock', the most sampled record in hip hop, was the first Bambaataa release to make full use of Soul Sonic Force, particularly the stuttering raps of G.L.O.B.E., whose 'MC popping' technique it premiered. Any music encyclopaedia will tell you of 'Planet Rock's' debt to Kraftwerk, but just as conspicuous is the use of Babe Ruth's 'The Mexican' (a version of Ennio Morricone's theme to Sergio Leone's *For A Few Dollars More* spaghetti western).

Cool Lady Blue remembers the impact 'Planet Rock' had on the scene.

'Oh, my God! "Planet Rock" was awesome. It was just like – explosion! It just took everything to another direction because here you had Kraftwerk and hip hop coming together which sort of symbolised what the club [The Roxy] was all about, because it sort of fused those two sensibilities together. So, yeah, it was like our anthem.'

'Planet Rock' successfully married two or more disparate genres of music and invented a new one – electro. Grandwizard Theodore emphasises the connection between 'Planet Rock' and the subsequent development of dance music.

'"Planet Rock" opened the doors for house music and freestyle music because the beat got faster. It really opened up a lot of doors.'

Hundreds of records, including memorable efforts by Planet Patrol, Warp 9 and Man Parrish, followed, picking up on Bambaataa's fascination with video arcades and electronica. New DJs, notably Madonna collaborator John 'Jellybean' Benitez, started to take this new electro sound downtown. Grandmaster Flash remembers how the impact of 'Planet Rock' rubbed the slate clean for conventional hip hop.

'With the introduction of electro funk – that became the B-boys' mainstay of music, electro funk.'

One of Bambaataa's chief collaborators on the 'Planet Rock' project, Jazzy Jay, head of the Jazzy Five, was a veteran of the park and block parties of the 70s.

'"Planet Rock" took me to a level where I was in people's faces that normally I would never see. I was in Europe, I was in Paris, so it took me to a level that made me understand the world and know that no matter where you go, everybody's still basically the damn same.'

In addition to electro, which ruled the hip hop clubs for a couple of years, Jay also attributes the development of Miami Bass to the success of 'Planet Rock'. Indeed, hip hop's influence is threaded throughout contemporary dance music. Breakbeats subsequently became the springboard for Detroit techno in the late 80s and early 90s. Ask Liam Howlett to assess his global dance phenomenon the Prodigy and he will inform you that it all boils down to breakbeats.

## ➤ Hip Hop International

With punks and white America exposed to hip hop, a degree of cross-fertilisation took place. Bambaataa updated his set lists to include songs from the B-52s, the Banshees and the Clash. The latter group, major rock stars of the day, returned the compliment in songs such as 'Magnificent Seven'. Following international magazine and newspaper coverage, Bambaataa took the opportunity to export hip hop abroad. France proved to be the most receptive audience, although breakdancing was netting youngsters worldwide. Kid Freeze remembers with relish the new-found opportunities for a talented breaker as he travelled the globe, working with everyone from Liberace to Run-D.M.C.

'I can always remember [my father] saying: "You're going nowhere with that dance, you start to do that dance and you're going nowhere." And the first thing that he saw me do, they flew me out to Florida and I did Miami 1984 Miss Universe Pageant with Tom Jones, his favourite star. I took a picture of him and he was so – "That's my son!" He was so happy. But, Dad, I thought I wasn't going nowhere with this dance . . .'

In 1983 Jennifer Beals starred in *Flashdance*, an unappealing big budget Paramount film set in Pittsburgh. It featured Crazy Legs of the Rock Steady Crew performing in the street. Even Hollywood was waking up to hip hop culture.

## ➤ Respectability & The Chairman Of The Board

Breakdancing fans included some unlikely figures, not least the late Frank Sinatra. The CBS Kennedy Center Honors was an annual TV extravaganza saluting those with distinguished careers in the arts. Holman was working with Harry Belafonte and the New York City Breakers on the film *Beat Street*. Belafonte was asked to pay tribute to Catherine Deneuve, the

choreographer, but refused, because Ronald Reagan was part of the ceremony. The New York City Breakers stepped in and devised a piece based
loosely on *West Side Story*. Frank Sinatra was also being honoured that
evening, and was smitten with their performance, which won a standing
ovation. As a result, when he hosted Reagan's inauguration two years later,
he asked the New York City Breakers to take part. As Holman recalls,
Sinatra's mood changed.

'Frank Sinatra had become really angry because the press had dissed
his son, saying: "Well, he's no Frank Sinatra, he's just Frank Sinatra Jnr and
actually the breakdancers were better than him." I was there talking to
Frank Sinatra and wishing him well and being quite obsequious and polite,
as you would be with the chairman of the board, when Tino [Tino "Action"
Lopez of the New York City Breakers] walks up, puts his hand on Frank
Sinatra's shoulder and says: "So, Frank, what did you think of the show?"
This is just after he had yelled at the press for saying that the breakers had
been better than his son. And I am thinking, this isn't happening. And Frank
Sinatra looks at me, with this smile on his face and says: "Your career is
over."'

The engine of hip hop's global appeal in the early 80s was breakdancing, as Michael Holman attests.

'It was B-boying or breakdancing that was the element of hip hop
that spearheaded that subculture into popular culture, into the eyes of the
world. It was B-boying and breakdancing that introduced hip hop in general
to the rest of the country and the rest of the world.'

The reason the importance of breakdancing has been superseded by
rappers, states Holman, is because of corporate America's inability to
market it.

'There was nothing really to package it with. There was no special
breakdancing shoes that you needed to buy to breakdance with. There was
no special breakdancing floor you needed to buy. You could just get a card-
board box. There was no special outfit. There was no special merchandise
or product or material that you needed to do this thing. Because there was
no special thing that you needed to buy as a kid who wanted to breakdance,
there were no companies there to sponsor it. Unlike skateboarding or BMX
bikes. BMX bikes and skateboards exploded and are still huge. They are
huge because you have companies who recognise that there are kids out
there who will buy $500 BMX special effects bikes, or who will buy $100
skateboards. [With breakdancing] there was no corporate sponsorship or
corporate backing that made it a viable thing for them to sell to the general
public.'

# chapter five

# hip hop gets the message

> ### It's Like A Jungle – The Story Of Sugarhill Records

Sylvia Robinson, flushed with the success of the Sugarhill Gang, produced 'Freedom' and 'Birthday Party' for new recruits Grandmaster Flash And The Furious Five. The breakthrough record, however, was 'The Adventures Of Grandmaster Flash On The Wheels Of Steel'. Highlighting Flash's quick-mixing skills, it was the first hip hop record to employ samples. Written by Duke Bootee, it set the scene perfectly for 'The Message', the first record to move rap away from simple party lyrics. There had been records with an agenda beyond the dancefloor previously. Kurtis Blow's 'The Breaks' was one example. Others included Sweet Tee's 'Vicious Rap' and, in particular, Brother D's 'How We Gonna Make The Black Nation Rise?', which attacked the Ku Klux Klan. But in terms of impact, 'The Message' was a seismic shift of emphasis.

The song was written by Duke Bootee, the Sugarhill percussionist and later solo artist, as Melle Mel recalls.

'He was the percussionist in the Sugarhill band, and he had "The Message" and he had a record called "Dumb Love". He wanted to do both records but thought that "The Message" would be better done by us, being that we was from the city. We had that tough edge. So she [Sylvia Robinson] thought that we would do the record better. She got us to do the record because she said that if he'd let us do "The Message", she would let him put out this record called "Dumb Love" and he went for it. She didn't just bring the record to us, she brought it to the Sugarhill Gang – I just found that out recently, because I was touring with them – they threw the tape away. None of us wanted to do the record, 'cos everybody was doing party music. So it was like, this is a little bit too serious, we don't know if our fans will get into something like this.'

Bootee, real name Edward Fletcher, a classically trained musician and sometime English teacher now studying for his doctorate, had just returned from England with Edwin Starr. Hip hop was an entirely new departure for him.

'I was walking down Broad Street. The record store had a sign in the window: "We sell 'Rapper's Delight'." So, I'm saying: "Well, they don't do that for a whole lot of records, what's this 'Rapper's Delight'?" So the guy who owned the record store, who I eventually became partners with in a business called Beauty and the Beat Records, he said: "Yeah, this is the biggest thing since cornflakes, this 'Rapper's Delight'." So he played it for me and I said: "Hey, man, that's [Chic's] 'Good Times' and just some guys talking over it." He said: "Yeah, but it's selling like hot cakes."'

Despite his initial consternation, Bootee ended up working at rap's first home, Sugarhill. By this time, Sylvia and Joe Robinson had set up a production line-styled enterprise, based on Berry Gordy's Motown model. The musicians included Jiggs Chase and Connecticut trio Skip McDonald, Keith LeBlanc and Doug Wimbish.

'What would happen is that people like Flash and some of the DJs and some of the rappers, Rodney C from Funky Four (Plus One), whoever, the informal leader of the group – we'd go to wherever the club was, Disco Fever, and they'd hear a song they liked and they'd bring it back to Sylvia or to the musicians. They'd say: "Look, we want to do this, but we don't want the whole song, we just want the dope part. That one part that the DJ plays over and over again." So we would take it and sort of bend it, change it enough, so that we didn't have to pay nobody. We would cut these tracks and a lot of times it was like what I heard Motown was like. Artists would be outside. We had two studios going. So the artist would literally be in the parking lot, waiting to hear tracks that we thought were hip.'

## ➤ Sugarhill's Engine Room

Keith Le Blanc first met Doug Wimbish and Skip McDonald in Dayton, when both were playing with a successful Connecticut group, Wood, Brass And Steel.

'We used to play a late night club called Leo's Welfare Disco in Newhaven, Connecticut. They called it Leo's Welfare Disco 'cos it was right next to the welfare office, and you could get in with either two dollars or some food stamps. I guess the place was totally illegal. It wasn't licensed and it was open all night and the whole inside of it was painted black, so you never knew what time it was. Rick [Weiner, Wood, Brass And Steel's manager] always went there. He would inevitably pick a girl to dance with. He would ask girls all night long till someone said yes. But what Rick called dancing looked like someone having an epileptic fit. We would just wait every night for him to get a girl out on the dancefloor, just for the laugh, 'cos it was just incredibly funny. The girls would always just run away, they'd think something was seriously wrong with him. So he was about to do his mating dance when we heard "Rapper's Delight" come over the system. Rick didn't even exist any more. The record was a shock, and Doug immediately looked at me and said: "That's an All Platinum record." All Platinum was Sylvia Robinson's record company before it was Sugarhill Records. So we immediately went over to the DJ booth to have a look at the label on the record. It didn't say All Platinum, but Sylvia's name was on it for producing. Harold [Sargent, previous Wood, Brass And Steel drummer] had come by about two weeks earlier and wanted Skip and Doug to go up to All Platinum Records, 'cos Sylvia had called him looking for Skip and Doug. I heard the words recording studio and money and records on the radio, and I was dying to go. But Skip and Doug didn't want any part of it, 'cos I guess they'd had a bad experience there before.'

Doug Wimbish maintains that Sylvia Robinson had a soft spot for Skip and himself, following their work with All Platinum. But he was wary of re-committing to her new label.

'In August of 1979 I got re-involved with them. They had already recorded "Rapper's Delight", which was cut by a band called Positive Force, and Sylvia Robinson had been calling my house to try to reach us. We were with the label, then we left, and the only number she had was my number. So she tried to call us to cut this song, and I wouldn't take her call. It was a lot of history from before, and I was like: "No, this is the place I wanna be right now." But she kept calling. Keith LeBlanc had never been in the studio before. He heard "recording studio" and was like: "You guys got somebody calling you up to talk about they wanna record, let's go! I'll drive you down there."'

Nevertheless, the impact of 'Rapper's Delight' forced his partners to reassess, according to Le Blanc.

'When we saw this new record with Sylvia's name on it, all of a sudden going up there looked a little better. So we went up there and that's how we got started with Sugarhill. It wasn't very long before we were playing together that we became the house band there.'

While Wimbish and McDonald knew the Robinsons of old, Le Blanc was not too sure what to expect.

'I remember hearing stories the whole drive up to Sugarhill, when finally everybody had decided we were gonna go there. Everybody was telling old stories. I didn't know quite what to expect. And we went up there and didn't meet Sylvia right away. We walked in the door and met a guy named Nate Edmonds who used to play with Jimi Hendrix. That was his claim to fame. Nate knew Skip and Doug from before. He immediately starts saying to them: "Everything's changed. Sylvia's found the Lord. Whole new thing here now." Which I thought was a bit weird. We went into the studio and then we met Billy Jones, who played in several of the bands that were on All Platinum Records. He was one of these guys that played every-thing. He was engineering the session, and he liked me because I hit the drums hard. After we recorded a few things, Sylvia came walking into the studio. I remember Billy Jones was just going on and on about how great we were and how the white boy was really good – I got used to the name "white boy". It was just something that was easy to call me, 'cos no one really knew my name at that point. Sylvia didn't say much and we said our hellos and goodbyes and she took Skip and Doug away for a chat. Then I went outside and waited in the car with a guy named Craig who did a lot of vocal work at All Platinum and then Sugarhill. So we sat out there for a while and then Skip and Doug came out. The reason why she had a chat with them in private was 'cos she wanted to pay me less, 'cos I wasn't "down", so to speak. Skip and Doug stuck up for me, fortunately, and we got paid $300 each for a couple of tracks. I mean we were broke when we went up there so $300 was great for doing something I loved.'

Many artists, both at the time and subsequently, would bemoan Sugarhill for underpaying them or not paying them at all. But Duke Bootee is philosophical about the remuneration.

'It's like a jungle, sometimes. I look at my training, my four years at Sugarhill, as being sort of the Harvard of the music business. You were working for people who had been around quite a while. There wasn't an overabundance of money being paid out, shall we say. But there's an oppor-tunity to get in the producer's chair, to get in the writer's chair, to learn more. I was one of these people that every time I went in the studio, I wanted to learn something new.'

Rodney C of the Funky Four is less charitable.

'I have to tip my hat to them in one respect, they were a label that actually gave us the opportunity to make a rap record and have inter-national fame and whatever. But on the other hand they fucked us off, straight up and down. They were just crooks. Not only did they take our money, they took our spirit. They sucked us dry. We were the sacrificial lambs that went into their slaughterhouse and they slaughtered us.'

One of the attractions for Le Blanc was that he could record something and hear it playing on the radio within a few days of the session.

'They were really incredible at getting a record out quickly, probably the fastest I've ever seen. The major record companies didn't have a clue as to what was going on. They were all panicking, trying to get a handle on it. It was a pretty amazing time, if I think back on it now.'

Le Blanc believes that the reason the Robinsons were so keen to get Doug and Skip on the payroll was because, in the early months of 1980, they needed an album to capitalise on the Sugarhill Gang's success.

'That's why I think Sylvia was looking for Skip and Doug. So we immediately started recording some things. Sylvia didn't have anything written down so it was basically wanting us to write the tunes by playing in the studio. So no one was really giving up anything good. Consequently the album was just a pile of garbage, but it sold like crazy. It was such a massive hit it really didn't matter. And then they put us on the road forever. We were supposed to go out for a week and we ended up being out for a year before we came home again. The first gig we did was in Harlem World and I was pretty excited to play there. It's like a dream come true for me, coming from Connecticut, and the best musicians in the world came from there.'

The Sugarhill Gang were a hot commodity. At one performance in Washington a near-riot occurred as punters desperately tried to gain entrance to the oversubscribed venue. But that was a long way from being Le Blanc's worst experience.

'One of the first rap gigs ever, where they had all the crews from New York, Skip McDonald dubbed it "the 145th Street Massacre". It was held at the 145th Street armoury and it was really the first big rap gig where they had Grandmaster Flash, the Furious Five, Sugarhill Gang, 'cos by this time it had progressed. They had Sequence which were these girls from South Carolina, the first girl rap group. 20-20, the TV programme, was filming it. It was a big deal. And we made the mistake of playing a ballad. I don't know what we did that for. I think one of the groups wanted to play a ballad but we should have never done that. All of a sudden you hear: BANG! BANG! BANG! Could have been firecrackers, could have been a gun. But all you could see was people breaking from the back of the auditorium, coming forward. Skip and Doug, they didn't even turn around, they just yanked their guitar cords out and ran for the dressing room and I was still playing. By this time the crowd was completely madness, so I jumped under the drum riser. Ed Fletcher was under there, alias Duke Bootee, and he had a little .22 pistol he used to carry with him. I don't think he's ever

65

used it, but he had it. And there was a girl under there as well, that somehow climbed up from the stage. I remember asking Fletcher: "What are we gonna do?" And Fletcher said: "What do you mean *we*?" Afterwards all you could see was shoes, people's clothes, you know, everywhere. It was just a massacre.'

Not the least of the problems attending the Sugarhill Gang's backing band was suspicion and outright hatred from established R&B musicians.

'The only band we got along with was Parliament/Funkadelic. We got along great with them, but everyone else was always trying to do us in. Cameo, the Gap Band, all these bands, things would happen to us like the power cord would be cut in the middle of a performance, or the house lights would come on. Stuff like that would happen. It was sabotage, 'cos those gigs, it was really serious competition for who was gonna rock the crowd. And with a hit like we had and the genre being a pure vocal thing that anybody could do, it just took all the stuffing out of the audience. By the time the rest of the bands came on to play, the headliners, the audience had nothing left.'

While Joe Robinson ran the business end of Sugarhill, Sylvia adopted a hands-on approach to producing and nurturing the music, according to Hank.

'People don't know how much time she spent in working for their diction, so at least it could be understood somewhere. You know, she did a lot of polishing.'

You'll get a different answer should you ask Doug Wimbish what he made of the couple.

'Do you really want me to answer that question? Well, they were businessmen. They were black entrepreneurs. There's a lot of talent that existed between Joe and Sylvia Robinson. Joe was a very streetwise businessman. He had a nightclub that he ran and other organisations that he was involved with, and Sylvia was an artist. They were very aware of what was happening with the record business, with the industry. Joe and them realised: "Look, let's give our stuff an independent vibe, so that we can actually monitor and assess all the different funds thats coming in towards us." And that's exactly what they did.'

In terms of personalities, Wimbish remembers how well they complemented each other

'As far as people, Joe's a very raw person, very streetwise, very point blank. You deal with Joe Robinson, dealing with anybody else is like eating cheese – a very, very interesting person and a very strong personality. Sylvia Robinson, on the other hand, has that same magic, yet knows how to put together the right people at the right time, and knew how to disband the right people at the right time. She was truly a work of art.'

Wimbish remembers the feeling generated when Grandmaster Flash and his crew came to Sugarhill's studios for the first time.

'They were the real goods. Finally, the real goods were coming to the plate. Grandmaster Flash was a whole different ball game compared to anybody else that had been at Sugarhill, anybody. They were the real deal. Flash would thrash everybody, nobody could even come close to what they were doing. They had stage charisma. Melle Mel was one of the baddest rappers on the planet. They had steps, the whole crew, and the look. They were geniuses on stage, they'd thrash anybody. When we cut "Freedom", which was the first record we cut for them, that record took off so big. All they needed was a start and they just turned into a snowball effect. It was unbelievable, amazing the energy that Flash and 'em had live. Two turntables, no band. It was good for us, 'cos we were the band for them.'

## ➤ Don't Push Me, 'Cos I'm Close To The Edge

The development of 'The Message' was a good example of Sylvia Robinson's benevolent touch when it came to Sugarhill's 'creatives', as Duke Bootee notes.

'I had done an African-sounding track, beating [the rhythm] out on a bottle. Sylvia said: "Well, try to get a little hook for that track." I had come up with – "It's like a jungle, sometimes it makes me wonder, how I keep from going under" – 'cos it gave it that feverish, jungle feel. So I took that verse and that hook that she liked and put it over a new track, which was more commercial.'

Bootee added the verses about broken glass in the neighbourhood, which Sylvia loved, and laid down a reference vocal track. Then Sylvia took it to Grandmaster Flash's rappers. According to Bootee, they were universally reticent.

'She tried all of them, Rahiem, Cowboy, Melle, Creole, all of them tried it. They were so into their style of rapping that they couldn't get with it, and they didn't like it: "This record ain't gonna sell, don't nobody want to bring their problems to the disco. We're a party group, we about being nasty and having parties." Sylvia believed in the track. She knew something was there. So after they were fed up and didn't want to do it, Melle came back to me and said: "Man, I got a verse that seems like it just go right with that record." I said: "Well, what is it?" He went into – "A child is born with no state of mind, Blind to the ways of mankind." I said: "That's it, that's the close! I love it!" So we ran it by Sylvia and she said: "Yeah, I like that." She recognised that it had been on "Super Rappin'" [previous Furious Five single for Enjoy]. So she talked to Bobby Robinson, did whatever she had to do and cleared it.'

'The Message' also featured other innovations, according to Bootee.

'I did everything but play the guitar, which Skip [McDonald] did. That was the first record that we used the drum machine on. It was the first record that was bass synthesizer instead of Doug [Wimbish] on bass. It was a change from what we'd been cutting at the time and kind of foretold what was going to happen in the future.'

Melle, for one, was amazed at the success generated by 'The Message'.

'When she put the record out, it turned out being the biggest record at that time. It took rap into a totally different dimension. Like the first kind of hardcore rap and street rhymes, and talking about the ghetto and whores and pimps. So it took rap into another dimension. That record made the whole hardcore scene. It was the turning point for everything and it came from a record that nobody even wanted to do.'

Flash had little involvement in the recording, despite his name adorning it. According to Wimbish, that was a jolt for him.

'What that record did was cause a little bit of a rift between Grandmaster Flash and the label. That was one of the first records where it wasn't all Flash on there, in fact Flash isn't even on the record.'

Despite his reservations, Flash was still pleased with the final product.

'The record just opened up another viable subject matter that you can talk about, as opposed to just party records. It was totally the other side, which a lot of people, to our surprise, was very interested in.'

However, this political awakening, he thought, should remain only one branch of hip hop's growth.

'It's important that you have rhymes that talk about social commentary, it's important to have rhymes that talks about bullshit and life. It's all about the beauty of hip hop. There are no constraints with this art form.'

While some reacted immediately to the scope and challenge of 'The Message', others were initially non-plussed. Jazzy Jay:

'"The Message" was a puzzle to everybody when it first came out. It was like they're putting out a slow song at a time where everything is kind of upbeat, uptempo, whatever. But the content of "The Message" is what caught everybody. Melle Mel was one of those lyricists supreme.'

Nelson George, at this time black music editor at *Billboard* magazine, recalls the impact of 'The Message'.

'[There was] still a lot of scepticism by the mainstream about this hip hop thing. I got "The Message" in the office on a Thursday or Friday, and I put it on the turntable. We had a little listening room. I was like: "Wow! Listen to this!" I was going around to all of the white writers – "You got to hear this record!" A couple of them really got it, because it was sophisticated, powerful social commentary in hip hop and it just hadn't been done before. It spoke very powerfully for what was going on underneath Reagan's America. It spoke for that other kind of economy that was beginning to develop underneath the Wall Street boom.'

'The Message' not only connected with black audiences, but mainstream America, as Melle notes.

'"Don't push me, 'cos I'm close to the edge, I'm trying not to lose my head" – At that time, anybody could have said that. At that time, half the people in America probably wanted to say that.'

Although the creative force behind the record was Bootee, and, to a small extent, Sylvia Robinson, Bootee acknowledges its impact wouldn't have been the same without Grandmaster Flash And The Furious Five's name to promote it.

'I think that a smash happens when you have the right track, the right lyric with the right act, and at the time I think all of those things came together and we were able to benefit by that confluence of effects.'

## ➤ Stars On 45

Flash and the Furious Five became bona fide stars, feted throughout America, touring with everyone from the Commodores and Cameo to U2. They responded by sticking to rock 'n' roll convention and shoving most of the profits up their nose. Melle Mel:

'We was hanging out downtown, got into that drug culture kind of thing. We was up at Danceteria. You see somebody like Billy Idol. He's on one side of the bar doped up and we're on the other side of the bar, coked up. That was because of "The Message". We crossed over. We was hanging out with all the stars over in the Roxy, in the back rooms, doing drugs with the owner or whatever.'

Doug Wimbish noticed the changes that success engendered at Sugarhill, and within the Grandmaster Flash camp.

'A lotta cats were doing a lotta drugs. Everybody was getting high, which was taking the focus off a lotta things. Cocaine was a very big thing at that time, there was a snowball happening. There's tons of coke all over, not so much in the studios, but cats were started to get involved in things that would take away from the creative flow. At that particular point it started getting a little scary and everybody started getting angsty. They started losing the plot. "The Message" was so big, and it was just Melle Mel doing it. That created some tension. And like all groups, it's hard for one person to walk in a straight line, never mind seven. Everybody wanted to get their stuff out. Melle had a record, so I'm quite sure it was: "Well, you know what? I wanna do a record now." So Flash ended up doing "The Adventures of Grandmaster Flash On The Wheels of Steel" – that was Flash's own separate thing. Then Scorpio did a record. Sylvia did that probably to keep everybody cool, but in the process of doing that it separated the people. They were doing individual things as opposed to collective things.'

With success, alongside status and money, came debates over who was entitled to what. By 1984 internal friction had splintered Grandmaster Flash and Melle Mel. A problem the latter attributes largely to bad management.

'If we just had a bit of good management, top-flight management and a good agent. We wouldn't have been as big as the Rolling Stones, but we could have got close, because we had all the elements. We had the people, we had the charisma, we had a good stage show. It was just a couple of things that we was missing and we could have went to the Moon.'

Flash quit the band, taking Rahiem and Kid Creole with him, and attempted to sue Sugarhill. Scorpio and Cowboy stuck with Melle Mel and appeared on his subsequent recordings. Melle remained at Sugarhill because of what he terms 'ambition'. Sugarhill may or may not have been under-paying its artists, but Melle had a firm rationale for staying.

'The money thing was kind of secondary to the hits, 'cos I knew that if you make enough hits, you'd lose less money. So I was the one that, whatever it is, let's just make this next hit. Let's just keep the ball rolling like that. Don't shut it down, because once we shut it down, somebody's going to take your spot anyway. And then that's what happened.'

Flash, according to Melle, was also aggrieved at the loss of status for DJs as the stock of rappers rose.

'At one time his name was known all over the world, just from being on a record that he didn't even do nothing on. He should be happy. He should be walking around with a gold record on his chest or something. He should be happy.'

Before the upheaval, however, one further classic single was released – 'White Lines (Don't Do It)'. It was, claims Melle Mel, largely autobiographical.

'That was just me trying to stay ahead of the game. At that time, nobody was really talking about drugs and nothing like that, and everybody was into it. It was like the counter-culture of what rap was. You're a star, you got bitches and you can sniff coke. You give girls coke and you have sex with them, so that's what the whole game was all about. You go in the back of the Fever, sniff some coke, get a broad, take her to a hotel. That was the whole game. Turns out to be a good record, though.'

Sugarhill, too, bowed out of rap music, as it was superseded by new labels like Tommy Boy, who got their start with 'Planet Rock', Profile and Def Jam.

'They just figured if you make a good record, you're going to have a nice run. Up to a point, that was true. After Run-D.M.C. and them came out, it wasn't true. It was about videos and MTV. So the same thing that happened to Herc actually happened to Sugarhill.'

As much as the Sugarhill Gang, Grandmaster Flash, Afrika Bambaataa et al. were hip hop's first stars, Run-D.M.C. were, to use the correct vernacular, about to take it to another level.

# walk this
# way

# queens takes the throne

> ## Kings Of Rock – Run-D.M.C.

Others had laid strong foundations, but if one group was responsible for introducing hip hop to the mainstream of rock and pop culture, it was Run-D.M.C. Darryl 'DMC' McDaniels, Joe 'Run' Simmons and DJ Jam Master Jay (Jason Mizell) graduated together from St Pascal's Catholic School. DMC remembers the day he first heard hip hop.

'I remember clearly. I think it was maybe 1977 or 1978. I was in elementary school. It was a disc jockey who was on WFUV. His name was Eddie Cheeba and he had a radio show. I couldn't really receive it that well from my basement. I think it was AM radio. He used to play records and rap on them, talk and play R&B on his little radio show. What really caught me about rap, the first time I heard rap, was he said –

When you're messing round in New York town
You go down with the disco Cheeba clown
You go down, you go down, go down, go down
Now you keep the pep inside your step
Don't stop, don't stop, till you get on the mountain top.

Then he had a little round where he would do the call letters of the station, WFUV. That was the first time that I heard it. Prior to that, I'd hear people around me, basically the older guys, the eighth-graders and the high school kids, saying this rhyme of Eddie Cheeba.'

Via the widespread circulation of mix tapes, Queens was growing familiar with developments in hip hop's Bronx homeland. The ingenuity of founding fathers such as Grandmaster Flash was gaining widespread recognition. However, in common with other embryonic New York hip hop markets, Queens was also developing an indigenous scene and identity.

75

DMC, taking refuge in his basement, sought to emulate what he heard on these semi-legal recordings.

'I was a local DJ in my basement. I took my mother's turntable and brought another turntable and a mixer, and I used to just wanna emulate Flash and be Flash. I used to call myself Grandmaster Get High. I used to buy all the breakbeats that I heard on a Flash tape or a Theodore tape, go down in my basement and spin the record back for hours. Then came "Super Sperm", and I started learning about James Brown's "Funky Drummer", all these records. "Whoa, what's these beats and what's these sounds?" It came across rougher and darker and denser, and more real to me. All I wanted to do was be a DJ better than Grandmaster Flash. At that time my partner, Run, he was called "The Son of Kurtis Blow". Kurtis Blow was popular at the same time as Afrika Bambaataa, Flash and them. But Kurtis Blow was more of the showman-type rapper. Well, they wasn't rappers back then, it was MCs – Kurtis Blow, DJ Hollywood, DJ Flowers, Lovebug Starski. These were MCs that were coming to rock the party, [saying] "Throw your hands in the air" and "Toot on a horn, ring on a bell". They would come and excite the crowd.'

DMC taught Run how to manipulate the record decks. As a result, Run gravitated to becoming Kurtis Blow's DJ as well as warm-up act.

'Kurtis Blow used to call Run out at eleven years old. Run used to come and DJ for Kurtis Blow after I taught him how to DJ. And he used to rock on the mic. But me and Run went to the same elementary school, so when we started hanging out he would bring tapes to the shows that he was doing. It wasn't till I started hearing factions of Afrika Bambaataa, Zulu Nation . . . It was different from the rappers of "clap your hands and stomp your feet, get on down to the rhythm of the funky beat". It was more street to me. And when I heard the Funky Four (Plus One) and Sha Rock, who was a female, they really inspired me into this style that I picked up. I started realising that when Flash and the Sugarhill Gang started making their records, that's commercial. Even though Funky Four made records on Sugarhill and Enjoy Records, their tapes were completely different. I started realising: this is the real, this is what I wanna be.'

After hearing the Funky Four, DMC switched to MCing and began to write his first simplistic rhymes.

Apple to a peach, cherry to a plum
Don't stop rocking till you all get some
Get on the mic and all get dumb
Queens is where I'm from.

For DMC, part of the appeal of hip hop lay in its rebuttal of gang culture. It provided an arena in which to battle for regional pride without using fists or weaponry, as institutionalised by Afrika Bambaataa. For him, the gang threat was as true of Queens as it was the Bronx.

'The thing that was in my neighbourhood was the Black Skulls and the Black Spades and the Seven Crowns and all these names. All these names and those personas became these rapping DJ groups. It flipped into something positive. It changed it. When it came out, the gangs disappeared. I was too young to notice that but then as I look back, I just know there was a point when I got to sixth grade, I didn't hear about the gangs no more. But in fifth grade: "Oh, don't go up there, that's the Black Spades." We got colours and all of that stuff going on in New York. And Afrika Bambaataa, he was really instrumental in saying: "No, we're gonna be the Zulu Nation and we're gonna stop fighting and killing each other and we're gonna do something constructive and we're gonna have fun."'

Before hip hop, even in suburban areas like Queens, youngsters had to watch their step.

'Back then in the fifth grade: "Watch out for the Black Skulls. They might come and take your Adidas off you." Ghetto street gangs would take your new sneakers. They'd rough you up, take your lunch money, take your Kangol, take your warm-up suit. You'd be standing naked, coming home from school. Gotta get on the bus with all the people looking at you, naked, 'cos a gang robbed you.'

DMC found an outlet for his new interests in school.

'In English class, our teacher used to give us five minutes just to write, draw and be creative. I just used to write in rhymes. I used to just fill my books with rhymes and rhymes. When the teacher would check them, he would pull me out in the hall: "What is this? Where's this stuff coming from?" I'm like: "I'm an MC," and this and that.'

One particular tape, according to DMC, sparked local interest in hip hop, and crystallised what he wanted to do with his overflowing poetry books.

'The Cold Crush Brothers – the way they put their rhymes and routines together for this battle, the way they presented themselves . . . To this day, that tape sits in my drawer, and it's my most prized possession. The way that tape went around, the way people said – "You heard the Cold Crush?" That was the biggest moment in rap history, in hip hop history, rocking the mic and DJing. It was at a time where the rappers, the MCs, wanted to get into showmanship. They would dress up in tuxedos or they would dress up in leather and all that stuff that Grandmaster Flash, Afrika Bambaataa and them did. I'm not knocking them because that's what they did at the time, but what made Run-D.M.C. so different when we started – we took what they used to do on the tapes and in the parks and we put that on records. And we didn't rap over R&B records.'

Russell Simmons, elder brother of Joe 'Run' Simmons and Run-D.M.C.'s manager, credits the band with re-establishing authenticity as a prerequisite of hip hop.

'The thing about them was that there was no theatrics. A lot of the artists were theatrical. Their good point was, it was accentuated so much that it made it unreal and it was bigger than life, that was the concept. Whereas rap came from a more honest perspective and attitude. It was a representation of the rest of the community. What Run-D.M.C. did that was special, they made costumes out of their regular, everyday outfits. That leather suit that they wore was a suit that they wore in Hollis Avenue in Queens. That gave them an edge. Authenticity always sells, not over any short time, but when people get it and once it's really appreciated, it sells for a longer period of time. It's appreciated, 'cos it really touches a person. Run-D.M.C. brought the honest hip hop kind of street attitude to rap.'

The group were impatient to record. But Russell Simmons was more cautious, as DMC recalls.

'Run would always say: "Russell, let me make a record, let me make a record." Russell had enough sense to know this thing could end any night – "You're not doing nothing until you get out of high school, because if you put a record out, you gotta have a diploma." So as soon as Run got out of high school, has the diploma, he starting making demos. Russell was gonna have us be in a group called the OK Crew, because that was the thing at the time, you wanted to be a "crew". When Russell named us Run-D.M.C., it sounds cool now, but nobody will ever feel what me and Run felt. "The name of y'all is Run-D.M.C." "Oh, Russell, you're gonna ruin us. We wanna be the Sure Shot Two or the Funky Two or the Devastating Two. Oh, man, Run-D.M.C. . . . ." And we're crying like babies.'

Another of Russell Simmons's concerns had been DMC's voice, which he didn't rate.

'He didn't think I had an MC voice like Kurtis Blow or [DJ] Hollywood or even Run. One thing about Run, to this day his voice never changed. The way he sounded when he was eleven, he sounds now. But Russell didn't like my style.'

Luckily for DMC, his rhyming partner Run was not only loyal, but shared his devotion to 'real' hip hop.

'Once God blessed us with the ability and the privilege of hearing the Cold Crush Brothers, we was like: "Yo, we gotta do that. We're not gonna do nothing fake. We ain't doing nothing commercial. No producer is telling us how to rap and what to rap about.'"

After rejections from several major record labels, Russell Simmons finally hooked them up with Profile Records, who signed Run-D.M.C. for $2,500 and released their debut single, 'It's Like That'. As bluntly thrilling as that song was (it later became a UK number one when remixed by Jason Nevins), it was the b-side that took radio by storm. 'Sucker M.C.s', which first aired on Michael Holman's *Graffiti Rock* cable show, married abrasive rhymes to a harsh, elemental beat. An attempt to harness the power of the hip hop mix tape, the resulting sonic crunch was revolutionary. The rap party record, its rhymes bedecking deep-grooved disco and funk breaks, was instantly supplanted with dynamics based squarely on rock 'n' roll beats.

'At that time, "The Message" was a big record. Being from suburban New York, a middle-class neighbourhood, we had good values in us. So we wrote this record called "It's Like That And That's The Way It Is". It was optimistic and pessimistic. It was good and bad. And that was written out of "The Message" and "Planet Rock" combined. It wasn't a thing where we did it to please anybody. We just made this record called "It's Like That" because we knew the various styles that was out there. But the b-side was me and Run's chance to get what we liked from the [mix] tapes on a record. That was the turning point, 'cos every rapper when "Sucker M.C.'s" came out – I get amazed – 'cos when I watch documentaries and stuff, they say their turning point was "Sucker M.C.'s". It flipped the whole thing. It made way for all the great lyrics and beats of the rappers of the 80s.'

The single announced Run-D.M.C.'s sound – sparse, insistent, pummelling – and promptly took over the airwaves. Record buyers' perceptions and expectations of hip hop were short-circuited once again.

'Russell would just look at us and say: "Oh, do you know what we got here?" "It's Like That" was charting on all the radio stations across the United States, but bubbling under in all the ghettos and all the streets and all the parties and stuff was "Sucker M.C.'s".'

Run-D.M.C. pioneered the rock/rap crossover with songs like 'Rock Box', from their debut, and 'King Of Rock', the title-track of their 1985 follow-up album. Both featured the guitar playing of Eddie Martinez, an occasional associate of Blondie. DMC remains proudest of the video for 'King Of Rock', which featured the band staging a mock assault on the rock 'n' roll hall of fame, and effecting their own brand of irreverent chaos once inside.

'Busting into a museum with the guard standing there, saying: "You guys can't come in here!" And stepping on Michael Jackson's glove, and Jerry Lee Lewis, and dissing all the icons and symbols that made rock 'n' roll great like the Beatles. Elvis is not the king no more, we are.'

## ➤ MTV Opens Its Doors

It was the 'King Of Rock' video which saw hip hop gain access to MTV, a music broadcaster founded in August 1981 which was heavily criticised for its resistance to even the tamest of black pop songs. The station agreed to air Michael Jackson's videos only after his record company, Epic, threatened to pull their entire roster from the channel. Russell Simmons, however, decided against joining the pickets outside MTV, led by artists like Rick James.

'I didn't want to be part of that whole negative vibe. I mean we worked kind of hard on MTV, it's true, at making them appreciate what we did. But at the time we were "soft" enough to appreciate what they could do for us.'

Ted Demme, now a successful film director, started his career with MTV in the mid-80s. He defends the station's position, suggesting that if there was a colour ban, it operated because record companies weren't allowing their black artists the finance to make decent videos.

'MTV got slagged, I think wrongly, for not playing black music. But at that time there weren't that many great black videos out, because black artists weren't getting the cash to do videos. Pre-1985 the exceptions were Cameo's "Word Up", Michael Jackson and Prince and probably Diana Ross. You had to be a big name to get on MTV. The videos didn't have to be great because God knows back then the videos weren't that great anyway, but they just were sub-par. And that's because they weren't getting the cash from the labels.'

Hip hop wasn't entirely invisible on MTV pre-Run-D.M.C. 'Rockit', Grandmixer D.ST's 1983 collaboration with Herbie Hancock, was aired regularly by the station. But Run-D.M.C. played their part by offering rap records that were sufficiently rock-orientated to appeal to the broadcaster. Russell Simmons:

'MTV had this belief that all they could play was rock 'n' roll and they forgot that the black community created rock 'n' roll. What they meant by "only rock 'n' roll" was there was no black people. By the time we came along they had broken down that door and there was Michael Jackson. Michael Jackson, of course, doesn't represent the same kind of attitude. Run-

D.M.C. was like the anti-Michael Jackson. Their whole rap was about keeping it real and Michael Jackson was the last real thing in the world. But Run-D.M.C.'s honesty and their street authenticity crossed boundaries and went into places like rock clubs, mod clubs, the Peppermint Lounge, the Ritz, all those clubs.'

DMC soon found that, through tracks like 'Rock Box' and 'King Of Rock', they had acquired a whole new audience.

'White kids loved this. We played so many rock 'n' roll clubs back in '82, '83 and '84, it was ridiculous. Long-haired white kids, cut-off jeans, drunk . . .'

To author Nelson George, MTV made Run-D.M.C hip hop's first icons.

'I think the argument can be made that Run-D.M.C. serves the same purpose for hip hop that Chuck Berry did for rock 'n' roll and that the Supremes did for Motown. They were the artists who confirmed this was something powerful, something with longevity, something special. Not only did they have these qualities, but they can appeal to everyone, and Run-D.M.C. opened up tons of doors. They opened up the video doors at MTV, they opened up the airplay doors at certain rock stations.'

## ➤ Walk This Way

Run-D.M.C. were well on their way to becoming the first superstars of rap. Their eponymous 1984 debut had been the first gold-certified rap album. A year later *King Of Rock* repeated the trick. The trio toured furiously, joining Kurtis Blow, Whodini and the Fat Boys as part of the Fresh Fest package. The only thing the band lacked was what the industry loves to call a 'crossover single'. For *Raising Hell*, the group's third album from 1986, Rick Rubin was drafted in as producer.

'I produced the album *Raising Hell*. I had done a little bit of work with them on their album before that [*King Of Rock*]. I think I played guitar on a song or two, just as a friend and fan hanging out. They were my favourite band, and the idea of some day getting to work with them was a dream of mine. Based on the records I was making and how much Russell loved the records, he asked me to do Run-D.M.C. with them, which was great. We had a great time and that was the record that really broke them. I think their record before that probably sold about a million copies, and the record we did sold about five million copies, so four million was a big jump. It had the Run-D.M.C. duet with Aerosmith, "Walk This Way", which was really an afterthought. The entire record was done and I really wanted to do something different and special to add to it. I was going through my record collection trying to find a song, because in those days people didn't think of rap music or hip hop even as music.'

Rubin maintains that he had to introduce Run-D.M.C. to the idea of doing 'Walk This Way' gently.

'I remember playing the song for them and they were familiar with the intro because of the beat, which they used to rap over. Jam Master Jay would cut the intro, but none of them had ever heard the actual song. All they knew was that intro drum beat. I said: "We should do this song." I remember it was met with some question at first, but then they listened to it and wrote all the words down and started thinking: "We can do this. Let's do this." And then we recorded the track. The Aerosmith guys came down and played the guitars. Then Steven [Tyler, Aerosmith vocalist] sang his chorus vocals first and then Run did the rhymes and then Steven joined in. We did it all in a day and everyone had a great time and it was really a good experience.'

DMC was already familiar with 'Walk This Way' as a breakbeat song.

'"Walk This Way" was the beat that Theodore would use, Grandmaster Flash would use it. All the DJs had that in a crate.'

However, that was the extent of his knowledge. Rubin's suggestion was, indeed, met with some question at first.

'Rick said go home and learn Steven Tyler's vocals. We put the record on. Understand, me and Run had never heard the record past the drumbeat, never heard those vocals.'

When they heard the lyrics, they were horrified.

'We called Rick on the phone. "Yo! This is hillbilly, gibberish bullshit! You're trying to ruin Run-D.M.C., everyone's going to laugh at us." He said: "Calm down, y'all got to do this record." So we said, all right . . . Jam Master Jay said a simple thing. "Go in there and do it like Run-D.M.C. would do it." Then it worked . . . Even after we made the record, we went home mad. Me and Run didn't really care about that record or nothing . . . I don't care about bringing white people and black people together. I just want to be dope on the mic.'

DMC stands by the record, but is concerned it shouldn't overshadow the group's other achievements.

'We already had MTV in our grasp. "Walk This Way" came and just grabbed the world. It wasn't nothing new to us, but everybody started flipping. There was a couple of critics who said: "They wanna cross over now."

Even to this day, I could come out to Britain tomorrow and they'll say: "Was it intentional that you wanted to cross over?" The reason why we make rock records is because we rapped over rock records before we got a chance to make records.'

Rubin recounts how 'Walk This Way', a US number four hit in September 1986 and one of the most frequently aired videos of the decade, suddenly took off.

'I grew up on rock 'n' roll music and listening to rock records, always knowing that there was this connection between rock and rap. For me, they weren't that different. One had guitars, one usually didn't. Just the phrasing of the vocals – one was chord singing, one wasn't. But it really wasn't that different. I was listening to my records and I found "Walk This Way" and I realised "Walk This Way" pretty much was a rap record already. It had a funky beat, it had verses that were monotone, it didn't have a melody. I thought if Run-D.M.C. did this song, people who don't understand rap music would realise it's kind of the same. Because it would still sound like Run-D.M.C., and it did. So that was kind of why we did that, and it worked. It didn't work at first, people were really offended at first. Aerosmith are from Boston and the big radio station in Boston is WBCN. WBCN played the Run-D.M.C. version of "Walk This Way", they were the first station to play it in the country, and their phones lit up, people cursing at them: "How dare you! Take this shit off!" They thought it was sacrilegious that a black group that couldn't sing was doing an Aerosmith song, and they were completely offended. The station took it off the air based on the outcry of the audience, and by the end of that week it had become the number one requested song on the station – when they weren't playing it!'

Russell Simmons sees 'Walk This Way' as a record that opened up the pop market, but not something that was otherwise revolutionary in its own terms.

'"Walk This Way" wasn't that big a breakthrough. It was a big pop record in a way but I think that the development of rap music and Run-D.M.C.'s development was all that "Sucker M.C.'s" and "It's Like That" and the real records. 'Cos "Walk This Way" was something they always played, what they used to call *Toys In The Attic* [the name of the Aerosmith album "Walk This Way" was originally taken from]. They didn't know who Aerosmith was.'

For Rubin, however, the record was more than just a commercial triumph.

'I think it was important in that it brought it to the mainstream and it showed people that rap was "music", and if people had a wall up, here was a familiar reference that they could use and it allowed hip hop into homes where it had never been before.'

Rubin's wall analogy echoes the video for the song, which depicted the two groups in adjoining rehearsal rooms. Partially shot in split-frame, the separate parties antagonise each other before the walls come down for a show-stopping jam session. The symbolism was no less enjoyable for its heavy-handedness.

Run-D.M.C. became huge stars, susceptible to the same pressures that befell their forerunners, as DMC recalls.

'We started getting a little ego. We're at a point now – we're from Queens. They laughing at us, 'cos we're from the suburbs. Well, let's show them we're ready to diss them. At that point we was ready to battle the Cold Crush, Grandmaster Flash. We was ready to battle the whole Zulu Nation on a microphone.'

Despite Run-D.M.C.'s breakthrough, for many in the music industry, rap was simply a faddish street music. Worse, it was performed by vocalists who couldn't sing over records pirated illegally by DJs who were making honest musicians redundant. 'Artistic necrophilia' was one brickbat employed by detractors. There were also charges that rap music incited violence. Rubin confronted both prejudices on an expedition to the west coast. Following trouble at Run-D.M.C. concerts in Pittsburgh, Atlanta and New York, the band's performance at Long Beach on 17 August 1986 was cancelled after local gangs rioted. Simmering tensions between rival Bloods and Crips (the dominant LA gangs) erupted during a set by Whodini. Of the 14,500 crowd, forty-two were seriously injured. Although they'd not even taken the stage, Run-D.M.C. were scapegoated for the incident.

'I went out to dinner with a guy who ran a record company in LA. We had been having all the success at the time and he was clearly trying to woo me to come to his company. "Why do you think people like it? It's not music." I thought: "Wow, this guy is someone who is trying to be supportive and doesn't think it's music." It just kind of opened my eyes as to what people really thought, because I was so immersed in it that I didn't understand that to other people it was just noise.'

# chapter seven

# the def jam story

### ➤ Rick Rubin – Big Beats From The Student Dorm

Like several other interested white parties, Rubin came to hip hop via punk.

'I was really a fan of punk rock music. The white kids in my junior high school were closed-minded and I was the only punk. It was lonely and most of my black friends liked hip hop music. To me it had a very similar energy. It was really pure and it was really from the street and it wasn't about being a virtuoso at anything. It was about having something to say and anyone who had something to say could step up and do it. I really gravitated towards hip hop because of the alienation of being the only punk, being part of a community that really embraced something.'

At the time, for those living outside the Bronx, the main access to hip hop was provided by the WHBI radio show hosted by Mr Magic – the DJ later saluted by Whodini on their 'Magic's Wand' single.

'He was the first guy on the radio anywhere to play hip hop, and it was on WHBI. Everyone I knew who was into hip hop would tape that show, and that was their listening for the week. Just rewind it and play it over and over again and that was the only place to really hear this music.'

With hip hop sharing punk's spontaneity and headstrong DIY principles, Rubin oversaw the release of his first record while still a student.

'When I was in college I made my first hip hop record, which was T La Rock and Jazzy Jay's "It's Yours". I made it just from a fan's point of view. There was a club downtown in Manhattan called Negril, which was a reggae club. It held about 200 people, and I used to go there. One night a week was hip hop night, and it was the only place in downtown Manhattan where hip hop existed. I went every week and just really loved it. I would go to the Bronx to buy records, because you couldn't get them anywhere else.

At this time hip hop existed in very few places. It was really a small, territorial thing.'

Jazzy Jay was bemused by Rubin's approach to recording the single –
he was forever insisting that the bass sound be louder and deeper.

'He was just the "Bass Master". He used to have this pitch control.
He'd slow everything down. He used to record it slow and then slow it down
even further. I was like: "Mmm." But he gave you a different sound. The
harmonics on "It's Yours" were kind of lowered in.'

The success of the single brought an introduction to Russell Simmons.

'I met Russell when that record was having success and he was
shocked when he met me, because it was his favourite record and he could-
n't believe that a white person had anything to do with hip hop. In those
days it just wasn't the case, it was really alien. So I met Russell and we
became friends. He was a party promoter and a record promoter and a
manager. He managed Kurtis Blow and he already managed Run-D.M.C.
But I met Russell because his name was on a lot of records that I really
loved, either as producer or manager. His name came up a lot, even though
it was this tiny little business. He told me all these horror stories of dealing
with record companies and what it was like and how he never got paid, but
how he kept doing it. Which really made me feel good about him in that he
was doing this because he loved it and it wasn't a business thing, it was a
love thing.'

Russell Simmons, too, remembers that first meeting with Rubin.

'We had a lot of records on the radio at the time. We really were
representing a lot. Whatever hip hop bands were any good who were on
the radio were ours. There was a record on the radio called "It's Yours"
and that record was produced by Rick Rubin. Jazzy Jay and T La Rock were
the artists. So Jazzy Jay was my man. I was like: "How you made this
record?" And he told me about Rick and he took me to Rick's dorm. I found
out that Rick hung out in the same club, Danceteria, that I hung out in. We
talked and hung out and he was a DJ for another group, the Beastie Boys.
He was DJ Double R, and he was a kid in school. I went back to his dorm
and he played me many dope beats and back then all I wanted to hear was
a beat. I didn't want to hear any melody. Anyway, he had a whole drum
machine full of hit records and we became friends. I became the manager of
the Beastie Boys and Rick Rubin. Then Rick wanted to produce a record and
he wanted to put it out on an independent label. He already owned the logo
Def Jam – that was something that he owned when he put out "It's Yours"
by T La Rock.'

At this stage Rubin, never one for convention, had a unique way of roadtesting his releases.

'I had a little MGB car. I had the first big sound system. I had to bring my car to the Bronx and they cut holes in my car. This was unbelievable in those days. twelve-inch woofers in your car was an unheard of thing. That was just how we did it back then, we were committed to the big sound. You'd work on a song in the studio and then bring it out to the car and see how it worked in the car. Because that's the way most people would hear it. Most people didn't have woofers in their car in those days, but still the idea of it sounding good in the car was important. Often we'd bring it to a club and play it that night, even just off a cassette. Not so much to see the reaction, but to just stand out on the dancefloor and feel the energy of it.'

Jazzy Jay remembers fitting the speakers into Rubin's car, with disastrous results.

'I put a system in Rick's car, and the system was too powerful. He had an MGB and on the way home it blew his tail light off and his licence plate fell off. The bass was just phenomenal – his lights didn't work, everything. His car just totally failed, but he wanted this system because it was loud.'

## ➤ LL Cool J – Radio Star

Rubin and Def Jam's breakthrough came in 1985 with LL Cool J's *Radio*.

'LL's album was the first album I ever made . . . It was so stripped down and so raw and so different to everything else that was going on, and his lyrics were great. It just sounded different to everything else that was going on in rap.'

Born James Todd Smith in Queens in 1969, LL Cool J began rapping at the age of nine after his grandfather bought him a DJ turntable. Within four years he was preparing his own demos, one of which eventually reached Rubin, who persuaded Simmons that they should sign the young rapper.

'Based on the success of "It's Yours", I started getting demo tapes sent to my dorm room which was the address that was on the "It's Yours" record at NYU. One of them was from a guy named Ladies Love Cool James, who was sixteen years old. One of the guys in the Beastie Boys, Ad Rock, really liked that tape and listened to it a lot in my dorm room. He was the one who brought it to my attention. I called Ladies Love Cool James and asked him if he would come to the dorm to meet. He came over and we decided we were going to make records together. We made our first single and I brought it over to play for Russell and he said: "It's a hit,

I love it!" I said: "Well, do you know what I should do with it? How's this gonna work?" He was the experienced guy. I was a college student, he was already in the record business. He said: "We should give it to one of the labels that I put these records out with." I said: "Look, all you do is complain to me about how they don't pay you and it's terrible and it's frustrating and it's a waste of time – why don't we just do it ourselves?" And he said: "No, no, I don't want to do it myself, because I'm hoping to get a deal with a big label at some point and this would get in the way of that." I said: "Well, let me. How about if I make the records and I'll run the company and I'll do all the work and you can be my partner?" And he said: "OK." And the reason I wanted to do that was because I was a college student and he was somebody who was really in the record business. I also knew that with the success of things he would get more interested, which he did, and it was really good.'

Rubin's role was to help orchestrate LL Cool J's sound and his brilliant, but sprawling lyrics.

'I grew up on song-structured music, so I know LL's album is the first rap record where it's songs. He would come to me with just a verse and we'd figure out: "What's the main theme of this?" Then that would be the hook and then we'd say: "OK, now these are the best lines, make the best lines the first verse and these lines make the best second verse." We'd structure it. I would programme the beats then play them for him and we would figure out which lyrics fitted best on which beats. He was such a good writer that he could really write about anything. I would provide the music and LL would provide the lyrics and we'd figure out how to arrange them and cut them up, so that it would be the best song that it could be. It was really simple and we did them all really quickly. I think almost every song on that record was recorded in two or three hours and then mixed in a couple of days. The whole album cost $9,000 to make and it came out and sold 980,000 copies, which was a big deal. Everybody was very excited.'

LL Cool J was an immediate hit, his showmanship and preference for gaudy, outlandish clothing (not least huge gold chains) making him rap's first solo superstar. His breakthrough led to Def Jam cementing a major distribution deal with Columbia, thereby securing their future.

## ➤ *Fight For Your Right To Party – The Beastie Boys*

Strange though it seems in retrospect, New York's Beastie Boys began life as a hardcore punk band, their main influence being black rasta punks Bad Brains. Comprising Adam 'MCA' Yauch, Mike 'D' Diamond and Adam 'Ad Rock' Horowitz (son of dramatist Israel Horowitz), the Beastie Boys soon slipped tempos to reflect New York's burgeoning hip hop vibe, though they retained punk's snotty attitude. Their debut album, 1986's *Licensed To Ill*, became the first rap record to top the Billboard album charts. Together with accompanying single 'Fight For Your Right To Party' it made them international superstars. In keeping with Rubin's original concept for Def Jam, they set out to engender as much mayhem, outrage and moral panic as possible. Their stage shows featured half-naked, caged female dancers while their penchant for car insignia was copied by fans, resulting in a minor crime wave visited upon Volkswagen cars.

Rick Rubin, at one time a Beastie Boys' DJ, witnessed their rise with something approaching satisfaction.

'At the time that they broke they were perceived as – I guess the best comparison would be the Sex Pistols – outrageous, rude, outlaw, snotty, arrogant, didn't care. And not talented. They were as hated as they were loved. People would always say to me that when they had success they were such jerks and assholes. But that's what they were always like. It's not the success that made them miserable, they were just kinda obnoxious and that's what made them who they were. We were all obnoxious and we all have grown through it and come out the other side. I don't mean it in a negative way, they were just precocious kids and they always thought they were the greatest thing in the world before they ever sold one record. I think the closest thing you could compare it to today would be Oasis. People who love them think they're the greatest and there are people who think they're just obnoxious and that's the same kind of perception that people had of the Beastie Boys.'

Joe Levy of *Rolling Stone* magazine, then writing for the *Village Voice*, assesses their impact.

'They wanted to be the loudest, meanest, baddest motherfuckers on the face of the earth. If you wanna be that way and somebody's pointing a camera at you, you'll be controversial. They wanted to drink from the biggest bottle of beer and wave around the biggest gun. That was their thing when they were eighteen years old. It's different now, but they talked a whole lot of silly stuff back then. They were fast and loose with their mouths.'

The Beastie Boys' whiteness gave some commentators a headache, but broadened hip hop's appeal.

'The fact that they were a white rap group didn't make any sense to anyone. I don't think real hip hop fans understood them to be a rap group.

I think the average person buying their record probably didn't even know what rap was. It was just these obnoxious kids screaming on a record and I think the Beastie Boys and Run-D.M.C. together really forged that path to turn people on to what hip hop was. I don't think people knew what they were getting into.'

Simmons notes that the band's breakthrough song, 'Fight For Your Right To Party', was a crossover success by accident rather than design.

'It was never even a planned single. "Slow Ride" was the single. I think they made that more to have a good time and as a joke. They wasn't thinking that this was going to be something that defines their career. It just did not sound like the rest of the album, or any other album they ever made. So that record was a lot of fun and they made it and then it got snatched off the album. Whenever an album sells like that, radio has to find something that makes sense for them, and "Fight For Your Right To Party" made a lot of sense and it became an anthem.'

The Beastie Boys, according to Rubin, weren't as pleased at the controversy surrounding them as some thought.

'I remember when the Beasties toured England. They were both well received and really not well received. The covers of daily papers were really against them. I remember I was thrilled, because I thought they'd made such a powerful impact and it was such a great thing. I remember talking to Mike or Adam. Me being so excited about how great it was that all of this good/bad stuff was going on. This for a new band, this kind of excitement and drama. And I remember them saying, it's different when you're actually doing it as opposed to reading about it. Going out and having people hate you is a very hard thing and it came very close to breaking the band up. I actually thought the band was gonna break up. I don't know if it was specifically the trip to England, but the overwhelming bad stuff that came with the good stuff was enough to make them step back and they didn't make another record for a long, long time. They didn't really function as a group for a long time. They had to re-invent themselves because they didn't like having the attention on them in that way.'

From humble beginnings in his NYU dorm, Rubin found Def Jam had turned into a sprawling business empire.

'The company was growing pretty quickly and things were out of control. As I said, none of us knew what we were doing. The company had existed for maybe two years at the time all the success started happening. I was just getting out of college and none of us really knew anything, or even understood that anything weird was happening, other than a lot of people were buying the records and coming to shows. You could kind of tell something was going on. It just all happened really organically and normally. There was just more to do.'

To many in the hip hop community, like DJ Bobbito, who worked at the label first as a messenger then on the A&R staff, the Def Jam logo signalled a product with class and hip hop authenticity.

'Def Jam in the 80s was the most reliable label. Def Jam found a way in the 80s to allow artists expression and creative control, first and foremost, and still wind up selling a million or two million records. That is so rare. He put out LL [Cool J] in '85, The Beastie Boys in '86, Public Enemy in '87, Slick Rick in '88, '89 was 3rd Bass, then '90 was EPMD. For six years they were putting out joints, and every single one of those records was either going gold or platinum, or double platinum.'

## ➤ *Party For Your Right To Fight – Public Enemy*

Rubin's next discovery became the jewel in Def Jam's crown. A sociologist's dream and infotainers in the truest sense, Public Enemy instantly rendered the tradition of easygoing party rhyming obsolete. Behind Chuck D's enraged yet eloquent narratives and Flavor Flav's linguistic acrobatics, rock riffs slammed against deafening shrieks, synthesizer stabs and digitised funk loops. The dress code was street-regular or militaristic, with the exception of Flavor's esoteric clock necklace. Public Enemy's 'scorched earth' musical policy took no prisoners and provided a powerful soundtrack to their unyielding advocacy of black values and autonomy. Whereas hip hop music previously had been enjoyably ephemeral, Public Enemy reinstated the tenor of Melle Mel's 'The Message' – the very existence of the black man was under threat, according to these self-proclaimed prophets of rage.

Like many others, Carlton Ridenhour, aka Chuck D, became embroiled in hip hop through his interest in the graffiti and artwork that accompanied it. He got his start by providing graphics for hip hop flyers.

'The whole New York metropolitan area before 1979 – it was insane because everybody was just participating in this thing that required two turntables and a microphone. The voices became multiplied and the styles of mixing these two records became more diverse. I got involved in this whole thing as a fan, somebody who just wanted to go to the parties and eventually designing the flyers. I became a flyer master. That was my first skill of trade in hip hop. A flyer master would do incredible flyers to bring the attitude and the feeling of rap and hip hop to a piece of paper, to try to make somebody come to the gig.'

Straight away, however, Chuck knew he was bored with some of rap's subject matter.

'If you have a song you should have a topic. If you have a topic that's just like the next person's topic, then your song isn't that much different from the next person's song. You really should be yourself and know what you're talking about and have it come from your heart.'

An acolyte of Long Island's Spectrum sound system, Chuck always wanted to work with its proprietor, Hank Shocklee.

'I was recruited by Hank in '79. I stepped to Hank to say: "Hey, look, man. I can do flyers because I admire your outfit. I just think maybe you need a little bit of marketing."'

Hank has bittersweet memories of their first meeting.

'I was doing parties, a bunch of gigs. I was in high school, and I took all my money that I was supposed to spend for my graduation yearbook, and I went out there and threw a party. The party was wack. I was sitting down on the kerb, trying to figure out what kind of an excuse I'm gonna tell my parents of why I didn't get a yearbook, 'cos I never got a yearbook or a ring and I couldn't even go to the prom or anything. So I was trying to figure out what kind of a lie I'm gonna tell my parents, why I lost their money, and Chuck sat down next to me and said: "You know why nobody came to your function? Because your flyers was wack." I didn't really wanna hear him because I was like: "Well, what's a flyer got to do with anything?" He showed me his flyers. My flyer was just typed out words. He said: "That's wack, people are putting graphics on it." Chuck showed me what a real flyer looked like. From that point we developed a relationship.'

They began collaborating together, first on the party circuit, then on Adelphi University's college radio show. Tapes of Chuck and Hank's show eventually reached Rick Rubin.

'The first time I heard Public Enemy, DMC [of Run-D.M.C.] played it for me. And it was a tape of Chuck. He was an MC at college, and he had this one song called "Public Enemy No.1", which was his theme song. He would play it at the beginning and at the end of his show, and I heard that song and thought it was the greatest and knew that he had to be our next artist.'

Chuck remembers how 'Public Enemy No.1' came about.

'I went to roller-rinks a lot. "Blow Your Head" [by Fred Wesley & the JB's] was a particular song they had. I dug the hell out of it because I just liked the fucking noise aspect. So, one day I got a copy of "Blow Your Head" and just slowed it down and spliced it together on two tape decks. I took this record and pause-taped it on two decks and rhymed over it with the other tape deck, and pretty much did an overdub and delivered it to WBAU where we now had three nights a week. We called this thing "Public Enemy No.1". Why? Because there was a cowboy character [a challenger to Chuck's MC throne] in the neighbourhood. I had stopped rhyming for two or three years and just took care of the radio and MC duties and throwing gigs. They thought I had fallen off. This was a message to tell 'em: "Don't mess with me." By the time Chuck D became an artist with Public Enemy, I was way past my prime. I'm like Satchel Paige – Satchel Paige was a baseball player that finally made it to the major leagues when he was forty-nine. But when I did that demo, which was at the end of 1984, it scared so many people. By the time it came out as a record [in February 1987] it was already dated.'

Rubin was determined to find out more about the originator of 'Public Enemy No.1'. Initially, however, he was rebuffed by Chuck, who felt he was too old to debut as an MC on vinyl. Legendarily, he once told his wife not to take Rubin's calls.

'I called him up and Chuck was already in college. LL was really hot at the time and sixteen years old. When I called Chuck and asked him if he wanted to make records he said he had already gone through that phase when he was a kid. He's too told and no one's gonna care and he doesn't want to do it. He considered himself a grown man, with a family and a regular job. I think he worked at a record store, and he thought he was very straight in his path and that was what he was gonna do. I put his phone number on a post-it note and stuck it next to my phone and I called him every day for six months saying we really have to make a record. I finally tried again in about six months' time and he said "maybe". At some point during that period he decided that he would do it, and he came in with Hank and Flavor, saying it's called Public Enemy. Because none of this existed before, it was Chuck D. It was all I knew and that's all I'd wanted to sign, Chuck D. And he said it's gonna be a group, it's gonna be like a rock band and it's gonna be called Public Enemy and we're gonna do this. And it was great. Another component to that is Bill Stephney, who was the first employee that we ever hired at Def Jam. He was friends with Chuck, so he was also always trying to push him along to do this. We were all happy when he came around.'

Chuck eschewed the simple twin MC/DJ or solo format for a larger team of contributors. The idea was partially inspired by his fondness for old school hip hop crews like the Furious Five.

'I always dug the numbers that Flash and the Furious Five presented, but I wanted to see if I could present the same amount of numbers with different obligations and different duties. When people first see you, they use their senses of sight before they hear you. So it was very important. I went to one of the guys doing the mix DJ tapes for Spectrum who I worked with, Norman Rogers, who became Terminator X. Flavor Flav also had a show on WBAU and we had actually done a bunch of different things together. I brought him along together with Professor Griff. He had an organisation called UV Force and they did the security for our gigs for the radio station. They had an organisation of fifty people that did the security and they had a certain look that bordered on a Black Panther, Islamic look. So we said: "We'll bring this along and try to mould this image to what we are already doing on Long Island."'

It was from this idea of collectivism and musical community that production specialists the Bomb Squad, Public Enemy's sonic masterminds, evolved.

'Before it had a name, it was actually a bunch of us cats that actually made the music. Eric Sadler, I called him Vietnam because he always wore this army jacket and these shades that looked like they was out of *Apocalypse Now*. He was a musician that had rehearsals downstairs. Hank, Keith and I were DJs, so we had a superior knowledge of records. Hank and Keith more than me, but I did about two or three years of catching up and archiving and I was the archive keeper as well. Our recall of the records became instrumental in how we were going to make records in the future. So the four of us together, along with a lot of musicians that were in the area, combined to make the music.'

Hank Shocklee sees the Bomb Squad as:

'Basically just four guys that made records. We loved music, and we just got together for the project. Basically, the project was making the Public Enemy record. The Bomb Squad basically consisted of myself, Keith, Eric Sadler and Chuck. We've had what I would call additional members, such as Terminator X and Flavor Flav.'

Chuck developed an idiosyncratic litmus test for the music he deemed suitable for Public Enemy.

'I wanted to make records that girls hated. You had Luther Vandross and love songs. I loved R&B when it was in the 60s, but by the time it got to the 80s it was garbage. So whatever my girl liked at the time, if she was saying turn it off, I knew that I had some shit. So my whole thing was, don't make anything that your woman likes, but make some rugged, real hip hop. And that was our formula, our plan, our goal at that particular time. Make something that people cover their ears to. It's "love at first hate" and that was the whole key in Public Enemy.'

Public Enemy's debut album, *Yo! Bum Rush The Show*, was released in March 1987. Rick Rubin remembers the scepticism with which the hip hop community greeted it.

'It didn't do well at the time. It was the least successful Def Jam record at the time. When we put it out to people in the hip hop community, DJs would only play the instrumental versions of Public Enemy records. They thought Chuck couldn't rap because he didn't sound like the other rappers and there's actually a reference to that on the second album ["Rebel Without A Pause"]. That was about the fact that they didn't accept Chuck. They felt the beats were good, but he wasn't. Then finally everyone came around.'

Among those who did not share Rubin's instant love of the group was business partner Russell Simmons.

'When I played the first Public Enemy album for Russell, he thought it was a waste of time. I remember him saying: "Why? Why do you waste your time with this stuff? No one's ever gonna like this. This is black punk rock, and this isn't what people want." At first he wasn't wrong, he wasn't wrong. But he eventually came around.'

Nowadays, however, Simmons is fuller in his praise for Chuck D and the band.

'Public Enemy defined the sound of Def Jam in a really good way, because the Beastie Boys and LL Cool J were worlds apart in a lot of ways. "Fight For Your Right To Party" and "I Need Love" were worlds apart. For me, Public Enemy was the epitome of Def Jam – "Rebel Without A Pause" and "Miuzi Weighs A Ton", all the records were anti-R&B. They were totally black and totally alternative and totally rock 'n' roll and totally everything that we stood for. All the things that Def Jam was. So they were the turning point because they defined the sound.'

Though he has always been keen to spread the credit, Rubin believes Chuck D was the creative force behind not just Public Enemy but also the Bomb Squad.

'Chuck doesn't take a lot of credit for the production. Obviously, the Bomb Squad played a big role, but it was always really Hank's vision. He was the former DJ and really knew what was good. He always knew what was good and other guys would present stuff to them and they'd work on a lot of stuff, but really, those are Chuck's records.'

For Rubin, it was when Public Enemy's second album came out that the whole picture came together and the group began to realise its potential.

'I was listening to it [*It Takes A Nation Of Millions To Hold Us Back*] on an aeroplane. It was the first time I heard it. Chuck had sent me a copy of it because he knew I was leaving and he'd just finished it and he gave it to me. I was on the aeroplane listening to it and I remember I cried. I was so proud. Because to me it just took it to a whole new level, and I remember crying, thinking that this is just such a beautiful thing that's evolving and growing. But for me it felt like that was the last one like that. That's what I always wanted from music, and I wasn't getting it from rap at that time, and it probably wasn't until N.W.A., which was years away, until another thing came along where I really felt like: "Wow, this is the new shit, this is real, this is exciting." It was really sad, really sad.'

By 1988, Rubin and Simmons had dissolved their partnership, with Rubin going on to work with a predominantly rock-based roster at Def American. He simply felt that *It Takes A Nation Of Millions To Hold Us Back* was such a colossal achievement, it would be impossible to equal it.

'I think *It Takes A Nation Of Millions* did several things that hadn't been done in rap before. For one, the musical production was really hyped up and chaotic, and so much of the Def Jam sound had been slow and low. Not about uptempo chaos and not about changing beats, but about jamming around one beat. That was a very explosive change from a musical standpoint. And that was the album where Chuck really started getting political. There hadn't really been that voice in rap before, so that combination made it a really stunning, stunning statement for rap.'

For Chuck D, the day *It Takes A Nation Of Millions* was released was the day hip hop left the cradle.

'Making *It Takes A Nation* was to expound upon – there's a world outside your head, and understand that there's a lot of people out there that are just like you, trying to figure themselves out, but we on the same team. And throughout *It Takes A Nation* there's topics that we're going to tackle and topics that a lot of people can relate to and topics that are not going to be covered by a lot of people on the outside. Basically, *It Takes A Nation* was, I guess, the first piece of grown up rap. You didn't have to be fourteen to feel it. If you was fourteen and you felt it, you'd probably pick it up later or take whatever you can take out of it and get to that next level. It was also the first album that showed to all the major companies that rap was an album format. It was the final straw in 1986. You had *Raising Hell* doing what it did and *Licensed to Ill* doing what it did. But *It Takes A Nation* was the final straw, especially coming out of the Def Jam camp . . . We wanted to make our albums like Led Zeppelin. When the rock guys came out with an album format it wasn't predicated on singles, which has been a black mainstay even up to today. "You gotta promote the single." Suppose you don't have a single? It means you don't have good music? You can't tie it all together? You can't tie it all together with a theme that resonates?'

Public Enemy's entire career has been hallmarked by controversy, although they attracted substantial levels of support from unlikely sources. The reverential stance taken by many UK rock magazines, for example, came close to genuflection. By far the most damaging setback to Public Enemy's reputation occurred in May 1989, when Professor Griff (Richard Griffin) conducted an interview with *Washington Post* reporter David Mills in which he allegedly pronounced that: 'Jews are responsible for the majority of wickedness that goes on across the globe.' Chuck was forced to sack his 'minister of information' (minister of ignorance, according to others) and found himself the subject of intense personal scrutiny. This is Chuck's recollection of events.

'We had done blistering interviews in parts of England and Europe, where we were really speaking of us as black people. Then you would have antagonistic approaches, like: "Hey, you guys are black." We were like: "Damn right." We was heavily topical by 1989, winning journalists' awards and stuff like that. And one particular interview that Griff did with a *Washington Times* reporter, they got into a tit-for-tat, talking about religion and backgrounds and stuff like that. My whole philosophy is, when you talk about religions and things like that, 6,000 years old, these debates go on and on. But here was a music reporter. He thought it was a topic to cover, and he took some of the isolated Griff comments and highlighted and spotlighted them outside of the context for which they were delivered . . . And once those isolated comments got blown up in a United States paper, it created a whole 'nother firestorm. Not to agree upon the statements at the particular time, which even Griff admitted were out of character . . . It got to a point where I don't think Griff was happy with the situation at the particular time, 'cos we had a hierarchy problem. He recognised that there was nothing I could do . . . It was a wild and crazy time. But I would tell you this. Even through all that we went through, with a bunch of statements, it paled in comparison to the amount of derogatory statements that these same record companies would allow coming out through their companies about black people. No matter what we went through in 1989 with the industry controversy, anti-Semitism, anti-white, whatever, it paled in comparison to the amount of accepted negativity in "nigger-ism" at the same record companies and industry that these journalists were silent to during the early to mid-90s. It wasn't so much I'm blaming the artists as the companies, who profited from it. So that endorsement of black hate, to me, overshadowed the reputed reports of us being anti-white or anti-Semitic or whatever.'

As well as press rebukes, the group were subjected to death threats. According to Hank Shocklee, Chuck bore the brunt of these attacks.

'Chuck is a very brave person because those bullets and arrows – whatever you wanna call it – was all aimed at him. I was in the background, Flavor was a side man. Chuck was the front man. He was the guy that had to do the answering. When he made the decision to pull his brother out the group, that was a very, very hard, long-debated decision.'

Chuck, for his part, believes that the reason some elements of the music industry conspired against them was because Public Enemy were redirecting black anger at corporate America.

'There was a whole lot of gunplay inside rap music, but what we did is that we didn't point the guns at each other, we pointed the guns at them, and that was scary to them.'

Public Enemy's third album, 1990's *Fear Of A Black Planet*, was another hip hop milestone, a powerhouse collection of searing noise, resentment and sharp-witted punditry from America's underbelly. There were three cornerstone tracks. '911 Is A Joke' attacked emergency service response times in black neighbourhoods. 'Welcome To The Terrordome' reflected bitterly on the band's treatment at the hands of the media during the Professor Griff affair. Most importantly, 'Fight The Power' was used by director Spike Lee to soundtrack his masterful movie about inner-city racial tensions, *Do The Right Thing*. Hank Shocklee remembers the album being recorded in a pressure-cooker atmosphere, but he remains proud of the finished product, particularly 'Fight The Power'.

'Public Enemy first started out by identifying the problems. "Fight The Power" was starting to move into solution-oriented rap. That record was very big because of the inspiration and the message that it was delivering, it was more uplifting.'

# chapter eight

# renegades of funk

> ### The Tommy Boy Story

Aside from Def Jam, the other label who did most to propagate hip hop in the 80s was Tom Silverman's Tommy Boy. They'd scored their break-through success with Afrika Bambaataa's 'Planet Rock', but paid a high price for it. Although Kraftwerk themselves were pleased with the record, publishers No Hassle Music did anything but live up to their name, claiming 200% of the publishing. Silverman recalls the label's first tentative steps.

'In 1980 I was thinking about starting a label. I was trying to come up with a name, and I wanted to have a name that had a nice feel when you said it, that had the right number of syllables. Sugarhill was really hot at the time, and I loved the flow of the word Sugarhill, just the way it rolled off your tongue and the way the syllables flowed. So I was looking for some-thing that had that same kind of syllabic rhythm to it. When you come up with names the most important thing isn't the intellectual part of what it means, it's actually how it makes you feel. One day I was in my grand-father's basement, and he used to make his own wine. He had grape boxes from California and they had labels on the side of them. There was one that had Tommy Boy on the side of it, and it was the name of the grape company. This is the actual inspiration for the logo of Tommy Boy.'

Like other would-be hip hop moguls, Silverman found himself having to move fast to stay in touch with developments with the advent of 'Rapper's Delight'.

'I said: "Well, if Sugarhill can do this, there must not be that much to it. I'm sure I could figure it out." It's a lot more complicated than it seems, but I did figure it out. It's all about getting the right record though, still to this day. So that made me wanna do it, the excitement of that was so great.

I just never thought I was qualified. But then seeing other people be success-ful, who didn't have any more credentials than I had, if not less, that I thought I could. I definitely had the connections and the knowledge and the intelligence to be able to try, so I said what the heck.'

Silverman was joined by Monica Lynch, who eventually rose to a senior role in the company but from the outset did everything from answer the phones to talent-scout.

'I got involved in hip hop when I answered an ad in the *Village Voice* for a "Guy/Gal Friday". Tom Silverman had just started Tommy Boy and I became his first employee. Prior to that I was waiting on tables and going to different clubs around town. Once I started working for him I became exposed to the DJ culture in a more direct way, and he brought me up to the T-Connection [club] in the Bronx and I met Bambaataa and used to go to Harlem World and a lot of the older clubs.'

For Lynch, there was a sense of camaraderie as much as competition among emerging rap labels like Def Jam, Jive and Tommy Boy.

'Back then it was really a cottage industry. I don't think we viewed each other so much as competitors as maybe compatriots in bringing this new genre to the forefront. There was no real precedent for this with the established major labels, who were still riding the wave of whatever was left of disco at that time. Primarily their heart was beating with rock music. I think we're more like brothers-in-arms in many respects. Certainly the busi-ness has changed quite a bit since then, and everybody's in the rap game in some way, shape or form.'

## ► De La Soul – Daisy Age Rap

After establishing itself with 'Planet Rock', one of Tommy Boy's hottest acts of the 80s was Brooklyn group Stetsasonic. Their producer, Prince Paul, brought Monica Lynch and Tom Silverman a demo of a Long Island group he'd been working with. Posdnous, aka Kelvin Mercer, together with Trugoy the Dove (David Jolicoeur) and Pasemaster Mase (Vincent Mason) formed De La Soul in Amityville, Long Island, in 1985. Lynch and Silverman instantly fell in love with Prince Paul's discoveries.

'He brought in a tape that he had produced with a bunch of friends from Long Island. It was De La Soul, and when we first heard it we thought it was the most bizarre thing. We loved it, and we knew that it was either gonna be nothing or be gigantic, but we thought we'd take a chance and try it. They had a refreshing attitude and their personality was wild and kind of fit Monica's and my personality. We had no idea how big it would be. It went on to sell almost a million albums. Actually, it was our first gold album. And "Me, Myself And I" was the single that really propelled that.'

Posdnous recalls the group's origins.

'Myself and Dove, we were in an earlier crew called Easy Street. I was the DJ and he was just the beatbox, but we both rhymed. So that crew didn't really go nowhere but we just stuck together and then Mase moved from Brooklyn . . . I spent all night thinking of a name. I just felt that everything we try to do will be from the soul, and I was like: "Yeah, man, let's call ourselves From The Soul." Dove said: "All right, that sounds cool, but the name sounds kind of corny. Let's spice it up, instead of From The Soul, let's say De La Soul." I was with it and that was it.'

Although Prince Paul took the demo to Tommy Boy, there was also interest from several other labels.

'Prince Paul, we went to the same school together. So after him hearing the tapes, loving it, realising we had somewhat of a common bond in the way we think and the way we put together music, we just started working on tapes and doing a lot of recording . . . We had three songs on the demo, we had "Plug Tunin'", "Freedom Of Speak" and a song called "De La Game" which eventually became "D.A.I.S.Y. Age" on *3 Feet High And Rising*. We got interest from Profile, Warner Brothers directly, First Priority. There was a lot of different labels and we was just overwhelmed. That was our hardest decision. Here are these labels that wanna sign us: who to go with? It was like a dream come true, but we figured [Prince] Paul was on Tommy Boy, and perception is everything. I mean it was cooler to be on Tommy Boy then.'

Prince Paul had originally been keen to take them to Run-D.M.C.'s label, Profile.

'Profile was interested, Geffen was just getting into rap and they really loved De La Soul. But De La Soul really liked Tommy Boy because of the vibe. We met with Monica Lynch and she was really feeling the tune. I think they liked that more, so they went for the feeling of the label as opposed to the money factor and everything. That's how we started off with Tommy Boy and started making records. From that point on I helped to define what their sound was. They had an idea, but it was always me who made clear the idea that they already had. Our sounds and our ideas fitted so perfectly, I don't think any other producer would have worked as well. I don't think any other artist I've worked with could make me define who I am as well as De La Soul.'

De La Soul opened a new chapter in hip hop. Skipping around their resolutely un-macho videos wearing colour-uncoordinated clothes, they were effortlessly refreshing. Their records offered a pick 'n' mix selection of obtuse samples and beats (ranging from Hall & Oates to Steely Dan), the kaleidoscopic musical contrasts and junctions counterpointed by unhurried, conversational rhyming. De La Soul's Day-Glo hippy chic felt like someone had opened the shutters on rap. Posdnous:

'I think what made our sound so distinct is that a lot of other rappers who loved the same type of music that we might sample from were too scared to do it. We never thought like that. I'm not saying that's the only part of our sound and what made our sound so successful, but I think a big part of it is that a lot of people, they had access to the same type of thoughts but they followed behind other people or played it safe and we never thought like that.'

Posdnous acknowledges Prince Paul's role as a conduit to their success.

'Paul was like the God, who came down and sped up these primates. We definitely had the talent to be where we were and where we are now, but Paul definitely came in and sped all that up . . . He taught us pretty much everything within the studio and he helped instil in us the whole level of never being scared to try anything.'

Silverman loved the change of direction that De La Soul brought, though the 'daisy age rap' tag with which the band were saddled proved ulti-mately restricting.

'The whole visual imagery of the daisy age and that whole hippies of hip hop – you can do something besides the gold chain, leather-wearing MC, which up to that point was the dominant paradigm in hip hop.'

The big single from *3 Feet High And Rising*, like so many other hip hop classics, was an afterthought that nearly didn't make the album, according to Posdnous.

'Literally, "Me Myself And I" was the last song recorded. So I was not even thinking that was going to be a single or whatever. Then it wound up being the song that we can't ever escape.'

## ➤ *Sampling – The Art Of Creative Theft*

Though Silverman had been careful in clearing samples for *3 Feet High And Rising*, there were still problems over one song. 'Transmitting Live From Mars' contained an unsolicited excerpt from the Turtles' 'You Showed Me'.

'It wasn't that damaging, but it was upsetting, because it was such a small usage. It was only on a skit. They took a 45 and they took about three seconds of it and they slowed it from 45 rpm to 33 rpm and they looped it. It was the most minimal usage to have a fight over it . . . We had errors and omissions insurance that covered the loss for us and for De La Soul, so there was just a small amount that they ended up having to pay. But De La Soul really got us to be the best label at clearing samples. We had one lawyer on staff then, and we were pretty expert at clearing. But we didn't know that sample was there. We had to clear hundreds of other samples, for both publishing and master use on that album. That was the first album that had such intense sample use.'

The sampling debate lies at the heart of conservative rock critics' objections to hip hop. Its detractors believe that however inventively it is employed, it feeds parasitically on the creativity of others. More enlightened commentators believe the practice is validated not only by the quality of the music it has produced, but also the way it has revived interest in the careers of sampled artists. Sampling, which hastened the decline of the traditional hip hop DJ, became a major copyright headache after rap records started to achieve serious sales. Posdnous believes Tommy Boy took their eye off the ball because they never expected *3 Feet High And Rising* to become a million-seller.

'Tommy Boy didn't think we were gonna sell the amount of records we sold, so why clear half of the stuff? Why tell these people? They are never gonna hear it. Obviously, they heard it because [the success] was phenomenal and it just took off. The Turtles heard this song and they was like: "I'm coming after you!"'

According to Posdnous, the litigation was not about straightforward remuneration.

'The only thing that pissed me off about them is that legally, they turned around to say: "We won't sue you if you perform on our new album that we have coming out. We're a bunch of people who really can't do it right now, so if you help us we won't sue you." That means that you will compromise your stuff. "No, no, go ahead, sue us, whatever. We'll fight you in court." So that's what it came down to.'

Unsurprisingly, Posdnous defends his right to sample the work of other artists, although he also sympathises with the parental feelings of the work's originators.

'I honestly have nothing against anyone who created something feeling like that, because I'd feel that's your child, you have that right to feel that. Someone like George Harrison may not appreciate people sampling his work, because he spent so much time crafting it. They may be saying words that he don't want said over his music. That's your right. But a lot of people have been very, very creative in sampling. It's no different to pulling a thought from your mind and then translating that harmony you hear and putting it down and then playing it. It's the same thing. We took a note from your life, put it with the note of this person's life and we played it and we made something totally different out of it.'

To Posdnous, there is a difference between sophisticated interpretation of an original idea and more rudimentary sampling approaches.

'There are some rappers who have sampled a big chunk of a record, whether it's famous or not, and just rhymed over it – the drum pattern that was on the record, the music that was on the record, they just rhymed over that. But there are rappers as well, or those same rappers on another record, they can easily take a voice of someone and put it with a harmony of something else and change it around totally. Within that actual sample itself you can manipulate the harmony, play it on different keys and play that harmony over. There's so many ways of being creative. Definitely, there are a lot of rappers who are musicians. They are musicians. They respect the music . . . We've always had the necessary sampling forms and everything and handed them in. It's all about them being clear, so after that first album we administered our own sample clearances. Anything that we knew that was an outright sample, we had no problem with asking these people for permission. It was cool. Get on the phone and talk to Daryl Hall [Hall & Oates]. Or the gentleman [Donald Fagen] from Steely Dan. We weren't trying to just take someone's music and not respect it.'

## ➤ Native Tongues – A Shared Language

The geography of rap was becoming more defined. At the same time as the west coast discovered its own identity with the hugely controversial N.W.A., the east coast brought us the Native Tongues. It may be an oversimplification to state that while Los Angeles was advocating get-rich-quick schemes and profanity, New York chose positivity, but the contrast between the cities was alarming.

The Native Tongues were a loose coalition incorporating the Jungle Brothers, De La Soul, Queen Latifah, Monie Love and A Tribe Called Quest. They were friends first and collaborators second. As attention began to focus on them, the press scrambled to write articles about the group's 'Afrocentricity'. In 1989 they released 'Buddy', a funny but frank look at issues surrounding sex.

Arguably the most influential group in this charismatic coterie was the Jungle Brothers, whose 1988 debut *Straight Out The Jungle* melded infectious rhythms with accomplished rhymes on the status of black people in contemporary America. The trio comprised DJ Sammy B (Sammy Burwell), and MCs Mike G (Michael Small) and Afrika Baby Bambaataa (Nathaniel Hall), who recalls their formation.

'We met in high school, as two brothers coming up under the hip hop influence. That was the undertone, the common bond between most kids at that time period in the mid-80s. Hip hop was showing its face in the mainstream. When I hooked up with Mike G, he was writing rhymes. He was listening to tapes from back in the days in 1979, 1980, 1981. Listening to tapes of Grandmaster Flash, Cold Crush Brothers. I was listening to the artists of the time like Run-D.M.C. and the Fat Boys and Kurtis Blow. It was just a casual thing, but it was something that me and him had in common. His uncle was (radio DJ) Red Alert, which I found out later after hanging out with him for maybe two or three years in school.'

The group concept developed through appearances at school talent shows.

'The school talent shows are a tradition. It's just that when we came on the scene, we added something new to the tradition, which was hip hop. Here's a stage where we could do something that ninety per cent of our peers know what we're doing but our elders don't. We can get on the mic and we can perform our lyrics and be just stars in the high school. It doesn't have to be a real super big thing. Block parties were starting to die down at that time, and contests were starting to die down. That was the only way to bring young music to the public, bring it to your peers and show them you got skills. The motivation behind that was – I'm going to be a star in front of my peers. Then there were prizes. When me and Mike did the school talent show, we won a prize which was to go see Run-D.M.C. at the Apollo.'

Inspired by the Zulu Nation, from whose leader he adapted his name, the Native Tongues records were Baby Bambaataa's initial idea.

'That came from basically seeing the Zulu Nation as a cultural organisation – seeing all these MCs and DJs somehow related by this culture called hip hop. So with the Native Tongues, we were separate groups to begin with. A Tribe Called Quest was being influenced by us 'cos Q-Tip went to school with us. He was always around when we were doing our first album. And De La Soul was working on their album and they were hearing us on the airwaves when Red Alert was playing, and they were influenced by us because nobody else was doing what we was doing and nobody else was doing what they were about to do. So they used us as inspiration and as we worked together more and more. I just sat back and said: "What is the thing that brings us all together? It's native tongue – we speak our own language." It's a language that only we can understand and the people that you saw come into the Native Tongues were people who could understand the tongue we was speaking in, the metaphors we used, the abstracts and lyrics we used, and those people became Native Tongues. What Tribe brought to the table was the jazz element. What Jungle Brothers brought to the table was the funk and the dance element and what De La Soul brought to the table was the pop element.'

Posdnous recollects how the Native Tongues idea came to fruition.

'We were sitting in Afrika [Baby Bambaataa]'s house one day in Brooklyn and he said: "When we do these songs together, and they're coming up so good, instead of having to be the Jungle Brothers or De La Soul, let's have a name." He had already told Tip [Q-Tip of A Tribe Called Quest] the idea. So I went back and told my crew and they was willing and Tip went back and told his crew and they was willing and I told the Jungle Brothers and they was willing and that's how we became Native Tongues from right there. From there we were just like a magnet, we just kind of attracted people like Monie Love and so on.'

Monica Lynch witnessed the idea's evolution.

'In the case of Native Tongues, you had a group of young men and women based here in the north east, who really sort of bonded together, 'cos they had similar views about doing some cool and very offbeat types of music. I remember when De La Soul and Latifah and [A Tribe Called] Quest and the Jungle Brothers did the video for "Buddy" and the "Buddy" remix. That was really the defining moment for Native Tongues. It really brought together all the major members of the Native Tongues and, philosophically, I think it presented what Native Tongues was about in a great way. And they were all friends and they liked to work together and play together.'

## ➤ *Monie Love – The UK Connection*

Posdnous was introduced to Monie Love by the Jungle Brothers, who had met her on tour in England. It was a shock to find an MC from Battersea, London, who so easily fitted what the Native Tongues-affiliated New Yorkers were doing.

'If you're talented, don't matter where you're from. But this female MC, and she's from London and she can rhyme like that – she just made such an impression.'

Monie Love was born Simone Johnson in 1970. She had been working with underground British hip hop labels since 1987, her early career fostered by DJ Tim Westwood.

'Hip hop came to England in the form of graffiti art, breakdancing, body popping, the whole dance form and the art form. I was thirteen or fourteen at the time. Sometimes we would do poetry in English class and I had an exceptional love for that, particularly so by the time hip hop came to England, via movies such as *Wild Style*, *Breakdance* and *Beat Street*. I started body popping, started breakdancing. There were other kids that were good at art anyway so when hip hop came over and we saw all the graffiti and stuff, kids that were good at art took to that.'

A video of Afrika Bambaataa's 'Planet Rock', featuring the Soul Sonic Force in their full regalia, piqued her interest. She became part of a tight-knit London hip hop community who would regularly practise their breakdance moves before bemused tourists in Covent Garden. The required listening was pirate radio DJ Tim Westwood, who also ran a Saturday lunchtime jam session on Tottenham Court Road.

'It was a nice club, it had video games in there and stuff. You could sit and lounge. It was like a meeting point, the town meeting, so to speak, of the hip hop community. Everybody would go there and socialise with each other. After seeing *Beat Street*, everybody started going into either DJing or rapping. I chose to be an MC because I already had a love for words, so I just found a way that I could bring across my words to music. A couple of friends chose the DJing side of things, hence you got DJs coming out of England like DJ Pogo, Cutmaster Swift, DJ Biznizz.'

Love made her transatlantic connection via a fan letter to Public Enemy.

'When Public Enemy came out, I wrote a letter. I looked on the back of the album and I saw the address for the fan club and I actually wrote a letter explaining that I would like to know more about what they're about, the whole political standpoint that Public Enemy took. I knew nothing about it. Being a black person living in England, I didn't have the same struggles as black people living in America, not on as big a scale. I was actually genuinely interested in knowing more about it so I wrote them a letter, sent it to the address that was on the back of their album. I didn't think I was going to get a reply, but I actually did. Professor Griff personally responded to my letter and went even further, saying that they would like to meet me when they come to England. They called me as soon as they got to England and I became this seventeen-year-old tour manager, taking them around and stuff like that. And they were schooling me on what they were about and giving me literature and giving me books and I was reading up on it and I was beginning to understand what they were trying to deliver.'

She subsequently met the Jungle Brothers and Queen Latifah on their UK tours, whilst also honing her MC skills, rapping at Tim Westwood's club nights.

'I got signed to Cooltempo in England. At the same time I was making friends with Latifah and the Jungle Brothers and people like that, I ended up putting three or four singles out in England, before I even came to the United States.'

> ## Ladies First

As well as the Native Tongues cut 'Buddy', one of Love's most enduring contributions to hip hop came when she joined Queen Latifah on her 1989 debut album, *All Hail The Queen*.

'When we recorded "Ladies First", I actually didn't realise how powerful a tool it was. It wasn't until it came out and we started doing shows and little girls aged eight, nine or ten and upwards all the way to my mother's age group would approach us. They'd want to shake our hand and say: "You're really putting women on the map." Then other teenage girls that were aspiring MCs, would come to us and say: "I really feel like I can do this now. I really feel I can contribute to hip hop. I'm not scared any more. You've helped to clear up any misunderstandings that I had about women in the rap industry and the hip hop community." It wasn't until I started getting that type of feedback that I realised how important "Ladies First" was, 'cos when I wrote it I was just enjoying myself and I was just expressing myself and doing what I love to do, which is writing poetry. I had the opportunity to put it to music.'

Queen Latifah was by now an established star. She made an instant impression on Monica Lynch.

'She came to the office and at the time she was still at Irvington High School in East Orange, New Jersey. It's one of those times where someone comes in and you know that there's something very special about them. She was a high school girl, so on the one hand she had all the gangliness and goofiness that high school kids have, but on the other hand, she definitely gave off the sense of worldliness and wisdom that is part of her. And she had a real charisma about her. I could tell from the way other people in the office were responding to her that she had something pretty special and unique. And she sounded great on her demos. She was hard and came off in a very confident way and it was a very different sound and style for female MCs.'

One of the producers on Latifah's debut was The 45 King.

'At the time Latifah was: "I am woman," a Helen Reddy-type gal. She wanted to make a "Ladies First" record and Monie was available, and there you go.'

Love remains proud of "Ladies First" and the way it challenged the roles of women in hip hop.

'I was addressing the lack of women in the industry, the lack of women standing out in the industry.'

Hip hop, though hardly a bastion of equality, had at least provided a level playing field for women. Sha Rock of the Funky Four (Plus One) was the first widely visible female MC, followed in short order by Sequence, the Mercedes Ladies and many others. The first true gender discourse came in 1985, when hip hop was dominated by a series of answer-back records. Brooklyn's UTFO released 'Roxanne Roxanne', an account of a cocksure ghetto girl who wouldn't make their dates, built over Billy Squier's ever popular breakbeat record, 'The Big Beat'. It was answered by a fourteen-year-old from Long Island, Lolita Shanté Gooden, who christened herself Roxanne Shanté, and struck out with 'Roxanne's Revenge'. More records followed, credited to the Real Roxanne, the Original Roxanne, etc. There were an estimated 102 themed releases in all, which said something about rap's pre-Run-D.M.C. insularity, but just as much about simmering gender tensions.

Monica Lynch at Tommy Boy believes that much of the criticism of misogyny in rap arises from ignorance and misunderstanding.

'Misogyny in hip hop has definitely been a question that I've been asked about many times. I would say that it's yet another example of why I think rap gets a disproportionate amount of media criticism, or it used to, I don't think it does any more. But it's sort of silly to hear about all the misogynist overtones in rap when you look at the history of rock music, or go back to earlier genres like the blues and listen to the lyrics in those records. Are there misogynist lyrics in rap? Yes, there are. Are there a lot of other exaggerated lyrics in rap, be they violent or exaggerations of wealth and fame? Always. I'm not saying that it's right or wrong, but I always have said that rap is one of those genres where if someone says something that's particularly threatening or exaggerated, you always have an opportunity for a rebuttal. And a lot of the women have fashioned their own rebuttals over the years.'

Salt-N-Pepa provided the breakthrough success for female MCs in the pop market in 1986 with the likeable *Hot, Cold & Vicious*. In the best traditions of Roxanne Shanté, they got off the blocks with an answer record. Under their original name Super Nature, 'The Show Stopper (Is Stupid Fresh)' hit back at Doug E. Fresh's kiss-and-tell narrative, 'The Show'. They remain unique as female rappers, having broadened and sustained their popularity into a second decade of existence. Others to taste long-term success included the aforementioned Queen Latifah, now a mainstream TV star, and the more hardcore-styled MC Lyte, whose 'I Cram To Understand U (Sam)' superbly documented a lover's descent into crack addiction. But 'Ladies First', Latifah's duet with Monie Love, remains the definitive feminist hip hop statement of the 80s.

Although the Native Tongues soon disappeared from the media's radar, Baby Bambaataa believes its concepts live on in contemporary hip hop.

'Everybody just started building on top of each other, building and building and building. If you could get it, you was in, and thus you had Black Sheep, Queen Latifah, Monie Love and other groups. The Roots, Pharcyde, Souls of Mischief, Del Tha Funky Homosapien, the Black Eyed Peas – I always regard all of those groups as Native Tongue groups. They don't fit in any other category but Native Tongue. Because they're all about art. Their music is about art and skills, be it with a band, a DJ, on the mic, beatboxing. It's about culture, that's their source. So I regard all those groups as Native Tongue.'

# chapter nine

# westside story

## ➤ California Rap

West coast rap, very much the poor relation to New York's hyper-creative hip hop expansion, finally began to stir in the late 80s. The first west coast hip hop song credited with reaching wax had been Disco Daddy and Captain Rapp's 'Gigolo Rap' in 1981. Afrika Islam of the Zulu Nation was one of the pivotal east coast activists who helped spread hip hop west. He toured with Soul Sonic Force in 1980, and returned two years later with the Rock Steady Crew to work on the big budget dance movie *Flashdance* (an inferior, candy-floss descendant of *Wild Style*, featuring breakdancing but no hip hop music). Alongside Grandmixer D.ST and Chris 'The Glove' Taylor, plus local DJs Henry G and Evil E, he DJ'd at the Roxy-styled Radio club in downtown Los Angeles. D.ST was in Los Angeles to work with Herbie Hancock on his groundbreaking 'Rockit' single – the first fusion of jazz with rap. California also boasted a highly visible dance scene, the west coast styles of popping and locking gradually being pulled under the umbrella term breakdancing. Sugarpops, Poppin Pete and Skeeter Rabbit featured in the original west coast dance documentary, *Breakin'*, as did rapper Ice-T.

There were also block parties, though more orchestrated and formal than their New York counterparts, as groups emerged like Uncle Jam's Army, a collective of DJs and promoters led by Roger Clayton. Local MCs honed their skills, rapping over imported Sugarhill/Enjoy records. One early sponsor was KDAY, credited with being the first rap-only radio station in 1984. Programmer Greg Mack promoted tours by New York talent, including Run-D.M.C., the Fat Boys and LL Cool J. The prevailing musical influences in this embryonic hip hop scene were funk supergroups like Parliament, Funkadelic, Zapp and Cameo. California also picked up on the electro boom, with a series of records that betrayed the influence of 'Planet Rock'. Other LA pioneers included Mixmaster Spade and Toddy Tee, whose mix tapes (particularly Tee's 'Batteram') inspired many of the practitioners of what would become gangsta rap. Mention should also be made of

Oakland's prolific 'pimp rapper' Too $hort, and the San Francisco Bay area scene, recalled by *Rap Pages* editor Alan Gordon.

'When you read magazines or watch documentaries on hip hop, when they talk about the west coast they're only dealing with LA, which is not really fair to the Bay area. The Bay area is really the creative engine of west coast music, from E-40 to Digital Underground and Too $hort. The Bay area has its own independent scene and this is something that LA's never had, which is a reason why LA hip hop hasn't grown much. LA pretty much depends on the record labels in Los Angeles to get a deal, whereas the Bay area has created their own scene by either financing their own albums and going independent, or somebody will get one of the bigger drug dealers in the neighbourhood to give them some studio time and put out an album.'

As Monica Lynch of Tommy Boy recalls, the launch of *Yo! MTV Raps* in 1988 had an enormous impact on spreading hip hop to the west coast.

'I think probably the moment where hip hop reached middle America in a very efficient and very significant way was when *Yo! MTV Raps* came on the air. Up to that point it took quite a while for things that were going on in the city to make their way into the suburbs. And in fact it took quite a while for things that were happening in New York to make their way to California. Things didn't happen so instantaneously. When *Yo! MTV Raps* came on, the power of these videos was amazing. All of a sudden you'd go to some place in America and start hearing some kid talking like Fab Five Freddy. So that, I think, was probably the most significant way that rap started hitting middle America, all the videos.'

## ➤ Ice-T – Original West Coast Rapper

The first widely 'recognised' west coast rapper was Tracy Morrow, aka Ice-T. A former military man, and subsequent gangbanger (which says much about the redemptive experience of army life for young men), he was among the many aspiring west coast rappers who monitored the development of hip hop in New York.

'The first time I ever heard a rap record I was in the military. It was the Sugarhill Gang: "Rapper's Delight". A lot of cats that were in the army with me were from the east coast, and they had underground tapes of Grandmaster Flash, Cold Crush Brothers, Treacherous Three. At the time the hottest underground tape was Busy Bee battling. And those tapes were out before the Sugarhill Gang's record came out, but I wasn't aware of them.'

The Sugarhill Gang's impact was immediate, and like many on the west coast, Ice-T's first efforts were improvised rhymes over east coast records.

'I was familiar with rhyming. The hustlers would do the street poetry and I had been making rhymes up, dealing with the LA gangs. Coming from LA, I knew how to just say rhymes. But the theory of doing it over music and to a beat was something totally different to me. The first day I heard "Rapper's Delight" I turned the record over, because the record had an instrumental side and I tried to rap. But my rhymes weren't really based around the syncopation of the beat, it was just more like story telling. But I knew something was there and I dug it, I learned. I think I memorised "Rapper's Delight" in about two days.'

He took the name Ice-T after the author Iceberg Slim, the pen name of blaxploitation writer Robert Beck, whose books like *Pimp: The Story Of My Life* and *Trick Baby* serve as a mandatory read for hustler MCs.

'Iceberg was my name in high school because I used to call Iceberg Slim words out of books, so the girls would call me Iceberg. They said: "Ice, you so cold, if a bullet came through a party it wouldn't do nothing but part your hair."'

After the army, and inspired by 'Rapper's Delight', Ice-T decided on a career as a DJ.

'At the time I was in the military and my agenda was to come home and become a DJ. Everybody that goes into the army usually comes home with a bunch of stupid stereo equipment, because you could buy stuff with no tax. So I came home with all this Pioneer stereo equipment and these big speakers and I was gonna do parties and clubs and venues and just basically make money like that. I didn't want to work for anybody, but when I started doing my parties everybody was fascinated with the rapping. So I said to hell with all this equipment, all I need to do is show up at other people's parties and rap and I could get some fame, make a little money. And this is what I started doing.'

Ice-T can lay claim to one of the earliest west coast hip hop records. In 1982 he improvised a few lines over a Terry Lewis/Jimmy Jam rhythm, which saw release as 'The Coldest Rap'. Other records followed, but as Ice-T concedes, these were essentially carbon copies of New York styles.

'Those were still more like New York raps. Everybody is like: "Look, dude, rap about what you do. You get on the stage and you rap these party raps but then in the dressing room, you are talking about bitches and you are talking about guns. Do that on a record." And we did a record called "Six 'N The Morning" and that was attributed as the first gangsta rap record. That really gave the west coast an image, because as long as we tried to rap like New York it wasn't anything special. Until we actually claimed LA and said this is where we're from and this is how we do it, then we found our niche.'

'Six 'N The Morning' was released in 1986 and, according to Ice-T, was inspired by Schoolly D. Jesse Weaver, to give Schoolly his real name, was a Philadelphia rapper and former shoe salesman who introduced the world to what was then termed 'gun rap' – effectively a precursor to gangsta. He was announced by the single 'PSK – What Does It Mean?' PSK was an acronym for Parkside Killers, a notorious North Philadelphia gang. It was a landmark release, though some later claimed the rapper's connections with the Parkside Killers were tenuous, if not wholly invented. Schoolly D had upped the ante, flying in the face of the benign hip hop tradition established by Afrika Bambaataa and others, by glorifying gang violence and drug scores. But according to Ice-T, records like 'PSK' didn't go far enough.

'It was vague. It wasn't like: "I got a gun and I'm selling dope." So I was like: "That's the vibe, that's the vibe." I just said: "Let's do that, let's cross that with a story." And it took you on a story of a street kid running from the cops, running into some girls talking crazy, knocking the girl out, jumping in a car, rolling with guns, going to jail, and it just had never been done before like that, so blatant.'

Suddenly, whatever the negatives were, west coast rap had something new to offer.

'I think the big break doing west coast rap was us just getting our own identity. I think that's the key to any hip hop, you have to be about where you're from. You cannot be in the south trying to rap about New York. If you are down with Master P, rap about the south. When you're from Miami, rap about Miami, which 2 Live Crew did. [Sir] Mix-A-Lot came out rapping about Seattle. You have to get your own fans or your own neighbourhood to like you and that pushes you through. If you're from Brixton, rap about Brixton, don't rap about LA. You're not gonna get respect and once you get your credit from where you're from, then you move across the world.'

Yet some, like Alan Gordon, believe Ice-T's rapping style always betrayed the New York influence.

'Ice-T was always important, because he was the first gangsta rapper in California, and his rhymes were really hard. But he was always seen as a New York rapper in terms of the way he delivered a rhyme. It was gang related, but it was more the solo individual criminal, 'cos when Ice raps about crime he never really had people around him. There was always himself on a mission, so that was an interesting thing because he was just another character in this world we were creating for ourselves, this one big comic book. Ice, he's an icon out here and will always be remembered for that now his popularity has dwindled [in terms of] album sales. Ice-T will always be recognised.'

## ➤ N.W.A. – *Straight Outta Compton*

Another of the earliest west coast hip hop records was the World Class Wreckin Cru's 'Cabbage Patch', released in 1987. The extravagantly-attired Wreckin Cru employed old school-styled showmanship and featured DJ Yella (Antoine Carraby) and Dr. Dre (Andre Young). From competing LA group CIA came Ice Cube (O'Shea Jackson) who joined with Dre, Yella, Eazy-E (Eric Wright) and MC Ren (Lorenzo Patterson) to form N.W.A. – an acronym for Niggaz With Attitude.

Dre first heard 'The Message' at the age of sixteen. Growing up in the Wilmington Arms district of Compton, which was dominated by local Crips, he elected to steer clear of the gang life and devote himself to music instead. He DJ'd regularly at high school parties, before joining Wreckin Cru, a loose coalition of DJs who worked regularly at venues like Eve's After Dark. One of his colleagues in the Wreckin Cru, Alonzo Williams, sold Dre his BMW in 1986. Dre promised to repay him in instalments, but quickly ran up a lengthy list of traffic violations. Dre was arrested, and when Williams refused to post bail he rang old friend Eazy-E, who agreed to put up the $900 if Dre signed on as producer for Ruthless Records.

As MC Ren relates, this story, and the others behind the formation of N.W.A, were symptomatic of tough inner-city adolescences in Compton.

'If you grow up in any black neighbourhood, they got gangs, I ain't been to one of them have no gangs. So you gotta deal with that. You go to public school, you're going to deal with a variety of gangs in school. It's bad, I'd say, Compton. I ain't gonna say it's the worst place in the world. Compton's the same as every black ghetto I've been to. That's the bottom line.'

Ice Cube, the group's lyricist and most potent rapper, reckons that though the group were community-based, the set-up was also an artificially manufactured one.

'N.W.A. was actually considered an all-star group. I had a group called CIA – Criminals In Action. So we were all spread out and we used to make tapes to sell on the street. It was doing them how we wanted to, real raw. And the tapes start catching on. Everybody wanted to get their hands on the tapes we were selling, so we decided the all-star group gonna make a couple of 12-inches and see what they do. It was just a side thing. When it ended up happening, it blew up so big, we ended up leaving the groups that we were in just to make sure this thing was together and make sure we had our roles set. It was no use to go backwards.'

Those roles within N.W.A. quickly solidified.

'I was mainly a writer and I had ideas as far as production goes. I would kinda write the song, have ideas for inserts, scratching and all that. Dre would do the music and he would take our ideas and apply 'em and put it all together, which was what he did best. Yella was basically helping Dre do that, he was more of a technician type of person in the group. Me and Ren used to write the rhymes. Eazy was the businessman, he had the knowledge and the know-how to make it happen when we could put it out on the streets. So that was everybody's individual role in the group.'

MC Ren was a friend of Eazy-E's from school days.

'Eazy-E wanted to get into the record business. So him and Dre had a DJ group. They used to do house parties called High Power Productions. Dre was already into the game with Wreckin Cru. Eazy put in the money and started his label. He wanted to get these dudes from New York [a duo entitled HBO] to do "Boyz-N-The Hood" [the first song written by Ice Cube when he was sixteen years old]. They didn't want to do it because they said it sounded too west coast, it don't sound like east coast rap. So Eazy was forced to do it, 'cos he had paid this money for the studio and everything. He didn't have nobody else to do it, so he did it. He weren't even going to rhyme, he just did it 'cos he had to.'

Despite Eazy-E's discomfort as a rapper, the single became a moderate local success.

'It was an underground success or whatever, so in the end he tried something else. He said: "Well, I'm gonna do a record with Cube, Dre and some other people, just put it out locally, call it N.W.A." And he used to always say it was going to be "our" style of group, the people that we knew or whatever. So he put it [*N.W.A. And The Posse*] out independent. And it blew up. I wanted to do a solo thing, and I stayed around the corner from him and he knew that. Cube was writing a lotta his material before I got there to write. So Cube, I guess he didn't think it was gonna pop, so he left and he went to school in Arizona. When he left he got a deal with Priority to distribute his records or whatever, and weren't nobody here to write. So he [Eazy-E] brought me in and let me write three or four songs. So that kinda took off. Cube got back, we all got together, and we got a deal with N.W.A.'

Although Eazy-E contributed little in artistic terms to N.W.A., according to Ren, he was very much the motivation behind the group, despite nearly being side-tracked into a career as a postal worker.

'Before Profile, he put all his stuff out through Macola, an independent. He would go up there all the time. He would come pick me up every day from my mother's house, and we would go up. He would walk in and talk to 'em, try to play it off. He would talk to the people at the front desk: "Yeah, yeah, how my record doing?" They'd just look at him. Then me and him would go through the back. He'd take a lotta boxes of his records out the back, because he had a jeep. We used to go around all of those spots, selling 'em off to the core [hardcore fans]. He used to do that all day. Before the group, he was about to go and work for the Post Office. A lotta people don't know that. He had money back in the day, hustling and all that. But he didn't wanna do that no more. He was going to get a job at the Post Office. He was thinking: "This shit ain't gonna work." I went with him. He took his test, but I'm saying: "God, let everything happen." And it took off, so it was cool.'

After his turbulent relationship with Macola, at that stage better known for releasing Mexican 'ranch' music, though they also had Hammer and 2 Live Crew on their books, Eazy-E established his own imprint, Ruthless Records.

'It weren't no lawyers, nothing involved like that. It was more on the street level, the whole company. Whatever we wanted to do, we could do it, anything. Not just music but any other thing. And people that was in the music business out here, there was a lotta R&B people, a lotta rappers. So if you was on a label, you couldn't do a lotta things – you had to do what they wanted you to do. You had to act this certain way, you had to wear these clothes. But we wore what we wanted to wear. We had it all, man, we did everything we wanted to.'

MC Ren remembers that the band members wanted to produce something that measured up to the east coast, but nothing that merely imitated it.

'It was hard, because the only people you had over here making records back then was Ice-T and the [LA] Dream Team. So a lotta people thought that everybody on the west coast was just like the Dream Team. The Dream Team were wack compared to groups like Run-D.M.C., Whodini, LL Cool J. All we had was Ice-T, really.'

Although they recorded *N.W.A. And The Posse* in 1987, it was with the advent of 1989's *Straight Outta Compton* that N.W.A. became a byword for rap rebellion. The statement of intent was laid out an introductory rallying call: 'You are about to witness the strength of street knowledge', and continued through Ice Cube's caustic, amoral tone in 'Gangsta Gangsta' – 'Do I look like a motherfucking role model?' Here was an album that was unashamedly seditious, misogynist and contemptuous of mainstream America. It revelled in its profanity and bloody, violent narratives, but packed a sound so streamlined and brutal that it was impossible to ignore its impact, no matter how difficult it was to gloss over the subject matter.

Ice Cube describes the build-up to its release.

'We were releasing twelve-inches and they were catching on, so it was time to do an album. We put together Eazy-E's album, *Eazy-Duz-It*, first. Then we was going to do *Straight Outta Compton*. We kinda felt each other out and we knew how to put a good record together. We were in our groove going right into *Straight Outta Compton*. The song "Fuck Tha Police" was originally a solo song for me. But me and Ren and Dre decided to make it into a group song, which was one of the best decisions, to make that a group song. That was one of the first songs we start putting together. *Straight Outta Compton* came along when we just wanted to show our skills on the mic over a beat, but rap like nobody has ever rapped before. Just straight from the heart, just saying things that we felt that nobody would say. It was something that the world hadn't seen before, but it was all pure. We didn't know what we was doing, it was like kids playing with dynamite. We were just doing what we felt.'

According to Ren, the album took just two months to complete at Audio Achievements in Torrance, California.

'Every day we met there at 12.30. We don't wanna waste no time, we'd go in there, lock the doors, then just start working.'

'Fuck Tha Police' was the song that thrust N.W.A. into the headlines, and the bad books of the American authorities. But Cube is anything but apologetic.

'The FBI wrote us a letter saying that law enforcement [agencies] didn't like the song "Fuck Tha Police". My record company, they were real scared and nervous about it. But we're so young, we didn't really care. As long as they don't got us in handcuffs, we don't care. And as long as they don't arrest us for this, who cares what they say. That's always been a part of rap as long as I've been in it. Most of my music is controversial, so it kinda goes with the territory.'

For Ren, too, N.W.A.'s use of profanity was rooted in the way they lived their everyday lives.

'Everybody out at that time, you go to their show, they'd be cursing in the show. Then they'd do a record. They don't wanna put out no records cursing, they don't curse. We was like: "They're hypocrites." We're gonna put out something that we feel that everybody can relate to, just like old Eddie Murphy records and Richard Pryor records when they do the concerts. We wanted to do something like that. We wanted to stand out, and that did it.'

Police authorities around the country sent faxes to their colleagues warning them of N.W.A.'s impending arrival. At a show at the Joe Louis Arena in Detroit on 6 August 1989, MC Ren witnessed the first direct police intervention.

'Before we got there, they was trying to ban our concert. All these preachers and people, they tried to ban the show. So before we got there we had to fly there for a press conference. They was telling us, don't do "Fuck Tha Police". If we do "Fuck Tha Police", we're going to jail and all this kinda shit. So we had to have meetings with the city council – and I remember that shit – me and Cube went there. We sat down with the mayor of Detroit and he told us don't do "Fuck Tha Police". We're going to jail if we do it. So we weren't going to do the song. They kept on and kept on, blowing it up, blowing it up. We're back at the hotel waiting to do the show, and we see it on TV, how they're pumping it up, pumping it up. We was like: "Right, let's do the song, that'll sell more records." So we just did the song . . . BOOM! BOOM! Sounded like gunshots, and the crowd started running. They rushed the stage, everybody ran off. They was looking for everybody. They just gave us citations, little tickets, and we left. After that they had it on the news, MTV News. Probably helped sell 500,000 more records.'

Ted Demme, producer of *Yo! MTV Raps*, attended the concert along with Fab Five Freddy and hosts Ed Lover and Dr. Dre (a different Dr. Dre to N.W.A.'s beatmaster). He relates what happened next.

'Backstage it's just this chaotic experience. At least fifty cops, all with their badges out and their guns drawn and I am scared shitless. They've got guys against the wall with guns to their heads and I see Eazy and Dre kick a door open and go flying out the back door. I had it all on video tape. N.W.A. escapes, no one finds them, and they are arresting all kinds of managers and people. Just as I am ready to put the camera away I get spotted by a cop and put into the back room. They go call my boss. I'm thinking: "Oh, God, I'm gonna get fired, I can't believe this." They take the tape, rip it up and go to the hotel and arrest N.W.A. They got arrested that night and they got released later on, but it was scary.'

Some speculated that Eazy-E might have masterminded the whole gangsta rap enterprise to sell more records, a charge that Ice Cube utterly refutes.

'It was done very unconsciously, because we were just being us. That's how we dressed, that's how we looked, that's where we were from, that's what was going on in our neighbourhood. So it wasn't thought out, we were just hoping to get on. We were just hoping to sell some records, people would like us and the west coast would gain some respect. That's all we were really digging for. That's why it came out so good, because it wasn't a scheme, it wasn't a plan. It was just us being who we are.'

The facts bear Ice Cube out. *Straight Outta Compton* became the subject of national exposure only when 'Fuck Tha Police' was condemned by the Fraternal Order of Police and an FBI representative. It was an independent release that went platinum with minimal airplay and TV exposure. Ted Demme relates how MTV considered it too hot to handle.

'I get on the phone and Eazy introduces himself. "Hey, Ted, my name's Eazy-E. I'm calling from California and we got this video we want ya'll to play." I was so blown away when I saw "Straight Outta Compton". It was the best video I had ever seen. I had never been to California. I'm a total New York kid, went to vacation in Florida, never went to California. I showed it to my boss. "Do you believe these guys? They've got crazy jheri-curls, they're wearing gang stuff like bullet-proof vests. This is unbelievable, we gotta meet these guys." Of course, the minute that I set up an interview for him, MTV says they can't play the video.'

Demme was forced to conduct his interview without showing N.W.A.'s video. He took Fab Five Freddy along for the trip to Compton and found the members of the band to be incredibly engaging and funny, if a little intimidating.

'I wasn't sure where the line was drawn, how hard are these guys? Are they messing with me now? There was just an energy about them that I loved. I will never forget driving through Compton on a flatbed truck and all these guys are waving to us and Freddy got up and waved back. "I wouldn't do that Fred, that was just a gang sign." Freddy hit the deck. I will never forget that, it was so funny. That was my introduction to N.W.A.'

Alan Gordon saw huge creative potential in the set-up Eazy had formulated.

'Eazy-E was just a conceptual person. He had an idea. The thing with N.W.A. was that everybody was very talented and very creative and especially everybody they had underneath their umbrella, including the D.O.C., who was probably the most fantastic writer in all of hip hop. And the group members of Above The Law. When these guys would collaborat you never knew who was in the studio, you just knew that Dre was there all day, every day, and all the other members would come in and collaborate, throw ideas around. You never knew what was going to be on each person's album. But Dre had the ability to take your idea and make it that much better. Cube had the same ability to conceptualise or have an idea for a skit based on things that they saw on TV or that they wanted to mimic, or things that they just naturally created for themselves. These are very, very creative individuals. And Eazy had a lot of ideas as far as what he wanted to do and Dre and Ice Cube would be able to crystallise those.'

Ice-T looked on as N.W.A. stole his thunder, but he was impressed by their skill and audacity, and fascinated by their fatalism.

'I had two albums out before N.W.A. hit and when N.W.A. hit, they just came out like BLAM! It was like six Ice-T's on stage, buck wild, and they took it to the next stage. Whereas my records were about crime, but at the same time I just tried to show you the balance of it. If you do it, you might end up in jail. N.W.A. is like: "Fuck it, we're *going* to jail."'

Ice Cube believes N.W.A. finally afforded west coast rap a definition and identity.

'With N.W.A. we just came in with a style all of our own that swept the whole world. So I think that was the ultimate thing the west coast had to do, was create a style for the music that we were doing.'

However, with the success of *Straight Outta Compton*, the group ethic suffered. Ice Cube's departure followed.

'I don't know if it was success, because things went sour quick. It was too quick. I think the group was more successful as far as reaping the benefits of their success after I was gone. We did our album, we put it out, we were doing our tours then everything went sour. It was too quick, too big. It was all the money issue. I had no personal problems, not even with Eazy or anybody in the group. So it was all just financial issues. Two or three years before we were all from totally different places in the world anyway, so it wasn't a thing where we were these brothers. We was a group of all-stars. So it was probably inevitable that we was gonna split at some time.'

A war of words erupted between the former members of N.W.A. and Ice Cube, who reserved special contempt for Ruthless Records' Jerry Heller. Several of these attacks concerned his Jewish origins. In return a skit entitled 'Benedict Arnold' on N.W.A.'s *100 Miles And Running* EP featured Dre threatening to violate Cube with a broomstick.

'So I came back with "No Vaseline" on my record and it got real ugly, to the point where it was getting physical . . . It was a couple of fist fights between my crew and his crew. None of the members ever got to each other but if we could have, we would have. We're all from the streets of LA and Compton, so we take it to the streets, that's how we do it . . . But time heals all wounds. We realised there was no future in us fighting, especially in the street. We all came too far for that and we was thinking about us trying to do a record together and getting it back together. It never came to pass, but that was on people's minds.'

Alan Gordon remembers how the unravelling of N.W.A. occurred.

'The fact that [Ice Cube] was successful outside the group may have caused friction with other people. When they put the album together, you've got a bunch of young guys who are filled with testosterone. They're mad and so they made a diss song and he came back with his diss song on the *Kill At Will* EP. Then he [Dre] came back with more disses throughout the *Efil4Zaggin* album and then he [Ice Cube] came back with "No Vaseline". Then it was over until Dre made *The Chronic*. The only people that responded were Da Lench Mob on the *Menace 2 Society* soundtrack. After *The Chronic* it was over with. "This is silly, we really don't have any beef. You're successful, I'm successful. Let's go on and do our thing." And it never resulted in any physical altercations, except for the New Music Seminar of 1991 where Above The Law and members of Da Lench Mob got into a big fight at a hotel. Cube knew he was a star and he was anxious to do his thing and there were just other factors, people whispering in each other's ear: "You should go solo, get your own record deal, blah, blah, blah." A lot of outside forces, because had these guys stayed together they would have been Death Row in that day, which they already were, but there would have been no Death Row probably. There would just have been Ruthless Records and they might have had every rapper in California underneath their label.'

Gordon points to one specific incident that may have triggered Cube's departure.

'Ice Cube was supposed to have a solo album come out, and Jerry Heller interrupted a studio session and wanted the Above The Law album to come first, and Cube could wait. And they wanted Cube to write another Eazy-E album and another N.W.A. album before they put out the Ice Cube album. Since he wasn't under contract and they were trying to get him to sign a contract, he had to sit back and look at what he had received the total time that he had done this stuff for N.W.A., which was $75,000 maximum. So he evaluated what his situation was, and Dr. Dre was the first person he told because that's the person he was probably closest with. They knew each other before N.W.A. got together.'

N.W.A. were never the same proposition without Cube's lyricism. Nevertheless, the group continued its commercial ascent with the *100 Miles and Runnin'* EP (1990) and the *Efil4Zaggin* LP (1991), which entered the charts at number one under the newly instituted SoundScan system of chart monitoring.

Ice Cube hooked up with Public Enemy's Bomb Squad to work on his solo debut.

'I felt Dre was the best producer on the west coast, and I couldn't have him, so my whole logic was to get the best producers on the east coast, and that's what I did. It was just the right thing for me to do, to try to find the best music available. I went out there and in one month, thirty days, we put together *AmeriKKKa's Most Wanted*.'

Dre, too, eventually dissolved his partnership with Ruthless and N.W.A. As far as Ren was concerned, that was the end of it.

'When Dre left, I was like: "Ain't no way!" No way we could do an N.W.A. album without Dre's beats.'

Dre had been lured away by the shadowy figure of bodyguard turned music mogul Marion 'Suge' Knight. But from Ren's perspective, the loss of his band was a blow that Eazy-E took personally, especially when Dre began to attack him on record and music videos.

'He was mad and hurt. You could tell if you talked to him, 'cos he wanted everybody around him.'

Eazy-E finally fell out with Ren too, when he refused to appear on an answer record attacking Dre.

'He wanted people to be in it, and I couldn't be in it 'cos they ain't did nothing to me. He couldn't take that.'

It is perhaps only fitting that N.W.A., whose achievements form one of the most compelling but morally unsettling bodies of work in modern culture, should implode with such viciousness.

# chapter ten

# rap goes pop

➤ *Tone Loc – Wild Thing*

In 1989, rap delivered its first quantifiable pure pop hit, 'Wild Thing', written by Young MC (Marvin Young) and performed by Tone Loc (Anthony 'Loco' Smith). The producers were Matt Dike and Michael Ross of Delicious Vinyl, one of LA's most distinctive early rap labels. It reached number two in the US charts and became, behind 'We Are The World', the second biggest selling single of the decade. Alongside samples from Van Halen's 'Jamie's Cryin'', this easy-going novelty rap featuring a memorable *basso profundo* performance from Loc, and set a new benchmark for hip hop's commercial viability.

However, Tone Loc attracted the wrath of media elements hostile to rap when the innocent party sentiments of 'Wild Thing' were confused with the term 'wilding', at that time a buzzword for black criminality. A white female banker had been brutally raped while out jogging one night in New York's Central Park by a gang of non-white teenagers. One of the accused youths dismissed the horrific attack as a recreational pastime called 'wilding'. Tone Loc was suddenly thrust into the dock simply because a journalist mis-spelt and therefore misconstrued the title of his song.

Tone Loc was perplexed by the fuss.

'It's a joke. Please, there's no comparison that they could put to the song or anything. I have nothing to do with that. That's way over in Central Park on the whole other side of the country, I have no control over that whatsoever.'

The song's author was Young MC, a successful rapper in his own right. The concept had been put forward by Delicious Records.

'They had given Loc a chance to write it and they didn't like what he wrote. They didn't feel what he wrote was appropriate for what they wanted to do. They asked me to write it, and first draft I gave them, they did their thing. I wrote the record in about half an hour, and out of the four verses I wrote they used three of them . . . There was a specific record that they wanted for Loc – he was a great writer in his own right – but they thought I would be better for him. So they just had me write those two songs ['Wild Thing' and 'Funky Cold Medina'].

Young MC believes the media hysteria was partially fuelled by resentment at rap's success.

'I personally think that there was a big element of that. There was a lot of jealousy from traditional musicians and traditional artists. Seeing kids that had very little or no musical training, they could not hold a note to save their lives, and they are selling millions of records. So there was a lot of disrespect.'

For Mike Ross at Delicious Vinyl, the scare stories over 'wilding' were just the bizarre outcome of ill-informed journalism.

'For a minute there the media tried to tell me to correlate the two things, but it was just for a moment and we didn't really feel it. It didn't really have any effect on what was going on because if you really paid attention they had nothing to do with each other. The whole incident, the whole sociology behind "wilding" is an ill thing and definitely needs to be dealt with. It was a scary aspect of life in New York, but it was a New York kind of thing, it had nothing to do with "Wild Thing".'

The Rev. Calvin Butts, soon to be an outspoken opponent of rap music, viewed the reporting as profoundly racist.

'I thought that was a terrible exploitation of young African American men. I thought it was a terrible exploitation of hip hop. It was a cheap shot, yellow journalism. It served to stigmatise not only the people, but the medium.'

After one further hit single, 'Funky Cold Medina' (according to Young MC an attempt to write a rap 'Love Potion No. 9'), Tone Loc retreated to obscurity and acting roles, as Ross recounts.

'It took a couple of years to make [follow-up album *Cool Hand Loc*] And after Hammer blowing up with "U Can't Touch This" and then Vanilla Ice – a terrible period of rap was at hand at that point. I didn't want to try and make Tone come out that way. So we went with this ballad, "All Through The Night". No one probably remembers the song. But at that time the scene was in a different place. We'd had our fifteen minutes of fame with Tone.'

Delicious Vinyl were then submerged by the west coast gangsta rappers, a movement they steered clear from, preferring to promote acts like the Pharcyde and Masta Ace. As Ross notes, this maintained the label's integrity, but might have been the wrong fiscal decision.

'We can't get arrested. Nobody wants to talk to me but you guys now!'

The success of 'Wild Thing' meant that major record labels were now on the lookout for malleable artists who could deliver some of that market.

## ➤ U Can't Touch This – MC Hammer

In 1990, the music industry was turned inside out with the emergence of two child-friendly pop stars, MC Hammer and Vanilla Ice. Both harvested unprecedented levels of criticism within the hip hop community whilst attaining astonishing sales figures. The careers of both have followed similar trajectories – huge success, followed by a sharp drop in their fortunes and sometimes farcical attempts to re-invent themselves. Both have had run-ins with Suge Knight, the notorious head of Death Row Records. Hammer released a new record in 1999 after his Death Row deal failed to materialise. Vanilla Ice, whose publishing money allegedly funded Death Row, is currently fronting a hard rock band.

'U Can't Touch This' was the summer hit which launched Oakland rapper Hammer, whose public endorsement of Christianity reflected his roots in gospel entertainment.

'I would actually rap in church, that was around '84 and '85. I started to write what would then become MC Hammer records. Previously our group was called the Holy Ghost Boys. There was two of us and I started to develop the MC Hammer style of rapping in my bedroom. It only took from '85 to '86. It took me about twelve months to get that record out because I did it myself. I pressed the record, I engineered the record, recorded the record, programmed the record and went to the recording studio. Did the whole nine yards and then began to market the record myself. So I started getting my record out at the end of '85, and mid-'86 it took off.'

The young Stanley Burrell had switched to rap from a promising career in baseball, but retained his sporting nickname.

'As a young kid I resembled Hank Aaron [Henry "Hammerin' Hank" Aaron] the world famous home run king. I worked for the Oakland A's as a bat boy so all the ball players, Reggie Jackson and all the Oakland A's, the world champions in those days, they called me the Little Hammer. So as a rapper, a friend of mine named Sam suggested I go by MC Hammer, instead of just the Holy Ghost Boy or so forth. So I became my nickname since I was a kid, MC Hammer.'

For Hammer, hip hop had lost the compositional skills evident in its earliest days.

'I was into the dance scene when I began to rap, so naturally I brought in that dancing element right through my performance. I was always a big fan of group choreography, way back in the days with the Jackson 5 and the Temptations and all the groups back then. I brought everything in it that I loved and of course the rappers at that time also brought in real music. If you listen to "Rapper's Delight", it's based on a Chic record, which was a musical record, very much so. Then you go into Grandmaster Flash and the Furious Five, those were musical productions. Grandmaster Flash and the Furious Five and the Sugarhill Gang and Melle Mel and Kurtis Blow – all of those rappers all had music, complete productions. Contrary to what a lot of rappers like to say today, music minus the real chords and music is not real rap. The real rap that came along before they ever even existed was put down with real music, before there was ever a so-called underground or what you would call hip hop today. Before some of the artists were eight or nine years old, this started off with real music.'

Hammer believes his appeal lay in those old-fashioned entertainment virtues which his main competitor, Michael Jackson, personified.

'My music is really grounded in performance, dance, responsible fun. Just having a good time and dancing. People like having a good time. Then, if you throw in responsibility and understanding, these songs touch a lot of people. You capture that through your music, then you are doing what I call soul music and that is what I am making. I'm making soul music. Hip hop reflects soul from a real perspective, good days, bad days, and expresses all of it within the concept of the album.'

Hammer's breakthrough single was 'U Can't Touch This', an innocuous, hook-dominated rap over a Rick James sample. The idea took shape while Hammer was waiting at an airport.

'The idea came from sitting on the runway thinking about music, being in a creative mode, and the phrase "U Can't Touch This" just came to my mind. Those creative things happen like that and being a big fan up to this very day of just about everything that Rick James has done musically – it was just an instantaneous marriage.'

Hammer became a fixture on global pop charts, dominating MTV with his flamboyant choreography and heavily stage-managed videos. His Capitol Records debut album, *Let's Get It Started*, sold millions worldwide. Alan Gordon believes he deserved the sales.

'He was received very well because there was no mistaking Hammer for, say, Ice Cube. There's room for every type of rap in hip hop. A lot of people didn't like it because some people just want their rap hardcore, but if you like to dance then you had to own a Hammer album. And the larger

### KOOL HERC

The expatriate Jamaican DJ and founding father of hip hop, constructing another breakbeat behind the decks in hip hop's homeland, the Bronx.

### AFRIKA BAMBAATAA

Former gang leader and the visionary force behind the Zulu Nation. Bambaataa's eclectic tastes in rock, pop and myriad other styles established hip hop as the jackdaw of modern musics.

### GRANDMASTER FLASH AND THE FURIOUS FIVE

The great technician behind the wheels of steel, Flash (seated) revolutionised the DJ's art, while the Furious Five provided hip hop with its first credible recording act.

## FAB FIVE FREDDY

A one-man hip hop industry, Fab Five Freddy gravitated from subway graffiti to downtown art galleries and was an actor, recording artist and MTV presenter before becoming one of rap's most prolific video directors.

## SUGARHILL GANG

Opportunists to some, the Sugarhill Gang nevertheless gave hip hop a vinyl identity via the release of 'Rapper's Delight' in 1979.

**RUN-D.M.C.**
The trio who took hip hop back to its roots, converted rock audiences
and made rap music a force on MTV.

**BEASTIE BOYS**
The first rap act to top the Billboard charts, the Beastie Boys employed traditional
rock 'n' roll shock tactics to make rap music a mainstream currency.

## PUBLIC ENEMY

The most politicised, challenging and articulate force in the 80s, Public Enemy made hip hop a legitimate medium for protest and social critique.

## DE LA SOUL

With their kaleidoscopic videos and disorientating marriage of musical reference points, De La Soul created hip hop party records that were both intelligent and enduring.

## ICE-T

The original west coast rapper. A man of much greater sensitivity and intelligence than his numerous detractors credit him for, Ice-T is also rap music's foremost raconteur.

## N.W.A.

Effortlessly controversial, Compton's N.W.A. gave the west coast rap scene an identity, and in Dr. Dre (second from left) and Ice Cube (fourth from left) boasted some of the most creative minds in the genre.

**MONIE LOVE**

A British expatriate with a natural grasp of hip hop aesthetics, Monie Love was a talismanic appendage to the Native Tongues movement and co-author of 'Ladies First'.

**MC HAMMER**

The biggest-selling rap artist of all time, whose baggy pants, frothy videos and quick-footed dance routines dominated MTV in the early 90s.

**MARION 'SUGE' KNIGHT**

A measuring stick for black manhood according to some, a public menace to others, Suge Knight's Death Row Records was the defining label of 90s gangsta rap.

## TUPAC SHAKUR

A flawed genius and frequent renegade of justice, Tupac Shakur packed enough into three days of his brief life to fill an entire book.

## BIGGIE SMALLS

New York crack dealer turned rap megastar, the Notorious B.I.G. proved a magnet for trouble – a status which belied his supreme abilities as an MC.

## WU-TANG CLAN

The loose coalition of Staten Island hip hop artists headed by genius producer Rza, the Wu-Tang Clan put New York back on the map in an era of west coast domination.

**EMINEM**
The first credible white rapper since MC Serch of 3rd Bass,
Eminem is a product of the hugely competitive and creative underground
scene revitalising hip hop at the end of the millennium.

**JURASSIC 5**
At the forefront of the new underground – Nu-Mark and Cut Chemist of the Jurassic 5
digging in the racks for second-hand vinyl treasure.

part of Hammer, besides just the music, was the live show or the video. Hammer made everybody upgrade their videos.'

Others, both inside and outside of hip hop, charged him with demeaning their art form. But for Hammer, being popular was not something he needed to justify.

'It is impossible for a rapper to make rap into pop. Pop is just short for popular, which means a lot of people love the record. Every artist that ever makes a record hopes to be pop. They hope that their record will be popular. Nobody makes a record saying: "You know what, I want an underground hit. I only want to sell 10,000 records."'

His credibility wasn't helped by the occasion when President George Bush adopted his 'U Can't Touch This' signature as a fighting slogan. Contrast this with Bush's 1991 response to *Newsweek* about Ice Cube's controversial solo debut: 'I've never heard of them (sic), but I know that rap is the music where it rhymes.' Military staff also employed Hammer's album for motivational purposes in the early 90s Gulf conflict.

'All the military guys were saying we were utilising the album out there to motivate us and things like that. So from the White House down to the jail house, people would quote different terms from the album, different phrases.'

## ➤ Vanilla Ice – Under Pressure

Hot on Hammer's heels came the first commercial white rap artist, Texan Vanilla Ice, who had opened shows on Hammer's tours. Before that, he claimed, he had won his spurs as an original hip hop B-boy.

'I went to this club called City Lights a lot, an all-black club. I just liked the music there and I was accepted there because I had so many friends that I knew that took me there. It was an all-black club. It really wasn't acceptable for a white guy to come in there. But I was embraced there, everybody knew me. I was always there. People accepted me there, it was really cool, I felt loved and comfortable there. I got drunk really bad one night and got up on stage, 'cos my friend dared me to at this little talent contest. I thought it was just a joke. So I got up there and I did my little thing, and the crowd went nuts. I kinda liked it. I was like: "Wow, this is really cool." And I did it the next week and then the week after that, and I just started really liking it. The response was great, the crowd was liking it, I fed off their energy. So I kept doing it and then all of a sudden, one day I did this one contest and Epic and Warner Brothers and Motown and MCA was in the house. I didn't believe these people. A lot of people come and see you and perpetrate and say: "Yeah, I work for this record company," or "I do this and that," and they really shine shoes or something, they're just full of it. So I didn't believe 'em, even though they had the cards and everything. So I landed a small record deal out of that with Ichiban Records out of Atlanta. So I had this record [*Hooked*] that I did at sixteen years old. I had this manager that wanted to change my image and change direction and all this stuff, so it wasn't so hardcore. But if you had heard the first version of *To The Extreme* – I had to take out tons of stuff and change the lyrics and all kinds of things, because it was just too hardcore, too X-rated. We sold 48,000 copies over three years. I opened up for Ice-T, Stetsasonic, EPMD, Sir Mix-A-Lot. I did the whole Stop The Violence tour.'

According to Vanilla Ice, he didn't expect things to turn out the way they did.

'I signed with SPK Records, and they said: "We're going to take your hip hop record and we're going to cross it over to this pop market." I said: "No way, man, I don't even listen to pop music. What are you talking about? It's not going to work." And they were like: "Well, we're so sure it'll work, to change your mind . . . here's a cheque for a million-five." And I saw it, it had my name on it and everything, a million-five. I was three payments behind on my car, and I was nineteen at that time. It was like I won the lottery, man, it was like "Fuck! What do you want me to do? I'll do whatever." So at that point I started playing a puppet. But I couldn't see, there was no way anybody could see selling fifteen, twenty, however many millions I sold of that record. No way I could see that. I didn't expect that, didn't see anything that was going to come from it.'

'Ice Ice Baby' was an amiable rap built wholesale on the bass line of Queen and David Bowie's 'Under Pressure'. Yet its success brought him to the brink of self-destruction.

'After my drug phase from '92 to '94, in '94 I found out that basically it wasn't about the money. Because I had millions of dollars in the bank. I had a million-dollar house, boats in the back yard, Porsches in the garage, and everything materially anybody could ever want. And I tried to commit suicide in '94.'

Chuck D, who before Vanilla Ice went pop considered signing him, believes much of the criticism he took was unjustified.

'White boy just doing rap. I wasn't one of the attackers. Matter of fact, I very rarely have attacked anybody in rap music. When he first came it was 1990, we're playing in the United States, yet another tour, and I'm in Jackson, Mississippi. I hear everybody go crazy over this cut. Nobody knows what this kid looks like, but they love the record. Everybody loved the record, until they saw this kid. And they saw this white kid actually rapping. Two years before, he had opened up for us. He was a white kid from Dallas with a whole black crew, and he had opened up for us in Dallas. Actually, we tried to sign him. 'Cos I said, if there's gonna be an Elvis in hip hop, I wanna own it.'

Alan Gordon was less impressed.

'Vanilla Ice never fit. Vanilla Ice had a great beat with the first single and he was a white dude that could really, really dance. Which was amazing to watch. But those album sales were generated outside of the hip hop community. He probably went gold with hip hop, but the rest of the nine million or whatever that he sold were to people who were just fascinated with the fact that it was a white dude that was dancing. But Vanilla Ice really couldn't rap, his rap was very, very weak . . . Vanilla Ice was a cartoon – the hair-do, the outfits. He was just trying to be like Hammer, which didn't really fit because Hammer was a far better rapper and his subject matter was more endearing to the black community. Vanilla Ice was what he was. He blew up and then that was the end of him. But Vanilla Ice was the worst thing that could happen to white rappers at the time, because MC Serch [of Def Jam group 3rd Bass] was a very good dancer and a very good rapper. On the first album they just came out and they were who they were, but on the second album they tried to distance themselves from Vanilla Ice to prove that they were a different type of white dude than Vanilla Ice. That's where they failed.'

Ice-T, who claims to like Vanilla Ice's new rock band, was nevertheless deeply suspicious of his authenticity as a rapper.

'Vanilla Ice's mistake – he should have never said he was street, that was his mistake. If he had just came out and said: "Hey, I'm a white kid trying to rap," he probably would still be around today rapping. But when you come out and you say street, street is a rite of passage. Every black person isn't street. When you say you're street that means you may have had to live on the street. That means you may have been homeless, you might have been out there really living. All of us didn't come from the street. I personally came from the street, I used to sleep in my car, I was out there going hand to hand, making my money off of the street, not a job, the streets. That's different. So when he came out, he insulted a lot of people by saying that: "I'm from the street." I'm like: "What street? *Sesame Street?*"'

As to the whole MC Hammer/Vanilla Ice competition whipped up by the press, Vanilla maintains that's all it was.

'We were friends. It was just the record company stirring up all this media, and it worked, and we both ended up selling millions and millions and millions of records. To this day we still have more hip hop records sold than any other artist, and I really don't think anybody's gonna ever match that, because that was a phenomenon.'

One of the principal reasons that Vanilla Ice became 'the most hated figure in hip hop history' had to do with his unfortunate comments at an American Music Awards ceremony, where he invited the audience to 'kiss my white ass'.

'That was a regret. I have ADD [Aggression-Driven Depression]. I'm very spontaneous. I said that because some guy in the balcony goes: "Wannabe!" And I go: "Kiss my white ass." I was kinda relating it to him, one guy. I didn't think all these millions of people are watching. It was an idiot moment for me, man. I look back at it and go: "Why did I say that?"'

Another high profile blunder was appearing in Madonna's *Sex* book.

'That was a regret too. I was going out with her on and off for a little period of time. I was over at this house she was renting. She said: "We're going to take some pictures." And I was like: "OK, whatever." I'm not think-ing too much about it and she starts taking her clothes off and everything and running out in the street and stopping traffic. I was kinda going along with it and everybody's laughing. The next thing you know, book comes out – metal jacket, hundred bucks, *Sex*. I'm looking through the pages and I'm going: "Oh, my God!" And there I am. She put me in her slutty package, and I just did not want to be a part of it. I have a lot of regrets. Taking the money and turning it into a puppet in a novelty act – that was a regret – instead of maybe staying with the roots, the hip hop thing, instead of going pop and all that you know, but . . . you can't change history, man.'

Years on, Vanilla Ice hasn't completely lost the arrogance that was a major source of irritation among his hip hop peers.

'People today that are selling hip hop records, like Puff Daddy or whatever, they owe a lot of their record sales to me. They really do, because I put hip hop in front of people's ears who really never considered listening to it at all. If it took a white guy to do it, so what? I still did it.'

Rumours about Vanilla being extorted for money by Suge Knight, in order to found Death Row Records, are common currency in hip hop circles. The story goes something like this. Mario Lavelle Johnson, aka Chocolate, was a young rapper befriended by the D.O.C., an artist whose career prefigured N.W.A's but whose impact was dissipated when he was involved in a car crash. The D.O.C. brought Chocolate to Suge Knight. In 1990, Chocolate heard a record on the radio he claimed to have written for Vanilla Ice two years previously – 'Ice Ice Baby' – while both rappers were working crowds at Tommy Kwon's City Lights venue in Houston. When 'Ice Ice Baby' became a million-seller, Suge Knight decided his client should be paid his dues. After a brief telephone conversation with Kwon, Vanilla Ice's manager, it was arranged that Chocolate would return to Texas to help write songs for Vanilla's album. However, despite selling eighteen million copies, Chocolate believed his authorship of seven songs wasn't fairly credited on *To The Extreme*. Vanilla Ice had a touring engagement in LA and learned that Suge Knight was keen to meet him. He tracked him down to the Ballage Inn in Beverley Hills. Knight asked Vanilla to sign over the publishing rights to *To The Extreme*. Whatever means he employed — rumours persist that he held Vanilla over a balcony fifteen floors up — Knight got his signature.

Vanilla has always denied these stories.

'Suge Knight and I have really not much of a relationship at all. I've only seen him a few times in my entire life. The rumours about him beating me up never happened. Rumours about him hanging me over a balcony never happened. I keep having to repeat myself over and over but I just don't want people to get the wrong impression, because I heard a lot of rumours going around and they're not true. You can look at it like I'm an investor in Death Row Records without a return on my money. And that's it, because it ain't about money with me, so there's no bitterness. He took a lot of money from me or whatever. No bitterness whatsoever, 'cos I ended up with way more than I ever thought I'd end up with.'

When pressed, Vanilla's explanation of events seems somewhat odd, as if he's attempting to excuse Suge's behaviour.

'He just approached me with some paperwork and I got the idea that he knew where I was at all times. He ran off a roster of people that pay him, from Eddie Murphy to so many other people. I was in LA, his town, and this is what he wanted from me. So I gave it to him. I pictured what was going on. I'm not an idiot . . . He knew where we were at all times. He showed up at the Palm Restaurant. I was eating there, he showed up at another restaurant. He had informers everywhere, in the restaurants, in the airport. They knew I was coming through, so . . . If I wanna play I gotta pay, so that's what I did. No big deal. I've no bitterness whatsoever.'

Whatever the truth, the tale serves as an indication of rap's descent into something altogether more sinister than the teenage innocents who bought 'Ice Ice Baby' in their millions could possibly have imagined.

# cash rules everything around me

# chapter eleven

# walking the line: rap and censorship

> ## The 2 Live Crew – As Nasty As They Wanna Be

On 6 June 1990, a federal district court judge in Florida deemed 2 Live Crew's *As Nasty As They Wanna Be* 'obscene'. It was the first album in American legal history to achieve such infamy. Many commentators would agree that it wasn't the most meritorious record ever released, but the obscenity charge marked a major departure in authoritarian responses to provocative art. Although the charge was eventually overturned by a federal appeal court in 1993, the original judgement temporarily laid artists open to prosecution over their lyrics. 2 Live Crew's case drew support from such unlikely sources as Donny Osmond, Sinéad O'Connor and Bruce Springsteen as they defended their first amendment rights to freedom of speech – no matter how objectionably they abused the privilege.

Rap acts were not unique in being subjected to censorship attacks. In the late 80s, extreme rock acts like the Dead Kennedys were scrutinised by the PMRC (Parents Music Resource Center). 'Washington Wives' Tipper Gore and Susan Baker (Al Gore and James Baker's 'better halves') were backed in their moral purge by TV evangelists Pat Robertson, Jimmy Swaggart and Jerry Falwell. One of their proposals was the labelling of offensive albums, an idea based on film classification. Hence the 'Parental advisory: Explicit lyrics' stickers which bedeck most modern rap albums, and a number of rock and R&B releases. That move ensured the records were instantly more attractive to younger consumers.

Comprising Luther 'Luke Skyywalker' Campbell, Kid Ice (Christopher

WongWon), Brother Marquis (Mark Ross) and Mr Mixx (David Hobbs), 2 Live Crew formed in 1985 in Miami, Florida. Their songs and skits were written in the tradition of foul-mouthed comics like Blowfly and Richard Pryor. Campbell, who was sued by George Lucas over his appropriation of the name Luke Skyywalker, was also their label manager.

They had released a number of records before *As Nasty As They Wanna Be*, employing the Miami bass sound of deep 'jeep beats' while boasting relentlessly of their sexual accomplishments. It was crude party music, and no one paid it much heed outside Florida. Then in 1989 they released 'Me So Horny', using a sample from the film *Full Metal Jacket* (specifically, dialogue from a Vietnamese prostitute). The album housing it, *As Nasty As They Wanna Be*, contained eighty-seven separate references to oral sex. Some of their other charming efforts included 'The Fuck Shop' and 'Face Down, Ass Up' (from their appropriately-titled 1990 follow-up album, *Banned In The USA*).

Brother Marquis began his interview by asking if he looked good, 'so I can get me some English pussy'. According to his colleague Kid Ice, 2 Live Crew was simply a reflection of what was happening in their area.

'We represent Miami, Florida, the south, and what the south was all about. It's all about partying and having a good time and at that time we were the only thing coming out the south. The criticism and the press and the people coming at us, we didn't expect that.'

Two retailers were arrested for selling the 2 Live Crew record, and the band itself was cautioning for performing explicit songs at a Florida venue. They faced a further court appearance over a skit on Roy Orbison's 'Pretty Woman' on the 'censored' version of the album, entitled *As Clean As They Wanna Be*. This time they ended up in the Supreme Court, defending an artist's right to parody the work of others. Like the obscenity case that preceded it, they won. Journalist Chuck Phillips notes that 2 Live Crew helped wake up the recording industry to the rap phenomenon, and also to the possible consequences of censorship.

'I think it galvanised the industry, because a lot of people didn't like rap at the time. A lot of white executives didn't like rap, the Recording Industry Association didn't like rap. They were forced to take a stand because this group was going to get arrested for these lyrics. They got arrested, in concert, and then a store owner got arrested – which was a real threat to the record industry. If the store owner gets sent to jail then he can't stock the records, he can't sell 'em, they can't make any money.'

2 Live Crew's most vocal opponent was Jack Thompson, a former golf pro turned high-profile right-wing lawyer.

'On New Year's Day 1990 a friend gave me the transcribed lyrics of 2 Live Crew's album *As Nasty As They Wanna Be*. I was stunned to find what was being uttered on that record was available in main street stores in America. I found out shortly thereafter it was being bought primarily by children. Because I'm a lawyer who has represented sexually abused women and children, that's why I had this concern about what I was looking at – this glorification of the abuse of women on this record. I contacted, ultimately, all sixty-seven sheriffs in the state of Florida and provided transcribed lyrics of the album. The first judge who found the album in the legal parlance 'probably obscene' was in Fort Myers. Luther Campbell, who was the head of 2 Live Crew, was contacted by the media and told that this has happened and Luther said: "Well, the judge is a racist and he must be a clan member." To which the news reporter pointed out, this judge is black.'

Thompson tested his theory that 2 Live Crew's 'pornography' was freely available to children.

'I asked a minor and his parents to go into one of the largest record store chains in South Florida and make the purchase. The album was sold, no questions asked, to this minor, there was no effort to "ID" the boy to see if he was a minor.'

Kid Ice and the rest of the band were unrepentant.

'They wasted their time trying to ban a record on 2 Live Crew instead of going after the drug dealers or something like that. It's ridiculous, but it helped in a way. It brought the group to the forefront, and we kept doing our thing and just kept having fun.'

Many in the hip hop community, like Rick Rubin, believe that without the controversy, 2 Live Crew would never have been heard of.

'When the 2 Live Crew record came out there was all this hubbub about it. I remember thinking: "I wouldn't put that out." But I wouldn't put it out because I didn't think it was a good record, not because I was offended.'

Joe Levy at *Rolling Stone* concurs.

'What happened to them arguably made their career, made them bigger and more important artists then they ever would have been otherwise. They're a "booty" band. It's about rump-shaking and champagne in a hot tub. That music is party music. But all of a sudden they were a first amendment test case, and they made one of the strongest records of their career in reaction to the controversy.'

Kid Ice denies the group were one-trick ponies, pointing to their sales profile prior to national exposure.

'Before they started protesting against us, we had gold records and platinum records. All they did was just brought us more media attention, 'cos we had our core fans.'

## ➤ Cop Killer – Time Warner Gets Cold Feet

The censorship debate exploded in 1992 when Ice-T's spin-off heavy metal band, Body Count, released their eponymous debut. Alongside songs such as 'KKK Bitch' nestled 'Cop Killer', with lyrics about the protagonist being ready 'to dust some cops off'. However, as Joe Levy points out, the song was more measured than some have suggested.

'"Cop Killer" included lines that clearly showed that [Ice-T] was not on a mission to wipe out every cop – things like: "I know your family's hurting/But I'm hurting too". He's a feeling, thinking man.'

Others saw it differently. Jack Thompson began to network with several right wing hard-hitters, including conservative poster boy Oliver North, who couldn't resist fuelling the debate with some ill-conceived moral indignation.

'Oliver North was the head of a group called Freedom Alliance which took certain public positions on issues of the day including the culture wars – the distribution of offensive illegal material through the entertain-ment industry. He called and asked me to represent his Freedom Alliance at the Time Warner shareholders meeting scheduled for June 1992 because Time Warner was distributing rapper Ice-T's album *Body Count*, the most offensive cut on that album being "Cop Killer", which describes how to kill police officers.'

In June, police groups nationwide co-ordinated a call to boycott Time Warner products unless Warner Bros withdrew 'Cop Killer' from the album. The following month, rap's old friend President George Bush weighed into the debate, calling the song 'sick'. The clampdown on Ice-T, according to the artist, was simply an act of corporate racism.

'When rock 'n' roll first came out, it was a serious problem because the white kids liked it. This is the issue that goes on with hip hop music – white kids like it. You think there is not going to be a problem in the south with little white girls singing "Me So Horny" with Luke Skyywalker on the stage? So forget about the words. The problem is not Luke or 2 Live Crew, it's your little daughter, the little white daughter looking at Eazy-E and saying: "I like him, Mommy." And taking down their little Donnie Wahlberg [New Kids On The Block] poster and putting Ice-T up, in shackles, over their bedroom. Back in the days, little white girls screamed for Chuck Berry, they screamed for Little Richard. Now they are screaming for DMX. This is dangerous, right. So I look deeper than the word "censorship". If you're gonna censor, then there's enough rock. I've been on tour with Cannibal Corpse and Crowbar. I've been on tour with death metal bands and black metal bands that are saying stuff that you can't imagine a rapper saying.'

An 'outraged' Charlton Heston read out the lyrics to 'KKK Bitch' to shareholders at Time Warner's annual general meeting. Jack Thompson recalls events.

'I sat there at this shareholders meeting watching Charlton Heston do a reprise of his role as Moses confronting a new Pharaoh, Gerald Levin (Time Warner CEO). It was the most stunning public oratory I had ever seen, because as Heston stood up he was booed and hissed because of what he was about to say and by the end of his speech he had captured the crowd and sat down to thunderous applause. I spoke after him, which was not a particularly enviable thing to be doing, but I made the legal point that what Time Warner was doing in distributing this was illegal. It was criminal, literally, and I predicted that Time Warner was opening itself up to civil lawsuits by people who would be third parties harmed by the advocacy of killing police officers. I mentioned specifically the likelihood that any trooper or police officer killed by an individual who could be proven to have been motivated at least in part by "Cop Killer" would have a cause of action to bring against Time Warner. The *Wall Street Journal* had an article shortly thereafter which said that although it was Heston's oratory which made the news it was my warning of what Time Warner was looking at in damages and possible civil litigation that persuaded the board to take my advice and pull the album off the shelves worldwide.'

Accountants began to look nervously at Time Warner's stock price. To many in the hip hop community, it felt like war was being waged. The theme of 'Cop Killer' was brought into sharp relief by the beating of Rodney King, and the acquittal of the four officers concerned on 30 April 1992, sparking the LA riots. Ice-T recalls how Heston's intervention escalated the furore.

'I thought he was dead first off, when he popped up out of nowhere bitching at me. Charlton Heston is nothing but a politician. The cat rails against me but at the same time he lobbies to keep a bullet called the Cop Killer legal, because he is the president of the NRA [National Rifle Association]. So he's got his shit twisted. But the problem with Charlton Heston is, due to the fact that he's been in a couple of wack movies, people think he's Moses. And if he says something really heavy, somebody thinks fucking God spoke. But he's a twisted old man, probably catch him at a peep [strip] show anytime soon, because I know he's not getting no pussy. But he's nothing to me. For him to step out and come up against me like he knew me, like he was familiar with my work, like he ever heard that record before, that was very wrong. He was brought in to go up against me politically. If I felt he, deep down inside, really felt this song, I might even have some compassion for him. If somebody calls me up and says they want me to go up against something, I'm like: "What about?" "Just go, because we know your voice carries." That's bullshit. I learned that when you speak up, if you start a fight, be prepared to fight it by yourself.'

Chuck Phillips interviewed Charlton Heston several times during the affair.

'He thought it was terrible that lyrics like this should be allowed to be put out on a record by a company of Time Warner's stature. If you're a company like Time Warner, which puts out children's literature and puts out supposedly good movies and things like that, their argument was you should not put out things that are filthy or encourage violence. They probably believe that. I have to give 'em the benefit of the doubt, if you look at their careers that's what they've always said. The problem with that argument is that, and I really agree with the rappers on this – it's a convenient argument for the rappers but it's true – Scorsese can make a very violent movie that can come out of mainstream production. Or a John Wayne movie can be a very violent movie, and no one really thinks of that. They separate John Wayne from the character he's playing, they separate Robert De Niro from the character he's playing. They never separate the rappers from the lyrics they're performing. In some cases it's the rappers' own fault because they promote that image, but in other cases – like Ice Cube – he's an artist, he's not a guy that's going out and shooting people. He's an artist that talks about things and writes about things and now does movies. So on that level I think it was hypocritical of Heston, I'm sure he was in a violent movie at some point in his life. If a sheriff gets shot in a cowboy movie, or a police officer gets shot in a TV show that's put out by Time Warner, then no one thinks that show should be taken off the air.'

Eventually, some sort of compromise had to be reached. There was talk of death threats against Time Warner staff, and Ice-T thought it was unfair to put the lives of his record company's employees at risk over his stance.

'It's not up to Warner Brothers to have the same political beliefs that I have, and if you are gonna be heavily political, be prepared, if you cross that line, for them to say: "Hey, we can't back you on this." I'm not mad at Warner Brothers. People get mad at Warner Brothers. Warner Brothers didn't do nothing. Warner Brothers put the record out. They got in trouble, so I said: "Look, I'm sorry. Let me get a release." It was a point in time where it was just out of control. The president was after me, they were talking about charging me with sedition. You know what sedition is? That's treason, it's punishable by death. So I'm like: "Yo! I'm not gonna die over no fucking record." Wasn't like "Cop Killer" was written as a rally call to go kill cops, it was just a song out of thirteen songs. It was just a move where I had to make a business decision, whether I was going to stand that ground and just totally be destroyed, because they was trying to take me out. I got tax audited three times, it was serious. It ain't really worth it. Simply because people aren't backing me the way they should be. So we pulled it. We wrote a letter to Time Warner and I said: "Look, Time, at this moment I feel I am a liability to you, but in the same sense I feel that you are a liability to me. Because if I change my stance that is my integrity and that is all I got. So, let me go, can I get a release? I owe you all three more albums, let me go my way. I'm not mad at you, just give me a release." And they released me. I put out *Home Invasion* on my own shit and we moved on. But the way the press interpreted it – like Chuck D said, if you ain't in the war, don't comment on the battle, 'cos you don't really know what's going on. The fact that "Cop Killer" was a rock record and they called it a rap record was definitely the way they were able to rally people behind. Because if you say a rock record came out called "Cop Killer", a lot of the white people with power would say: "Well, I like Aerosmith, I like Fleetwood Mac, maybe I like this song. But if you say rap, that means niggers, and I don't like it." Immediately.'

Events, according to Ice-T, went into a surreal but sinister spiral.

'We're sitting at the house one day playing Sega and a homeboy calls me up. He's like: "Yo, Ice, you on TV!" So we switch the channel and there is Dan Quayle, the vice-president, saying Ice-T this and Ice-T that. We're like: "Oh shit! It's on." I don't know how many people know what it's like to have the vice-president yell your name in anger, but it's at that point, and it was crazy to us. Because, like we said, it was just a record.'

Fab Five Freddy, like Chuck Phillips, widens the context of censorship to include mainstream film entertainment, and questions why rap has been the subject of such a witch hunt.

'It's inherently racist, because you have motion pictures with huge white stars that kill, shoot and maim dozens of people. Bruce Willis, Arnold Schwarzenegger, Mel Gibson, go down the list. With sound, as well as picture. And with just the sound from records, they wanna ban this thing. The same corporation, Time Warner, who have bad guys killing cops and doing this and saying whatever, but when it's the voice of young, black, angry youth, it became this whole nightmare.'

Ice-T is still bemused by the whole affair.

'I've been listening to Ozzy Osbourne my whole life. I ain't looking for no bats to eat, I ain't done no rituals. Some kids are weak and they will, but that's not the fault of the music. Johnny Cash said: "I shot a man in Reno, just to watch him die." Sounds like the Geto Boys to me.'

## ➤ Parents Just Don't Understand

2 Live Crew and Ice-T were the two most celebrated examples of rap's brush with censorship, but there were others. In July 1992 Tommy Boy dropped Paris, a highly politicised San Franciscan rapper. An employee had leaked details of his song 'Bush Killa' and the artwork for his forthcoming *Sleeping With The Enemy* album, which featured a scene best described as a Bush assassination fantasy. Monica Lynch at Tommy Boy concedes:

'We've had our run-ins with controversies in rap. Specifically the Paris album was something that was problematic for us. It came not too long after Ice-T's controversy. During that time there was this real sort of moral outrage and a lot of political pressure being directed towards what was perceived as gangsta rap. As a result there was a lot of pressure on corporate America to tone down its involvement in rap.'

The hysteria reached a farcical high point in June 1993, when the Rev. Calvin Butts pledged to steamroller 'offensive' rap records at a New York City protest rally. Having grown up in the South Bronx, Butts knew his hip hop – he can recall seeing the documentary *Beat Street* and enjoyed records by Grandmaster Flash (he incorporated parts of 'The Message' into his sermons), Kurtis Blow and the Fat Boys. But gangsta rap was a whole new ball game. It was 2 Live Crew who first caught his ire. Then members of his flock starting playing him gangsta rap records.

'This is not social commentary, this is not trying to bring people to a greater and higher awareness of some of the problems. This is a glorification of a gangster culture that we certainly don't need to be a part of. Now this is a money-maker to be sure, and whenever you appeal to the lowest element in a human being you're going to get a response. But this is not what we should be doing, this is a prostitution of the music.'

He stresses his distance from some right-wing conservative thinkers who have attacked rap.

'I'm not of the William Bennett school. I wasn't dumping on 'em. I didn't want to destroy their dreams and kill their music.'

One of his many confrontations came on a TV chat show when he was put up against Ice-T, the most eloquent of rap's defenders.

'I had a fight with Ice-T on a TV programme once – not a fight but a debate – and he agreed to appear with me. Ice-T said at first there would be some things we could work out. But then he started talking about his music and how he wasn't going to change. So I exploded and said: "It's my thing to shut you down then." And it's not my thing to shut him down, that's not what I meant. In the heat of that I probably spoke too soon. What I was talking about was, it's my thing to try to get you to see even more clearly.'

After Rev. Calvin Butts, the biggest advocate of censorship in rap music was Dr C. Delores Tucker – who adopted her title despite not holding any recognised post-graduate diploma. Tucker became the highest-ranking black woman in state government in the early 70s as Pennsylvania's Commonwealth Secretary. However, she embarrassed her local party with dubious financial dealings and real estate ventures. Eventually, after being accused of accepting large sums of money for speeches actually written by state employees, she was sacked by Governor Sharp. Her profile slumped, until she was approached by Dionne Warwick at the 1993 'brunch' of the Congressional Black Caucus. Tucker, previously ignorant of rap music, formed the National Political Congress of Black Women. Warwick and Melba Moore (a former R&B singer) became co-chairs.

Dionne Warwick initially connected hip hop with MC Hammer ('It was easy to accept and easy to listen to, and most pleasant to dance to.'), but her views quickly changed.

'Gangsta rap represented a very pointed, unacceptable idiom where my ears and my being – just as a civil human being – were being assaulted and insulted. Having no control whatsoever over the verbiage that was being used, with regards to descriptions of people – women specifically – graphic and demonstrative. Not only adjectives, but activity. Demonstrating what can and will and has been done inside the privacy of four walls, which should be confined to the bedroom and is nobody's business but those that are participating. The use of curse words, just liberally used, without any regard for the ears that were going to be listening to it, and the lack of responsibility of those who were perpetuating this. That's what it did to me and it still does.'

She has heard nothing since to convince her of the worth of rap music.

'I don't think that rap has become the new black American music at all. I don't consider rap [to be] music. I consider it as a form of communication. When you talk about American black music, you talk about Ray Charles and Gladys Knight and Aretha Franklin. You talk about those who are making music. That's American black music and this is rap. It has its own niche it has carved out in our world of entertainment and in the record industry. I really don't call it music.'

C. Delores Tucker can at least make a distinction between hip hop and rap.

'Hip hop music I have no problem with. Gangsta rap I do, because gangster defined by Webster [the dictionary] is "activity engaged in criminal behaviour". As we know, the media, especially music, inspires, it motivates. It's something that our children love to imitate and it has a powerful influence on them. You're teaching children how to become a gangster, because that's what gangsta rap does, it tells them how to engage in the culture of the gangster lifestyle. And that is criminal behaviour which leads them into places where they need not go and they are going at tremendous rates.'

These are legitimate concerns, some of which resonate with voices from within the hip hop community.

'No one should use any negative stereotypical images about anybody, and I support the Jewish people and I just condemn African American people for not doing what our Jewish friends have taught us – never let anybody denigrate you with these stereotypical images that you've fought for years to get rid of. Now you're gonna have children come back and use the term nigger, use the name bitch, call us that, when we are super women, what we had to do to raise those children.'

One of the old school originals, Melle Mel, is an example of someone who has concerns about gangsta rap's celebration of the ghetto and its perversion of the hip hop ideal.

'I ain't trying to go back to the ghettos, just to be in the ghettos and live in some fuckin' tenement with some roaches and all that stupid shit. I ain't trying to be out with niggers, drinking beer, smoking blunts – I did that. That don't get you from point A to point B.'

For Chuck Phillips, Delores Tucker at least came from the community which rappers attacked more than any other – black women.

'That was really the beauty of Delores Tucker in the beginning. There *are* very offensive, sexist, terribly misogynist lyrics in a lot of rap songs, and you had a black woman standing up saying that. That's a lot different than Tipper Gore saying it. You couldn't just say it's a white conservative going after a black rapper or black artist, you could say it's a black woman who had marched with Martin Luther King. She had a pretty good history, even though it was chequered.'

Whilst sharing some of her convictions, the Rev. Calvin Butts disapproved of Tucker's hectoring methods.

'Dolores Tucker is someone that I have great regard for, but I had another approach. My approach was to call the young men and women into conversation, because I believe that only through conversation, dialogue, debate, sometimes argument, will you really get to where each other is coming from.'

Tucker claims that her objections to rap music arose from observing her three-year-old niece's behaviour.

'We had her in a private school and we heard from the teacher that she was doing a lot of things that thirteen-year-olds were doing. She was taking little boys in the bathroom. Then she came home and asked me: "What is a bitch?" The little boys were calling her the "b" word. We even had to take the male Barbie doll away from her because as soon as she got the dolls, she's undressing them and putting them on top of each other. So it affected her in such a tremendous way.'

Sensible observers would dispute the logic of trying to explain her niece's experiments with Ken and Barbie simply by pointing to a rap record she may or may not have heard. Whatever the ideological aversions to censorship may be, the withdrawal or amendment of records is invariably counter-productive, as Kid Ice of 2 Live Crew can attest.

'Our records were meant for adults, eighteen and over with the explicit lyrics and stuff. We also made clean versions for the kids, but somehow the kids got hold of the dirty versions and they liked the dirty version more than the clean versions. So that's when the whole thing started, when parents got a hold of it. That's what started the censorship stuff against 2 Live Crew. We weren't going for that, but it happened, we accepted it and we moved on.'

Joe Levy of *Rolling Stone* believes that America has a pre-disposition to violence that gangsta rap simply exploited.

'Why was *Goodfellas* a big hit? Why is *Lethal Weapon* a big hit worldwide? Why does Sylvester Stallone still have a career? These are questions for the ages. I can't answer them simply, but people like violence. Americans like violence more than your average world citizen. It's sad but it's true. You put a gun on television, you put a gun in the movies, you put a gun on a record and people pay attention.'

# chapter twelve

# natural born killers

---

## ➤ Death Row – Jailhouse Rap

In 1991 pop rappers Hammer, Kriss Kross and the Fresh Prince (aka Will Smith) registered multi-platinum sales. A major factor in pushing the visibility of such artists was the introduction of SoundScan, a management information system gathering retail figures for pre-recorded music from over 15,000 stores in the United States. Mike Fine of SoundScan relates the changes that this new information gathering resource meant for genres like rap.

'Prior to SoundScan, there was basically one overall chart. They talked to store personnel who really didn't have any sales figures in front of them. What they tended to do was report items that were genre-specific to the genre charts, but not to the overall chart. So a store person may say: "OK, I took care of DMX on the rap chart, I won't mention him when I talk about my overall chart." So the pop type of artist tended to do well on the overall chart, but genre-specific artists tended to not come through with their actual sales.'

From SoundScan's introduction in 1991, rap artists started to receive the chart recognition and corresponding media exposure their efforts deserved. But by 1992 it was not the pop rappers who benefited, but the new hardcore gangsta movement. None more so than Dr. Dre, who was about to release his first post-N.W.A. project, *The Chronic*.

## ➤ Suge Knight – Gangsta Godfather

Before talking about *The Chronic*, one of the biggest-selling rap albums of all it's necessary to backtrack to the slow rise of Marion 'Suge' Knight in LA rap hierarchy. Indulged by his mother, Suge Knight grew up in a tough Compton ghetto around Blood gangs like the Tree Top Pirus. He was a sporting prodigy, rising to the heights of reserve linesman for the LA Rams. He then found a job as a bodyguard for swingbeat king Bobby Brown. At clubs and parties he kept meeting local celebrity the D.O.C., who was produced by Dr. Dre. The D.O.C. soon became his next client. In the meantime, his reputation as a no-nonsense arbitrator, someone who relished physical confrontations, increased tenfold.

One of the most persistent rumours surrounding Knight concerned his financing of Death Row from the proceeds of Vanilla Ice's publishing rights (discussed in Chapter Ten). Death Row publicist George Pryce is convinced Knight obtained the backing legally.

'The Vanilla Ice incident is definitely BS [bullshit]. The money that I know about came definitely out of Suge's pocket. I've no idea with the whole financial thing, but this money, as far as I know, came out of his pocket, and from Jimmy Iovine and Ted Field [of Interscope] who were spending a great deal of money on the development of Death Row when they signed them on. But Vanilla Ice was definitely not dropped over any balcony.'

Knight seduced first the D.O.C. then his good friend Dr. Dre (plus Dre's girlfriend Michel'le) to his management, after he made repeated claims that the members of N.W.A. were being underpaid by Ruthless, Eazy-E and Jerry Heller. The next objective was to get Dre, the golden goose, released from his Ruthless contract. Knight invited Eazy to a meeting. When Eazy arrived, Knight told him that the D.O.C., Dre and other artists including Michel'le, Kokane and Above The Law wanted to leave the label. Knight denies that any leverage was employed on his part to get Eazy to sign release forms. Eazy counters that Knight said he was holding Jerry Heller in a van outside, and 'knew where my mother lived'. Whatever took place, Knight emerged with the release papers. Knight clearly enjoyed the art of intimidation. *Rap Pages* editor Alan Gordon remembers his tremendous presence.

'Suge Knight was this ominous figure. Here is this 6ft 5in, 320lbs black man who looks like he should be in the WWF [World Wrestling Federation] running a record company, wearing all red and diamonds and jewels. He has this evil stare, but a very gracious smile. You wanted to know who he was and there were rumours starting: "Oh, he's a former Blood." But he just commanded a lot of respect because anything that Suge Knight wanted to do, he'd have had anybody following him. He was the measuring stick of manhood that black men in America would like to achieve. Here is somebody from the streets who burst his way into the entertainment industry and made himself successful and then showed that he had a high level of intelligence to start brokering record deals and film deals. So he was Superman for black men, until we found out that he got caught up in this celebrity and the vanity got to him and he started to become more of a figure than his artists. That's where the problem arose.'

In all his statements, all the way up to his committal hearings in 1995, Suge Knight emphasised the community ties that bound Death Row. Afrika Baby Bambaataa of the Jungle Brothers contrasts the family vibe of the Native Tongues with the mentality of the gangsta rappers.

'All these groups had the same profile as being family, like the Native Tongues people had, but they were more a sinister family. They were more of a ghetto-centric family, where Native Tongues was an Afrocentric family. We were good neighbours to each other, we had love for each other and that came across in the music and the way we wrote our lyrics. We were friends, not enemies. Everybody who could relate to us were automatically our friends. It was a creative movement, not a destructive movement.'

## ➤ Snoop Doggy Dogg – From Out Of Deep Cover

Calvin Broadus, aka Snoop Doggy Dogg, formerly dealt drugs as part of a large Crip gang based in Long Beach. Later, he would tell George Pryce about what informed his decision to move away from the drug trade.

'Snoop had been in prison for a brief time regarding drugs, and he told me while he was in prison, all of these older guys, some of whom were there for the rest of their lives, said to him: "Look, guy, you know you're talented." He used to rap for them and they were saying: "Don't follow this, you don't need to be like this. You get out of here. You're intelligent, you're good looking, you're young, you should be able to make it."'

In 1991 Snoop hooked up with producer Warren G (Warren Griffin), the hard-drinking step-brother of Dr. Dre. Together with R&B singer Nate Dogg (Nathaniel Hale), Snoop's classmate from Polytechnic High School, they formed 213, and tried to get Dre interested in their project. Although initially reluctant to endorse them, about a month before the release of N.W.A.'s *Efil4Zaggin* Dre heard a demo tape that impressed him. Snoop was invited to collaborate on a song Dre was moulding as the theme to a new film, *Deep Cover*. Snoop wrote a set of lyrics inside ninety minutes, in the process establishing himself as Death Row's most talented new asset. Among the other artists who joined the roster were Kurupt (Ricardo

Brown) and Delmar 'Daz' Arnaud, a Long Beach native and cousin of Snoop. Together they became Tha Dogg Pound.

The *Deep Cover* soundtrack became a major hit on release in May 1992, but unresolved legal problems surfaced. Ruthless sued Sony for using Dre without their permission, alleging that his release papers were signed by Eazy-E under duress. The case was thrown out of court, but bitterness on both sides escalated, as Dre's projected solo album, *The Chronic*, was held back from release schedules.

Further legal trouble stalked Knight, Dre and Death Row. Dre had already physically attacked Dee Barnes of Fox TV's *Pump It Up* programme, resulting in a rash of adverse publicity. Then at the Black Radio Exclusive convention in New Orleans, Dre and four others were arrested. There were other dangerous precedents. Aspiring rappers Lynwood and George Stanley were viciously beaten, and stripped, by Knight, after Lynwood had 'improperly' used Knight's telephone. Dre was also hit with another assault charge for attacking Damon Thomas on 2 June 1992. As a result he was shackled with a tracking device.

After allegedly using finance from imprisoned drug baron Michael Harris, Knight found more legitimate backers for his enterprise in the shape of Interscope Records, run by Ted Field and Jimmy Iovine. However, during negotiations in November 1992, Ruthless once again fired off a multi-million lawsuit alleging breach of contract over the *Deep Cover* soundtrack. A settlement was finally reached in December, whereby Ruthless agreed to release Dre on the proviso that his new employers would pay a royalty on all his subsequent production work. *The Chronic* was finally readied to hit the streets.

Very much a Death Row production, Dre's collaborators on *The Chronic* included Snoop Doggy Dogg, Tha Dogg Pound, the D.O.C., Rage and RBX. With repeated endorsements of marijuana use, proclamations about the stature of the Death Row family and attacks on Eazy-E, *The Chronic* featured some of Dre's most accomplished work. It subsequently became the biggest selling hardcore rap album of all time. It was in Billboard's Top Ten for eight months, confirming the commercial potential of gangsta rap.

Alan Gordon believes there was more than one genius at work on *The Chronic*.

'The D.O.C. rarely ever curses, he's an extremely good writer. He's almost like an English teacher, and when they were doing *The Chronic*, the D.O.C. was the principal writer for everybody on that album, Snoop Dog included. So when you listen to Snoop Doggy Dog after the D.O.C. left Death Row, you hear the difference in his raps now to his raps then.

Rappers really don't change too much even if they change their style, but Snoop used a lot more cursing than he did before. The D.O.C. spent much more time helping them craft their lyrics, and that whole teamwork ethic made N.W.A. what it was and actually made Death Row what it was.'

Writer Chuck Phillips recalls that, for all the album's advocacy of illegal drugs, Interscope were wary of Ice-T's situation with 'Cop Killer' and made sure anti-police lyrics were removed.

'There was a song on *The Chronic* that they changed the lyrics to and removed the cop references. They cut those things out because Interscope said: "No more." For a while you didn't hear anything on a Dr. Dre record about shooting cops.'

According to Phillips, *The Chronic* merits its reputation as one of the finest albums of the decade.

'*The Chronic* was a different album than had ever been made in rap before. It was a great record and it was really musical. There's so much creativity in that record by so many guys that nobody even knew. Dre was one of the few people anybody knew at the time, and it was a re-birth for him. It was totally different to anything he'd done. For my taste and I think, obviously, for the taste of a lot of people, it brought P-Funk's music back. It brought back George Clinton [a regular and consenting source of samples on Dr. Dre's work], it brought funk, it brought real piano, real guitars, real bass lines. He used the drum machine as if it was a real drummer. So it was music you could hear, with fantastic rapping and some great lyrics – not all great lyrics – but some very great lyrics. So on the level of music, this album was huge in the black community, and it eventually translated into the white community, but it took a while.'

If mid-80s hip hop was hallmarked by a stripped-down aesthetic to reflect a 'street' perspective, then the 90s saw the sound draw heavily on R&B and funk grooves. G-Funk was the term affixed to Dre's creation, and it quickly became the dominant musical motif of gangsta rap.

After the release of *The Chronic*, Death Row moved into an address on Wilshire Boulevard, near Westwood, adjacent to Interscope's offices. It was periodically populated with Bloods, Knight's favoured gang, but also rival Crips. Some of the stories that emerge of events there, ranging from intimidation to outright thuggery, would be hard to believe were it not for the number of such accounts. The store room was reputedly employed as a 'torture chamber' where those who had caused offence were taken to be 'slapped down'. Visitors regularly saw office menials mopping up blood from the floor at Wilshire Boulevard or Death Row's preferred studio, Can-Am, Tarzana.

By this time venerable publicist George Pryce had joined Death Row's staff.

'I went to his office and sat there for seven days round the clock waiting to see him. When he did see me, he passed by and said: "You've got to forgive me for the delay in interviewing you, but I'm having a staff meeting and as soon as that meeting's over, we'll talk. Better still, why don't you come to the meeting?" The first thing on the agenda – he stood up and said to everyone: "I'd like you to meet George Pryce. He's the new director of publicity for Death Row Records." We hadn't talked salary, hours, anything.'

Pryce is among those who feel Suge Knight has been misrepresented by a hostile media.

'Suge Knight was a brilliant person. I have a son the same age, and I used to talk very frankly to Suge. I was never afraid of him. Some people were, only because he's such a commanding guy, a commanding force. Not that he was some kind of monster, because he certainly wasn't.'

Pryce had never worked for a record company before, but sensed that Knight wanted him because:

'They needed someone that was versed in damage control, which I had done, but mostly on a corporate level prior to going there.'

His first major project was Snoop Doggy Dogg's album, the follow-up to *The Chronic*. Because of his age he was nicknamed Papa G by his co-workers, though Knight preferred to address him as Papa Hollywood because of his perceived affluent background. He quickly adapted to the volatile atmosphere at Death Row.

'I was working on the telephone at my desk and Suge's cousin came in. She said: "Papa G, you've got to leave right now." I said: "I'm on this call, I'll be off in a few minutes." She took the phone out of my hand and grabbed me by the hand and pulled me out. As we were walking out the door there were some guys coming in. I think they were armed and they were people that had been disgruntled by something that Death Row was doing, from some gang. So we left the building for a moment, and that was more or less my first experience with what could happen at Death Row.'

Pryce echoes Knight's statements about Death Row being a family. Yet he would occasionally caution the label's roster on bringing their vinyl personas into the office.

'I would tell them: "Don't start acting out that stuff with me, that's a role you're playing, but the cameras are off for today. Calm down and be who you are."'

Confounded by the violence, upset at delays to the start of his recording career and brave enough to complain about not being paid commensurate to his contributions, rapper RBX became the first member of the Death Row family to jump ship. Eventually he would release a solo album tellingly entitled: *AWOL: Escape From Death Row*. Long-time Death Row supporter the D.O.C. also departed, under the pretext of travelling to Atlanta to work with friend MC Breed.

For Snoop's solo bow, Knight co-opted two of Nate Dogg's songs, 'Ain't No Fun' and 'Regulate' (co-written with Warren G). As he'd done on *The Chronic*, Dre worked methodically, recording hundreds of songs before picking out the versions he preferred. Others contributed, including former EPMD alumnus Sam Sneed and Warren G, but Dre kept the credit for himself. Nate Dogg recalls how Snoop worked alongside Dre in the studio.

'Sometimes he'll write, sometimes he'll freestyle, but with "Gin And Juice", he just got on the mic and said what he was gonna say. And if you're having fun, it's gonna come out. If you mess up, hey, you're on a mic, go back and do it again. But that's basically how it happened that time, just in the studio messing round.'

He describes the origins of 'Ain't No Fun'.

'I was going to work one morning and I forgot something, and my cousin lived with me and my girl. So when I get back home my girl was touching her toes, you know? That's what I was thinking about when I was writing my poem, it ain't no fun. I was mad but I got it out of my system that day.'

Before the album could be released, Snoop found himself in enough trouble to end his career before it started. On 23 August 1993 he was upstairs with bodyguard McKinley 'Big Malik' Lee at his home in the Palms district of LA. Another friend, Sean Abrams, was standing outside when he became embroiled in an argument with neighbour Philip Woldemariam, who drove off with two friends. Tensions had been simmering for some time, and Snoop, Abrams and Lee resolved to end it, boarding their jeep and pursuing Woldemariam. They eventually caught up with the trio, who were eating Mexican takeaway in Woodbine Park. Gunfire ensued. Woldemariam was shot in the back by Malik, who maintains he acted in self-defence. Whatever the truth about Snoop's involvement, he found himself charged with first degree murder weeks before his album emerged.

Fab Five Freddy had interviewed Dr. Dre for MTV, and through that connection was chosen to shoot Snoop's video for 'What's My Name?'.

'We wanted to come up with something that had a visual hook and go some place that people hadn't gone visually yet. So I did some research into the technology around Morphing, which was still very new. So I did my research and the rest was that video, "What's My Name?". That video was done about six months after the LA riots, so you had a very tense situation. I was supposed to shoot another exterior shot, which was gonna be a Doberman sitting between a girl's legs, and it was going to move from the girl petting the dog's head into the girl braiding Snoop's hair. But we never got to shoot that set-up. Dre told me Snoop would be there that day, so I'd be able to get all the set-ups I needed to complete the video. I said: "Dre, what's going on?" He says: "I'll talk to you in a minute." So in between shooting we get a break to change the lighting set-up. I said: "Dre, what is going on? What time is Snoop gonna get here?" He says: "Yeah, we gotta little problem." I jokingly said: "Well, what is it, a 187?" [the police code for a homicide]. He said yeah. I was like: "What do you mean? Snoop?" He said: "Yeah, some guy had been following him around, putting up his gang signs and they bumped heads, got into it, shots were exchanged, he's dead." During that period of time he went underground. Coming up in two days was the MTV Music Video Awards, where he was scheduled to present an award. He went, gave out an award, and turned himself in.'

Chuck Phillips remembers how Snoop's murder case changed everything.

'People had been arrested for things, but never a guy that was right on the cusp of becoming a superstar. It made him huge in a negative and positive way, because he rapped about shooting people and getting in gunfights and fighting it out. And the very thing he's been arrested for, all of a sudden, is the very thing he's rapping about. It was a big deal because it looked like he could go to jail . . . It took the illusion of gangsta rap – which everybody had been saying before was just a story – now you got a guy that's talking about it who's arrested for murder. That made it a different thing and a much scarier thing for everybody in the record industry.'

Housed in an appalling cartoon cover drawn by another of his innumerable cousins, Snoop's album *Doggy Style* sold 800,000 copies in its first week of release, entering Billboard's charts at number one. Many sales were attributable to the massive publicity Snoop's murder charge had engendered. But as George Pryce discovered, the sales were coming from outside the LA ghettos discussed in the lyrics.

'The majority of Death Row sales were coming from young suburban Caucasian children, boys and girls alike. It made up a greater proportion of the sales. People in the ghetto all appreciated and all wanted the music, but in ghettos and urban areas people have other ways of getting it. I think other people thought it was damaging because it was going into all kinds of homes in Beverley Hills and New York and that kind of thing, where it hadn't before. Little white kids were walking around with their asses out and rapping. I think that's where it really became a problem, not for us, but maybe for certain factions in America.'

The success of *Doggy Style* seemed to ensure Death Row's long-term survival. However, all was not well. Warren G left the label after a series of provocations – he'd been slapped publicly by Knight, had his lyrics altered so they contained pro-Blood statements and finally, at the boat party for the launch of *Doggy Style*, his friends had been beaten up and thrown off the boat under Knight's direction. Warren lined himself up with a contract at Def Jam and found himself the latest multi-million selling G-Funk star. Suge Knight quickly identified the perfect replacement – Tupac Shakur.

# chapter thirteen

# murder was the case

➤ *Tupac Shakur – Thug Life*

Tupac Shakur, aka 2Pac, was the son of struggling mother and Black Panther activist Alice Faye Williams who later took the name Afeni. She gave birth to her 'prince' on 16 June 1971, taking legal work in Brooklyn to raise the child and Tupac's half-sister. As a teenager, his mother enrolled Tupac in the 127th Street Ensemble, a Harlem theatre group, before relocating the family to Baltimore. Contrary to his later persona, he attended Baltimore School For The Arts and studied acting and ballet. By the time he was eighteen, the family had moved again, this time to Marin County in California. Tupac turned to drug dealing, and through Digital Underground's manager Atron Gregory got a chance to join their stage show as a dancer. In 1991 he began making his first demo tapes, one of which reached Interscope A&R man Tom Whalley.

Tupac was chosen by producer Neil Moritz for a role in his feature film, *Juice*, about a Harlem heist gone wrong. Many believe the hard-bitten character he played informed his subsequent musical persona. His Interscope debut album, *2Pacalypse Now*, emerged in 1991. Sales of 500,000 were enough to encourage Time Warner to increase its stake in Interscope prior to the Ice-T furore. A year later Tupac moved to Los Angeles and had the first of a series of scrapes with the law. In Oakland he was ticketed for jaywalking, then beaten by the police (he filed a $10 million lawsuit). On 11 April 1992, a nineteen-year-old murdered a Texas policeman. The youth's lawyers claimed 2Pac's 'Trapped', from *2Pacalypse Now*, had triggered his actions. Chuck Phillips reported on the case.

'His name was Ron Howard, and he shot a state trooper while he claimed he had *2Pacalypse Now* on. The policeman walked up to the window and he just shot him, didn't ask any questions or anything. And his widow sued Tupac and the record company, which became a big deal. They lost that case, but it became part of the argument in [Howard's] criminal case. He was convicted, and he's on death row right now. Part of his argument was that the music influenced him to kill. He claimed the lyrics about killing cops were on when the guy was walking up to the car, and he shot him.'

In August, Tupac was alleged to have been involved in an incident in Marin County in which a six-year-old boy was shot in the head. A month later, vice president Dan Quayle declared that *2Pacalypse Now* had 'no place in our society'. George Pryce compares Tupac to his old friend and former client, Miles Davis, the legendary jazz trumpeter and another driven Gemini with a split personality.

'He had some old wounds, and I don't mean literally, even though he had them literally. Just wounds of the mind and heart from things that had happened in the past. When he finally got an audience, or he got an avenue with which to speak out, he did, and he did it in a very short length of time which overwhelmed people.'

Tupac attempted to upgrade his image as a tough guy with the release of his second album, *Strictly 4 My N.I.G.G.A.Z.*, in 1993. Despite its title, the overwhelming majority of buyers were white. Tupac's vendetta against the world continued. He beat up a limousine driver who accused his entourage of using drugs in his car. And after being upstaged by an MC who dared to battle him in Lansing, Michigan, Tupac retaliated with a baseball bat.

The dizzying pace of Tupac's life accelerated. After appearing opposite Janet Jackson in John Singleton's *Poetic Justice*, he relocated to Atlanta in the autumn of 1993. On Halloween he was involved in the shooting of two undercover cops. He was charged with aggravated assault, but in November he pressed ahead with a role in *Above The Rim*. It was now that Suge Knight moved in, knowing Tupac's innumerable scrapes had landed him with huge legal bills. Tupac agreed to give him a song, 'Pour Out A Little Liquor', credited to Thug Life, but refused to sign a full contract with Death Row.

Tupac couldn't keep out of trouble. On 18 November he was co-charged with the rape of fan Ayanna Jackson in his Parker-Meridien hotel suite. The adverse publicity was too much for Interscope's Jimmy Iovine, who now encouraged Knight's attempts to lure Tupac away to Death Row. Tupac again refused. His next court appearance came on 1 February 1994, after he was charged with attacking film directors Allen and Albert Hughes on the set of a video shoot for Spice 1's 'Trigger Got No Heart'. He received a fifteen-day sentence for the assault.

With artists like Tupac flagrantly ignoring the law and lyrics extolling the beauty of violence, rap was the subject of a series of scare stories in the mainstream press. On 23 February 1994, Representative Cardiss Collins and Senator Carol Moseley-Braun held government sessions concerning explicit lyrics in pop music, an event subsequently known as the 'gangsta rap hearings'. The campaign 'to bring gangsta rap to heel on Capitol Hill' was spearheaded by C. Delores Tucker.

'As a result of that, it made the industry know that they were being watched, and that further hearings would continue, and they did.'

If Suge Knight was being watched, he didn't care. There are a thousand stories. One of the most chilling was the disappearance of business competitor Happy Walters (manager of Cypress Hill, Funkdoobiest and House Of Pain). He went out one afternoon to withdraw money from a cash machine and re-appeared three days later, shaved and naked. When questioned about what had befallen him, Walters claimed he had amnesia. Others noticed cigarette burns on his arms. Then there was the *New Yorker* writer who arrived at Can-Am Studios to do a profile on Death Row. He made the mistake of asking Knight an impertinent question. For his troubles, he had his face held over Knight's office fish tank — containing piranha. Even the loyal George Pryce admits there were things that went on without his knowledge.

'If some of the things you read about went on, I certainly was never privy to them. Suge would tell me when it was necessary for me to be in meetings. I would say: "Oh, you're having a meeting, Suge, is it necessary for me to come?" "No, Papa Hollywood, you go on and do your work, we don't need you." And then I'd hear that maybe there was an incident.'

## ➤ Sean 'Puffy' Combs & Biggie Smalls – I Love The Dough

Sean 'Puffy' Combs started out as an intern at Andre Harrell's Uptown Records, where his first major signing was Jodeci. Demonstrating a keen eye for trends in black music, Puffy adapted their image to reflect 'the hip hop vibe' and was rewarded when Jodeci's debut album topped the R&B charts and sold three million copies. But his most important signing was Biggie Smalls. A crack dealer on Brooklyn's Flatbush Avenue, Christopher 'Biggie Smalls' Wallace (aka Notorious B.I.G.) weighed over 300lbs and took up rapping as a sideline to his criminal day job. One of his homeboys, producer Lance 'Un' Rivera, recalls his entry into showbusiness.

'Biggie came to me, he had rapped over Big Daddy Kane's record or something like that. This was the guy everybody was talking about, he was the nicest in the neighbourhood at rapping. So we went down to this studio, downtown Brooklyn, called Funky Slice, and tried to make a demo. One thing led to another, but I lost interest. Biggie still pursued a record deal.'

Biggie sent a demo tape to Big Daddy Kane's DJ Mister Cee, who forwarded it to the *Source*'s 'Unsigned Hype' column. It also reached Puffy's ears, who immediately fell for Biggie's laconic but booming delivery. Rivera would eventually set up the Atlantic Records-backed Undeas company with Biggie – a label that released records by their homeboys and friends Junior Mafia and Lil' Kim. Rivera says he was inspired to do so by Puff Daddy's arrogance when he dropped in to see how Biggie's career was progressing.

'One day Biggie asked me to come out to Jodeci's video shoot. We were sitting there waiting for Puffy to come. When Puffy showed up, he saw me with Biggie and he called Biggie across the street. I saw this smile turn to a frown on Biggie's face. Puffy asked Biggie: "Who is that guy?" Biggie was like: "Yo, that's my man from the 'hood." And Puffy set it down: "Nah, he can't come because DeVante [Donald DeGrate of Jodeci] don't know him, you can't be bringing him too." So I seen the expression on Biggie's face, he was upset about it. As I was driving home I called my brother and said: "Yo, man, I wanna be in the music business." He was like: "Yeah? What changed your mind?" And I said: "Puffy". That's why I'm in the music business. Just to get on Puffy's nerves.'

Although he continued to sell drugs, Biggie's debut single, 'Party And Bullshit', was issued by Uptown. But Puffy believed Biggie was the crucial artist if he were to make a success of his own label. Too ambitious to remain a deputy to Harrell for long, he launched Bad Boy Records with backing from Arista and signed Biggie, as well as Craig Mack. Puffy and Biggie spent eighteen months working on his number one debut album, *Ready To Die*.

On 29 November 1994, the first day of his trial for the rape of Ayanna Jackson, Tupac Shakur was invited to a recording session to guest on a new track by Little Shawn of Uptown Records. At the entrance to the Quad Recording Studio in Times Square, he was shot several times and robbed. Despite this, he still crawled into the elevator to reach the meeting, at which he found Biggie Smalls, Puff Daddy and other Uptown employees. It was only in the hospital that he discovered he had been shot five times. One shot had penetrated his skull, another removed one of his testicles (leading detractors to dub him 'Onepac'). Yet at 6.45pm the next day, he discharged himself. Wheelchaired into court on 30 November to hear the verdict on the Jackson case, he was found guilty of sexual abuse, but inno-cent of the more serious sodomy charge. He checked into another hospital under an assumed name, still fearful that those who wished his death would come looking to finish the job.

In February 1995, Tupac received a four-and-a-half-year sentence, and was taken to Rikers Island, then Clinton Correctional. His recordings, especially 'Dear Mama' and his third album, Me Against The World, which debuted at number one on the Billboard charts, were huge hits. But reports leaked out of jail that he was receiving 'special attention' from inmates and prison officers. All the time in prison he dwelled on who was behind his shooting. He believed Biggie Smalls and Puff Daddy to be the perpetrators. Also in February 1995, the Stanley brothers' case against Knight reached court. Pleading no contest, he was sentenced to nine years' probation.

Knight's old nemesis, Eazy-E, was dying of AIDS. By 9.30pm on 1 March his condition had worsened seriously, and in room 5105 of Cedars-Sinai Hospital he married his girlfriend Tomika Woods. Over the next two weeks he was placed on a respirator as his condition became critical. His attorney read a statement at the steps to the hospital which included the admission: 'Maybe success was too good to me'. Dre visited him in an attempt to reconcile, but Eazy never regained consciousness. By 26 March 1995 Eazy-E had died of AIDS-related pneumonia. He left seven children.

## ➤ East Meets West – Territorial Dissings

Tensions between east coast and west coast rappers intensified during the early 90s. The sudden rise of N.W.A. and its related artists, and the break-through of Death Row, had stolen the rap market from under New York's nose. On the east coast, the old school bemoaned the touting of gang affil-iations that hip hop had originally sought to destroy. Baby Bambaataa of the Jungle Brothers recalls the upset that the situation caused hip hop founder Kool Herc.

'I'm not going to name any names, but you had groups that went after it and said: "Look, we're going to hold it down for New York." They did whatever they had to do and New York was happy with it, but I don't think Kool Herc was. When I see Kool Herc today – and that's the found-ing father of hip hop – he's like: "I just wish they wouldn't be talking these gangsta tales."'

Conflicting opinions on the east-west divide were regularly explored in the Source, the highest circulation rap periodical. Alan Gordon of competitor *Rap Pages* believes the *Source* was distrusted by many on the west coast for what they saw as pro-New York coverage.

'The east coast/west coast beef started in the pages of the *Source*. East coast rappers were always getting better ratings than west coast rappers. That created a lot of hostility, that you had to prove something to New York. Rappers from the east coast had a forum to sit down and say what they did not like, but they would not use names: "I don't like that gangsta rap." If you say you don't like gangsta rap, you're basically saying, at that time, you don't like west coast music. That's where everything started, and it started festering more and more in the pages. Then when *Vibe* [magazine] came, they opened up another forum for that, with all the Tupac controversy. Then here come the articles: "Is there an east coast/west coast beef?" Then the rappers fall right in line and started making songs, even guys who were never really involved in any disses started making songs about New York and how your record will never get played out here, if you come out here I'll slap you, blah, blah, blah.'

The east coast/west coast resentment reached boiling point at the August 1995 *Source* Awards ceremony. Rightly or wrongly, Sean Puffy Combs had acquired a reputation for appearing in all his artist's videos, and for slapping 'executive producer' on records where his involvement was tenuous. In the company of newly recruited R&B singer Danny Boy, Knight took the stage and made a thinly veiled attack on Puffy. George Pryce recalls events that evening.

'Suge, in receiving an award that night, said: "Come to Death Row. You don't have to worry about your CEO being in all the videos and rapping and that sort of thing," which was taken totally out of context. It was picked up by people who hadn't fact-checked. But this went on and on and on, and from that, people started acting it out. Suge was just saying that he concentrated for the most part on what he did. Dre was the producer, he had his acts. It took me months before I could get Suge Knight to do an interview or go on television. He was a behind-the-scenes kind of guy, a true suit even though he didn't wear one. It wasn't an attack, it was a comment that was turned into an attack. All he said was if you want to be on a label where your CEO is not in the videos, is not this and that or the other, then come to Death Row. A very small thing. I'd guarantee you it was maybe not the right thing to say on television at an awards show, but that's Suge. He's a real person, meant nothing harsh about it. Then things started happening. People read about it and get angry . . . After the incident Puffy called me several times because he wanted to turn the whole thing into some sort of a unity movement and to get Death Row Records and Bad Boy Records to immediately do a big blitz advertising campaign and that kind of thing'

According to Fab Five Freddy, the host that evening, Suge Knight was simply bullying his east coast competitor.

'I was one of the hosts that year, when Suge got on stage and really kicked it into high gear. When he stood on the stage in New York, he came up there with one of his artists and said: "If anybody out there wants to come and get down with a record label, and doesn't want the executive producer jumping all around on your videos, then y'all come and get down with Death Row." Immediately the crowd was like "Oooh!" It was like: "Oh, my God! It could jump off right here!" Those were the volleys that got the crowd really riled up. But these weren't the artists that felt this way, these were the people in the peripheries around the different artists. Sadly, those were the people who ended up pulling the trigger on Biggie and Tupac, who were the two biggest casualties.'

Puffy, later in the evening, struck a conciliatory tone, pleading for the west and east coasts to work together as brothers. But, whatever Pryce says, the damage had been done. The paths of Puffy and Knight crossed once again on 24 September 1995, at Jermaine Dupri's birthday party in Atlanta. There was a shooting outside the club as Puffy tried to speak to Knight. Knight's friend and bodyguard, Jake 'The Violator' Robles, was shot. He died from his injuries a week later. Knight believed Puffy was behind the assassin's bullet, which he thought was intended for him. The feud entered a deadly new phase.

Death Row was now deeply immersed in gang culture. Suge Knight decorated his office in red, the Bloods' preferred colour. Dre was unhappy with the way things were heading, despite having been dubbed 'The Phil Spector of rap' by Newsweek. While Knight was trying to sign R&B acts and arranging soundtrack tie-ins to duff movies like Above The Rim, Dre wanted to complete his reunion album with Ice Cube and finalise a record by his girlfriend, Michel'le. In addition, he faced his own legal tangles. A high-speed car chase with the LAPD in 1994 led to six months in a Pasadena halfway house. By the time he came out, he had tired of Death Row's ceaseless promotion of gang life.

With Tupac locked up in prison, Knight made his move. Together with lawyer David Kenner, he travelled to greet Tupac on his release on 12 October 1995. Tupac's bond of $1.4 million was met by Death Row/Interscope. Knight had 'got his man', by now the most successful rapper in America. George Pryce remembers the initial impression Tupac made on him as 'delightful'.

'I had known his mother a good deal ahead of having met him. But he had so much energy. And a certain sadness, a certain suspicion of everyone around him, because of circumstances. This is an unfortunate thing to happen to a young person, to feel that they always have to be looking over their shoulder. But he did feel [safe] coming to Death Row, he felt protected. I think he looked at Suge as a brother, but also possibly a father figure, which he had never had before.'

Tupac immediately entered the recording studio, Knight passing him a handful of master tapes that Dre had recorded for his joint effort with Ice Cube. Friend and producer Johnny J Jackson worked alongside him. A more unusual collaboration developed with Faith Evans, wife of Biggie Smalls, the man Tupac believed had tried to have him killed. Their collaboration became 'Wonder Why They Call U Bytch', but they were forced to use Death Row R&B singer Jewell to voice the track due to contractual complications. George Pryce recalls the incredible energy Tupac possessed once he'd left jail.

'I felt that he knew how much time he had on this planet. He worked incessantly day and night. If he got an idea in the middle of the night, he'd call up Suge Knight and say: "I'm on my way to the studio, let's do this, this and this." And Suge was able to understand that creativity. He allowed him to do that, where some of the other artists were very structured. There was jealousy. There were people who had projects that were about ready to come out, that his things superseded. That was because he was on a mental timetable. This man came out and did *All Eyez On Me*, which was the double CD. None of that stuff was in his head in prison or anything, he came out and produced that whole album. He was in the studio the day after he flew here from prison. We had a party, we had a dinner in Westwood, and the next morning he was in the studio and when he came out he had a double CD.'

However, Johnny J also remembers a quieter, more reflective side to the man.

'There were times when he would come out to me and my wife's house, and just be quiet and enjoy himself. Have a sandwich, go out and read a newspaper. He was a real quiet, cool individual. He could be that party animal and be as loud as I don't know what, but when we got to our house he just wanted to rest up. You could tell he needed to take that break and lay his head down. He laid on the sofa and everything. I kinda look at it as a sentimental thing, my homie laid there, but he was a real quiet individual deep down. The man was so down to earth and so sincere. He would look at me and my wife and say: "One day I'm going to be like y'all. I'm gonna get me a wife, I'm gonna find me a good woman.'"

Death Row was consistently attacked by right wing extremists, religious bodies and maverick self-publicists like Delores Tucker. She now viewed all gangsta rap as 'pornographic smut', despite having heard very little of it. She bought Time Warner shares and campaigned vociferously that they should drop Interscope, thereby isolating Death Row. The release of Tha Dogg Pound's *Dogg Food* ('the filthiest of them all') was consequently delayed. It was not long before Time Warner bowed to the pressure and pulled out of Interscope, allowing the label to buy back its shares. Suge Knight claimed that Tucker's activities were a front for her attempts to establish her own 'clean' rap label. However, *Dogg Food* still hit stores on Halloween Night 1995.

In December, Snoop and Tha Dogg Pound (Daz and Kurupt) arrived in New York to record a video for 'New York, New York', a remake of the Grandmaster Flash track. They denied it was intended to diss the east coast, but given Death Row's reputation, few in New York believed them. Monie Love was asked to appear in the video, and harvested a torrent of abuse for her efforts.

'I went to that video shoot, 'cos a girlfriend of mine was dancing in it. The guy asks me: "Can we get a shot of you in this video?" With this whole east coast/west coast nonsense, this imaginary war going on, I can either be in this and get ridiculed by New York or I can choose not to for politically correct reasons. I said to myself: "What am I doing that for? I've never even met Tha Dogg Pound, much less have they ever done anything to displease me. If it was anybody else asking me to be in their video, I'd say yes." So based on that fact, I said yes. I was in the video, it came out, I did get ridiculed. All sorts of people came up to me saying: "How can you be in that 'New York, New York' video? They're the westside, they're dissing New York. You're supposed to be from New York." I was like: "Look, if you want to get geographically technical, I'm from England, so I don't know what the bloody hell you're talking about."'

On 6 February 1996, Snoop attended the LA Superior Court for the hearing into the murder of Philip Woldemariam. The crucial witness in the trial was Duchaum Joseph, Woldemariam's friend, who said McKinley Lee had fired in self-defence (even though Woldemariam was hit in the back). After nine days of deliberation, the jurors recorded a 'not guilty' verdict. Some were later invited to eat with the acquitted defendant, Snoop, at Monty's Steakhouse. One juror even attempted to impress Suge Knight with a rap about the trial. George Pryce remembers the toll the legal proceedings took on Snoop.

'He grew up a great deal during that time. I was with him every day, in and out of court. When we had a few moments to talk, it really did devastate him. But he grew up a great deal then. He started thinking about his family. He had the one son and he just became more family-oriented.'

When Dre was released from his Pasadena halfway house, he was disturbed by the changes at Death Row. Previously the label's big cheese, he was appalled at Knight's decision to sign Tupac and particularly Hammer. The former pop rapper had known Knight since he helped with security on Hammer's 1989 tour.

'We went back since '88, '89 as friends. So by '95, at the height of Death Row and me going through a transitional period, Suge gave me a call and said: "Hammer, you could make an album right now and sell fifteen million albums. Come down here with your homeboy and get in that studio and let's see what we can come up with." So we began to put some ideas together on how we were going to do this, and Tupac wrote a few tunes for me.'

Hammer still remains loyal to Knight, and admires his business acumen.

'When you felt that "gangsta image", a lot of that came from the CEO of the company. He really knew what he wanted to hear, contrary to what people might think. He wasn't just the "muscle" side. Suge cut a lot of business deals with a lot of people. He had a lot of movie things and a lot of soundtrack things going on. He was in the midst of diversifying his company. So while you had the other element that was obviously publicised, there was a very astute businessman working on the other side. Suge was after every dollar, make no mistake about it. If we were playing cards right now and we stacked that money on the table and I turned my head, my pile was gonna be short a few dollars.'

Dre swallowed his pride and started work on a new song, 'California Love'. Knight ordered the song be included on Tupac's new album. Then he tried to force Dre into producing an album for Hammer. Dre quietly struck a deal with Interscope to allow him out of his contract. Suge Knight didn't take what he saw as disloyalty lightly. Death Row artists began to spread rumours that Dre was a homosexual. Tupac was particularly vicious, writing two hateful anti-Dre raps in 'Toss It Up' and 'To Live And Die in LA'. Knight also paid a personal visit to Dre's home to recover some outstanding master tapes.

Producer Sam Sneed also departed after a confrontation with Knight because he had featured east coast guest stars in his video, 'Recognize'. He was to be punished. The industry rumour was that he was raped in an artists meeting, though Sneed admits only to a severe beating. Sneed considered his options, swore an affidavit about events and booked plane tickets to leave the country. Alan Gordon watched the whole edifice of Death Row begin to crumble.

'What went wrong was egos abounding. The thing that Suge Knight should have learned from Eazy-E, which was how he secured Dre and the D.O.C. and Michel'le from the roster, was that you had to treat your artists just a little bit better. Cater to their egos a little bit. A few hundred thousand dollars here, a nice car there, which he had done. But when they ask for it, you've almost got to "baby" them. At the same time, slap them on their wrists and say: "I'm daddy, I'm running the show."'

Tupac's 1995 album *All Eyez On Me* was a sprawling double set, replete with innumerable put-downs of Biggie Smalls and suggestions that he had bedded his wife, Faith Evans. According to George Pryce, Tupac was convinced Puffy, Biggie or both were behind his attempted assassination.

'He wasn't a liar. That's what he really felt. I wasn't inside his head and I didn't know his background. I didn't know what in the past had happened. I do know that he told me that he'd been very close to Biggie Smalls at some point in the past. They'd started out together.'

At the 1996 Soul Train Awards in Los Angeles on 29 March, Biggie was booed by Death Row staff and affiliates. A further confrontation was reported backstage, but as George Pryce relates, such incidents were often exacerbated by press hype.

'There was a *Hollywood Reporter* journalist at one awards. Tupac was all done up in fatigues, like Che Guevara. Of course, they had no weapon whatsoever, but we did see someone across the parking lot. He had something, I don't believe it was even a gun. This guy who was always drunk from the *Hollywood Reporter* came out, stood there for a minute and went back into the entire press corps and told them that Tupac's just pulled a gun on someone from Bad Boy Records. I called this guy and said: "Number one, you were drunk. How dare you? If you thought you saw that, write about it. Why did you go in and announce that to 250 people in the press corps which is going to put an incident that was blown totally out of proportion all over the world?" This kind of stuff really ate at me with reporters.'

Tupac kept up the feud by releasing 'Hit Em Up' – which targeted not only Biggie, but Puff Daddy and Mobb Deep. However, according to Lance Rivera, Biggie loved the song.

'In my opinion, that was a good record. Outside of what was going on, what the lyrical content was. Me and Big used to laugh about the record, because this record was hot. At the end of the day, it still was music.'

On 7 September 1996, Tupac flew to Las Vegas to attend the Mike Tyson and Bruce Seldon boxing match in the company of Suge Knight. In the lobby there was a fight, where the Death Row Bloods beat up on suspected Crip members. Afterwards their cars headed out to Club 662, Suge Knight's latest entertainment venture. As the convoy moved through the streets, a Cadillac with California plates pulled up alongside Tupac and Knight's BMW. The car was sprayed with bullets. Knight's head was grazed, but Tupac caught four bullets, two in the chest. Still conscious, Tupac was wheeled into the University Medical Center. While he was in surgery, his mother Afeni, boxer Mike Tyson and the Reverend Jesse Jackson came to the hospital. Tupac spent six days in a critical condition before being pronounced dead just after 4pm on 13 September 1996.

George Pryce was in Club 662, waiting in vain for the Death Row convoy to arrive.

'I had some major press people coming into the club for the party, who were not going to the fight. So I felt as though I should go ahead, or I would have been in that caravan. Someone immediately came and whispered to me in the club, and I had my son with me, and I immediately got into the taxi and went to the hospital. And I never saw Tupac again. I talked with Suge, and then the lawyers asked me to get on a plane to come back to Los Angeles to go into the office. They knew that I would have a great amount to do. So I handled things from this end and Suge's attorneys handled most of the press in Las Vegas. So I missed seeing Tupac again. I kept abreast of it until he died. I was glued to television sets and telephones. Then I had to go forward with trying to make arrangements for things after his passing. I still do not understand it. I think it's going to take me a lot of years before I really understand it. The world is a funny place in that he was respected and did very well, but he's an overnight icon now. Anything that he did will make lots of money for other people for many years to come. I was in a state of shock for quite a few days. I had to deal with other artists who were also very afraid for themselves. Because no one actually knew how this had come about. The incident that had happened after the fight was totally unrelated, I believe, to the reasons for the killing. I don't know, that's part of the mystery. I'm an amateur detective but I haven't solved that one yet.'

Tupac's producer Johnny J was at his wife's high school reunion when he heard the news. He rounded up some other friends and booked a plane ticket to Vegas.

'We got there, slept a little bit, arrived at the hospital and talked to his mum. Afeni was telling us: "My baby is gonna pull through, he is going to be all right." So we were relieved. Ten to fifteen minutes later, we're pulling out of the driveway. We were gonna grab a bite to eat, 'cos Tupac's mum is telling us he is gonna make it. Radio turns on: "Tupac has just died." We're not even out of the hospital driveway yet. The whole hospital turned into total chaos – helicopters, police cars, cameramen were chasing people. We got into the front of the hospital and we were all emotional. Everyone is breaking down and people was chasing us, trying to interview us. I went into a total wreck that night. I held the pain in all night and I just went totally crazy. Headlights were on through the whole day for 'Pac, in memory of him. I went and bought all the Tupac CDs I could get my hands on. I bought everything and they were just selling out. Vegas was crazy. That had to have been the wildest experience I have ever dealt with and I will never forget it. You know it was hard, man, it was hard for us. Broke my heart in half and I couldn't believe it and still, to this day, it's hard to believe that he is gone.'

Inter-gang warfare between the Bloods and Crips intensified as a result of Tupac's slaying. Meanwhile, Suge Knight was under investigation by federal authorities, who established a task force to investigate Death Row's links to the drug trade. Knight pounced on Death Row accountant Steven Cantrock, accusing him of misusing label funds for his own benefit. He was forced to sign an 'IOU' for the missing money, allegedly at gunpoint. The authorities believed that this time, Suge Knight had gone too far. Witnesses to the event were subpoenaed to give evidence to a federal grand jury. Knight injured his case by acting erratically. He failed to make two court dates requiring mandatory drug tests, violating his existing probation. A bail hearing was ordered for 28 October 1996, at which Judge John Ouderkirk remanded him in jail for parole violations. The net was closing in.

The court proceedings resumed on 14 November. On 26 November, despite the protests of Death Row artists and sundry henchmen, Judge Czuleger found Knight to be guilty of actively participating in the attack on Orlando Anderson, the Crip who was beaten at the MGM Grand immediately before Tupac's death. Knight read out a long statement, explaining how he had always acted for his community, but it was light on contrition. Suge Knight was going to remain in jail. Judge Czuleger withdrew his parole and ordered him to serve out his nine-year sentence for the Lynwood assault.

Alan Gordon saw Knight's downfall as inevitable.

'Suge Knight gave in to his own vanity. He started to become bigger than his artists, showing up on the cover of magazines. As Suge Knight, you don't want to be on the cover of the *Source*, even though it would be great for album sales. As Suge Knight you want to be on the cover of *Forbes*, you want to be on the cover of *Black Enterprise*. You want to be on the distinguished level, you don't want to keep it too street.'

George Pryce reflects on the tremendous success the label had engendered, and what he sees as deliberate misrepresentation by the media.

'We were tremendously successful. That's one part that I think the press was right about. If it weren't for certain circumstances, I would say it would still be. I have this funny feeling that some people in this country still don't like that kind of success for people who are not educated. They basically came with what they knew and it made money. There was a hunger for that "keeping it real" kind of thing. That's what we were selling – being real – and that's what young people the world over obviously wanted and still want.'

With Knight in a prison cell, Death Row was rudderless and adrift. Afeni Shakur began to question the value of her son's estate with Interscope. The creditors swooped on Death Row, as former producers like Johnny Jackson complained of non-payment of promised royalties. Nate Dogg believes Afeni Shakur's research stampeded others at the label into questioning their financial situation.

'Everything was fine, everybody was new in the game, so we weren't really tripping on royalties. I would say it got out of hand when Tupac passed. A lot of people started wanting to look into it. It's just the response Death Row gave his mother when she was looking for money. It made all of us want to go and see about our money. They said that Tupac spent all his money up on girls, which was mighty funny.'

Among other creditors were Solar Records' Dick Griffey, the D.O.C. and American Express. Michael Harris, the imprisoned drug lord, also wanted to know where his investment in Death Row had gone. Strangest of all, Delores Tucker filed a $10 million lawsuit against the estate of Tupac Shakur, alleging that his lyrics about her on *All Eyez On Me* had caused her personal humiliation and mental suffering. Due to Tupac's lyrics, she stated, her husband William no longer wanted to have sex with her. Prince Paul had seen one of his Gravediggaz records caught up in the censorship furore. For him, Tucker's actions robbed her of whatever dignity and integrity her position held.

'You're saying you hate Tupac and then trying to sue his estate? In other words you're getting all the bad rap money that he's made for cursing and all that and you're putting it in your pocket? It's still dirty money.'

With Suge Knight gone, his artists faded away. Nate Dogg remembers that a name change after Tupac's death seemed to bring the operation bad luck.

'We gave ourselves the name Untouchable Death Row. I think that jinxed us. You may be blessed enough to be on top of the world, but you were quite touchable.'

Other mainstays of the Death Row operation also quit, notably George Pryce.

'I left Death Row because the man that hired me and the man that was the only person that I really answered to at Death Row was not at Death Row. I was unhappy at the way things were turning. They all became Suge Knights overnight.'

A week after Suge Knight was sentenced, Biggie Smalls attended the 1997 Soul Train Awards in Los Angeles. It was followed the next evening by a party hosted by *Vibe* magazine. Puff Daddy, Little Caesar (of Junior M.A.F.I.A.) and Biggie, nursing a broken leg from a car accident, attended. Puffy and his entourage drove ahead of Biggie's car. When the convoy stopped at a red light, a car pulled up alongside them. Half a dozen shots rang out. When Puffy reached his friend's car, he found Biggie slumped in his seat. He was rushed to hospital (the Cedars-Sinai Medical Center, where Eazy-E died) but was pronounced dead.

Press stories raged about the identity of Biggie's killer, and whether it was a payback killing for Tupac's murder. Others speculated that the cause of the shooting was a disagreement with local Southside Crips, whom Biggie had previously employed for security purposes. Whatever the truth, Biggie's murder brought to an end arguably the most disturbing chapter in twentieth-century music. According to Chuck Phillips, Biggie's assassin, unlike Tupac's, left no trail.

'To this day I don't know who killed Biggie. I think I do know who killed Tupac and I think the police knew. To this day there's not one name I've ever got of a real person, and I really have tried. I spent hours and hours on who shot Biggie. So no one knew where that killing came from, and how did this guy disappear and never say a word about it, and do such an excellent job in front of so many people?'

Lance Rivera sums up the feelings of many in the hip hop community.

'Nobody deserves to die for reasons that they had nuthin' to do with. Biggie didn't have a beef with whoever killed him, he didn't curse out his mother, he didn't stick up his girlfriend. He was listening to music and somebody drove past and killed him.'

Hammer was among those best placed to observe the impact of the deaths of Tupac and Biggie.

'The deaths of Tupac and Biggie absolutely marked a turning point. It felt as though enough is enough of what I call the media rivalry. The east coast versus the west coast feud sold a lot of magazines and the magazines perpetuated a whole lot of it. I'm sure if you were isolated from the actual places, the west coast and the east coast, you would think there was a civil war going on. But outside of that entrapment and those devastating deaths, what was really going on? When do two people arguing make a war? But it was great for magazines and as soon as the deaths happened, the same magazines said: "We gotta end this. We gotta bring peace." And the peace sold a lot of magazines. It's just unfortunate that people can be exploited to the point of creating enough animosity through the media to cause tensions and hate and anger, enough to cause a death. Because in the end analysis, I blame the media more than I do the actual people who killed Biggie and Tupac.'

Monie Love observed hip hop's crisis of confidence.

'When Tupac and Biggie died, there was a lot of speculation as to: "Is hip hop going to survive? Will it survive the death of Tupac and Biggie?" And quite frankly, money survives everything. There's too much money in hip hop now for it to become stagnant, even though we lost two of the most influential people within hip hop.'

To Chuck D, the invidious glorification of black-on-black violence that dominated rap music in the 90s went unremarked upon because young black men were seen by the corporations as expendable. He believes that the deaths of Biggie and Tupac were, therefore, largely inevitable.

'One company came out and said: "We got the realest niggers' shit around." And this is a record company that is backing and endorsing it. They sit up in their white offices in New York and accepted it going on, because they say: "Hey, that's real." Yeah, but we know what's reality. Reality is somebody steppin' up in *your* office and blowing *you* away too. It dissipated with a situation that was predictable in the middle of the 90s. I said a couple of these kids are gonna come home in a box, and still make a profit for these companies. I said that in 1991, 1992, and the boxes that came home was Tupac's in '96 and Biggie's in '97, amongst a bunch of boxes that come home.'

For Lance Rivera, however, what the dual tragedies proved was that it was ultimately up to an artist's own conscience what they put on their records.

'It's not really up to the record companies or the people who market and promote it. It's up to the artists. If you look around and you see a child, what do you want your child to say? "Kill, Die, Smoke Weed, Fuck, Fuck, Fuck?" So then you have to ask yourself, is there some type of creative way that I can relate to the masses without using those particular words? People like Tupac did it with "Keep Your Head Up" and people like Biggie did it with "One More Chance". That's true artistry.'

## ➤ After The Fall

Before the deaths of Tupac and Biggie, gangsta rap had reached critical mass. Afterwards, there was less appetite for incessant lyrics about gangland gun battles. Ice-T, for one, felt that the glorification of violence had gone too far.

'I've been shot a couple of times, I know that shit hurts. It burns. I'm always gonna love groups like Mobb Deep, DMX, because that's hardcore stuff, but the problem is how close are you gonna play to your raps? We've had two tragedies with Biggie and Tupac and I think that basically is because they had a personal beef that they took on to wax. Biggie's got a million fans and Tupac's got a million fans, and that's very dangerous. I don't advise it. We felt the loss of them, because they were some of the greatest, and when they died we all learned. When Eazy died of AIDS, everybody learned. AIDS hadn't really touched me until Eazy passed. So, unfortunately, I think Tupac and Biggie and Eazy maybe died so that hip hop could live, and it's a much more peaceful game at this point. There's a lot more love shown between the east and the west coast, because we saw what stupidity could bring. I know them brothers is resting in peace, but we don't wanna see that happen again. You ain't never heard about Ice-T going to jail or getting caught for drugs or carrying guns or getting busted at an airport. The only time I ever got in trouble, I didn't break the law, so does that mean I'm fake? Or does that mean I'm smart? You answer that.'

Rick Rubin admits to boredom with the way gangsta rap had overtaken the genre.

'There were things about gangsta rap that I actually liked in terms of how "outlaw" its position was. But again, it was N.W.A. and the Geto Boys. It was a handful of groups that really did it well. Just the endless flow of records that were offshoots of those were a lot less interesting to me. I can't say that I was against gangsta rap as a genre, I'm just against bad records.'

Others, like Chuck D, take offence at the unscrupulous morals of some of those companies pedalling gangsta rap.

'These companies are profiting off the negative aspect of black life, profiting off black death. If you're gonna profit off it, at least you should be able to open the door to reality checks for the artists, train them on how to deal with the public. Maybe you can't change their art, we're not asking for that, but you gotta be more present to make contributions in the community for what you're taking the money from.'

On 20 April 1999 Los Angeles Police confirmed they were now treating Marion 'Suge' Knight as a suspect in the murder of Notorious B.I.G.

# chapter fourteen

# empires of rap

> ## Business As Unusual

As Death Row's influence dwindled, rap grew stronger yet. After a lull in their fortunes, Def Jam reclaimed their ascendancy first through LL Cool J's *Mr Smith* (1995), Jay-Z's multi-platinum *Hard Knock Life* and finally with hardcore rapper DMX – both of whose albums have topped the American charts. Puff Daddy's Bad Boy empire went from strength to strength with its owner enjoying international success with a hybrid of hip hop and R&B. Ruffhouse Records, formed in Philadelphia in 1987 by Chris Schwarz and Joe 'The Butcher' Nicolo, also hit a platinum seam. After the Fugees broke through in 1996 with *The Score*, increasingly successful solo albums from Wyclef Jean, Pras and Lauryn Hill followed. Master P's No Limit empire rose from nowhere out of a record store in California to dominate New Orleans. Its most significant acquisition was Snoop Dogg, in a deal negotiated with imprisoned Suge Knight.

Two of the more interesting empires arose from previously unheralded hip hop territories – the Wu-Tang Clan's many-tentacled Staten Island collective and Jermaine Dupri's Atlanta operation.

> ## Wu-Tang Clan – Enter The 36 Chambers

Arguably the most innovative force in hip hop in the 90s, the Wu-Tang Clan combine mystic gobbledegook with triumphant, cinematic hip hop. Impassioned, contradictory and unpredictable, this exotic brotherhood are as keen on playing chess, espousing arcane philosophy and practising martial arts moves as they are on assembling their genuinely unhinged records. They were single-handedly responsible for resurrecting the poor sales that east coast rap endured at the hands of west coast gangsta rap. It is little wonder that Suge Knight hankered after signing the band, who nevertheless struck a deal with RCA's Loud subsidiary allowing solo members to work 'freelance'.

Rza (Robert Diggs), the group's founder and producer, first encountered hip hop at DJ Pete Jones's Staten Island parties.

'I remember writing my first lyric in the fourth grade. It was sex lines – "See a girl with the breasts/You go have a squeeze and put your hand up her dress" – that kinda dirt. That'll be the beginning of my musical interests in hip hop. I started rhyming with other DJs. By the time you were twelve or thirteen, you was working a summer job selling newspapers to buy turn-tables and echo machines or a beat box.'

Rza would visit his friend Ol' Dirty Bastard (Russell Jones)'s house, borrowing his big brother's tape recorder to document their pre-pubescent sex rhymes. Before the Wu-Tang came to fruition, Rza released his debut solo single, 'Ooh! I Love You Rakeem' (as Prince Rakeem) for Tommy Boy. Prince Paul worked with Rza during this period.

'I knew Rza when he was Prince Rakeem, pre-Wu-Tang. We made demos in the 80s, which I've still got. We came up with the Gravediggaz – and that's my involvement with Rza. But I knew him more as an MC than as a producer. He did "Ooh! I Love You Rakeem", he produced that, but I didn't really focus on his production as much as his MCing skills. I thought he was way ahead of his time. I think Rza was going through problems. He had some legal things that he was going through, and we all used our pent-up energy and made the Gravediggaz. Then Rza played the first Wu-Tang record for me and it was really, really good. So he put it out independently while we were doing the Gravediggaz. 'Protect Ya Neck' did really well and that's what made it appear as though Wu-Tang came out first. Technically, yeah, they came out on wax first, but the Gravediggaz were there around the same time.'

Rza remembers this difficult period.

'I had to go to jail, had a baby on the way. I was fucked up in the game. I was really on a down, compressed at the bottom of this shit, but I was making music and shit.'

Rza set up a business plan and a collective ethos, borrowing liberally from the I Ching, Asiatic philosophy, kung fu films and the Koran. The music industry seemed to offer Rza a route out of poverty.

'I've done all that poverty shit, of being forced back and forth on situations. So when we got a chance to get into this music game and make some money, I said: "I'm never going to be poor again." A lot of people were saying there's a lot of money in this music business, billions of dollars. Blacks don't have none of it. We get maybe one per cent of it. I said: "No, we're the driving force of the industry." So I decided that I'll make a new industry. I'll make an industry within the industry. Also, I watched a lot of rap that was coming out, 'cos it wasn't real, it wasn't how New York was, it wasn't how we grew up, it wasn't our struggle, it wasn't reflective of us. I got that idea in my head, a determination and drive to just keep making this money and find different ways to make money. And I realised that people was interested in me, and my crew, and how our life was. I said: "In that case, that's what we're selling them."'

Pooling the collective's limited resources and borrowing money from his mother, his sister, his grandmother and a friend, he orchestrated the release of 500 copies of Wu-Tang's 'Protect Ya Neck' debut in 1992. Helped by college radio, the single took off and the Wu-Tang were able to take their pick of major label offers.

'I pressed them up. We often made demos in my house and took 'em to the studio to re-cut 'em. I just went to a radio station and pushed through the door – "Play this one. It's better than everything else out there, and if you like hip hop, you gotta like this."'

Rich Isaacson at Loud Records remembers the chase to pick up the Wu-Tang Clan.

'One of our street team, based out of Michigan, heard the record and he called our college radio guy in the LA office and said: "Man, you gotta hear this Wu-Tang record, it's incredible." So the radio rep brought it to Stephen Rifkind and he flipped. He got on a plane and flew to New York and hooked up with the group. Then we made the deal with Wu-Tang. What we did with Wu-Tang was unprecedented. In almost all record contracts, when you sign a group there's a paragraph called "the group provision". Basically, that says if any of the members of the group leave and start a solo career, they have to do that with the label. The record company's investing in breaking the group and if the guy's going to go off, the record company that funded him should keep him. That's sacred within the record business. Rza, particularly, had a vision of what he wanted Wu-Tang to be, and a lot of other record companies were coming to Wu-Tang, 'cos they had a hot record, and they were throwing real dollars at them for their album. He didn't really want to go to another record company to take the money because he knew he would have to sign a group provision to do that. We told him that if you come and sign with Loud for a lot less money, we'll let you take the solo artists to other labels. So long as we have the ability to match whatever offers you get, and if we match the offers you have to stay with us.'

Of all the records to emerge from the Wu-Tang family, none has surpassed the impact of their 1993 debut album, *Enter The Wu-Tang (36 Chambers)*. Sidestepping hip hop conventions, this was a frighteningly original creation benefitting from the multi-faceted personalities involved. The standout track was 'C.R.E.A.M. (Cash Rules Everything Around Me)', a reflection on the group's impoverished origins and a redefinition of hip hop values. Rza says much of the inspiration arose from the Wu-Tang's dissatisfaction at the status quo in rap music.

'When I put the first album together, I was in a real competitive state of mind, with real vengeance in my heart. "Fuck the music industry, fuck the hip hop game." I realised that a lot of these guys was corny, and they was acting like they was the best.'

Rich Isaacson relates one anecdote that typifies the Wu-Tang's anarchic streak.

'Right before their album came out in November 1993, RCA Records had a convention. Of all places it was a retirement community in Connecticut. Each night of the convention they fly in everybody from all over the country that works for RCA. Each night they have a different genre of music showcased. On the night of the urban department, we had Wu-Tang perform. Half an hour before the show, Rza calls my hotel room wanting to borrow my car. I said: "I lent my car out to someone, but what do you need?" He said: "We need to get some stocking masks." So I said: "I don't think it's a great idea for you guys to run into this retirement community and try to get some stocking masks," knowing the market that we were in. He said: "Oh, if you don't have the car, no big deal." So half an hour goes by, we're ready to go on. Steve [Rifkind] and I are standing to the side of the stage. It's a pretty small room and there's a little makeshift stage and the place is packed. It's all the RCA country people, the corporate executives from Germany, BMG's German health company . . . The place is packed, and they have no idea what they're about to see. All of a sudden nine guys come out with their heads covered with stocking masks. Me and Steve are standing by the stage watching the reaction of the crowd. You just saw everybody take two steps back. They don't know what the hell's going on. And Ol' Dirty senses, I think they all sensed, this was a different crowd than they're used to working. Ol' Dirty grabbed the microphone and we have no idea what he's going to say or do. He starts singing 'Somewhere Over The Rainbow'. And the crowd instantly changes their temperament, and they lighten up. Within twenty minutes Wu-Tang has the entire place chanting "Wu-Tang, Wu-Tang".'

Prince Paul watched Wu-Tang take off, though Rza honoured his commitments by working on the Gravediggaz 1994 debut, *Niggamortis*.

'Wu-Tang's influence on wax – you hear it everywhere. Mobb Deep is a very good example. Practically every kid who rhymes in New York copies Raekwon. Rza totally topsy-turvied the industry with his methods of business – "We're all gonna come under one label that's Wu-Tang, but as separate artists we can go wherever." That's incredible. I admire Rza a lot. All of the stuff that he sat and told me when we was doing the Gravediggaz stuff in my basement came to life. There's very few people who mean what they say and actually put plans into action and make them work. People talk about ingenuity, but to me he's really a genius, and not just in the sense of his business savvy, but as an artist in general.'

The Wu-Tang dynasty expanded with a series of memorable albums – Method Man's *Tical* (1994) and *Tical 2000: Judgement Day* (1999), Ol' Dirty Bastard's *Return To The 36 Chambers* (1995), Raekwon's *Only Built For Cuban Linx . . .* (1995), Rza's *Liquid Swords* (1996), Ghostface Killa's *Ironman* (1996) and Coppadonna's *The Pillage* (1998). All achieved at least gold status, both of Method Man's releases going platinum. *Wu-Tang Forever* (1997), the group's second collective effort, was a triple-platinum double set comprising over two hours of music. In 1998 it was estimated that Wu-Tang artists had sold more than thirteen million records – an industry within an industry, as Rza promised. The Clan, according to some counts, now boasts over 200 members – seemingly all of whom have a solo record in them.

'We've always been individuals anyway. We always had our own crews. We were part of one crew, but had crews of our own. So a person like Raekwon, his crew became more like my niggers, but he loved me so much they had to show me love . . . We always was powerful together but we also had the strength to do it individually. When I made a record deal I said: "Well, Raekwon does good without me. He's powerful within his own self." I couldn't take his power away by making his power be obligated to my power.'

For Rich Isaacson, the Wu-Tang re-established the east coast's identity and viability at a time of almost complete west coast domination. They were also a precursor to the spirit of entrepreneurism which engulfed rap in the mid-90s.

'All of a sudden east coast hip hop was back on the map, and that's one reason why they're important. Another reason is because of what they represented in terms of their entrepreneurial spirit. This was a group that had a very definite vision about what they wanted to do with their music, and what their brand could do globally, and what the power of hip hop really was. They knew it from day one. They knew that the Wu-Tang logo was ultimately going to be on the back of a T-shirt or a sweatshirt one day. They knew when they put that Wu-Tang logo on each of the solo members' albums, those albums were going to benefit from having that logo on there. They realised that they had the potential to create an industry, and they did. And because Wu-Tang was successful in doing that, that inspired countless other hip hop artists and young entrepreneurs who were in the hip hop culture and community to do the same things.'

## ➤ *Georgia On My Mind – Jermaine Dupri And So So Def*

Hip hop was never an exclusively New York or Los Angeles phenomenon, though those two cities are undoubtedly dominant. James Smith's Texas-based Rap-A-Lot Records, for example, scored huge success with arch gangsters Geto Boys and their spin-offs, so too Sir Mix-A-Lot's Seattle oper-ation. But the biggest rival to the east and west coast monopoly in the 90s arose from Coca-Cola's home, Atlanta, Georgia.

So So Def Recordings CEO Jermaine Dupri, by the age of 26, was overseeing a production résumé including Mariah Carey, Aretha Franklin, Usher, TLC, Mase, MC Lyte and Cam'ron. After starting off with child rappers Kriss Kross, Dupri has seen So So Def Recordings enjoy multi-platinum success with Da Brat and Xscape. By the age of five Dupri Jnr had learned to play percussion to funk band Brick's entire catalogue (his father was their road manager). As a pre-teen he immersed himself in B-boying, performing alongside Diana Ross before becoming the opening act on Run-D.M.C.'s Fresh Fest tour. He also started tinkering with studio equipment. Eventually he came across Chris Smith and Chris Kelly in an Atlanta mall, and shaped them into Kriss Kross, who became platinum sellers on the back of their 1992 crossover hit, 'Jump'. According to Dupri, that record only took about two hours to knock together.

'I made a beat, I just started writing the raps and came up with the first verse. I called one of the Chris's on the phone. I said: "Listen to this, this is going to be our single." He liked it, then I wrote the second rap and put it down again, gave him a tape or whatever. Recorded the song in less than two hours.'

Dupri used the proceeds to establish his own label, So So Def Recordings. Much like Puff Daddy at Bad Boy, Dupri has dabbled in R&B as well as hip hop.

'It's always been important for me to be a name in hip hop, period. 'Cos that's my heart, hip hop is my heart. But R&B is my heart as well. I just wanted to be like a young Quincy Jones. I just want to be classified as a producer. I want to be like the Wizard of Oz, you come see me when you need a fix, whether you're a rapper or an R&B artist, I'm going to fix you.'

With So So Def established, Dupri hooked up with Chicago's Da Brat (Shawntae Harris), the first female rapper to achieve platinum solo sales with 1996's *Funkdafied*.

'Brat was found by Kriss Kross at one of their concerts. At the time I was just so caught up in guys and the men of rap. I was like: "Girls? You've found this girl rapper? I don't want to hear no girl rapper. I don't care about girls rapping." She heard me say that and she was like: "What? I'm going to come down there and do what I've got to do." So she came, she did a little rap and it was her attitude and the way she came at me was something I had never seen before. I was sold from that point on.'

Da Brat tells the story in her own words.

'Ed Lover from MTV was hosting the show. They asked if anybody could rap or sing or perform and I ran on stage and took the mic and started rapping. I probably said every rap I ever wrote and the crowd, they were going crazy. I won $50 for winning and they took me backstage to meet Kriss Kross.'

Da Brat has carved out an image as an outspoken female MC, distinguishable from her peers by a less precocious dress sense but a mouth as foul as any gangsta rapper.

'When Foxy Brown and Lil' Kim came out, whatever rocks your boat. If they're comfortable dressing like that – do whatever you want to do. I love Missy [Elliott]. I still love Latifah, I still love MC Lyte, I still love Salt-N-Pepa for the way they paved the way for the female artist. I really give props to anybody that's trying to do their thing. I think we all need to keep positive people around us and in our corner because negativity ain't going to get us nowhere but either dead or knocked off the map or fucked like Vanilla Ice.'

Missy Elliott collaborated with Da Brat on the track 'Sock It 2 Me', from her 1997 album *Supa Dupa Fly*.

'Da Brat I had always been a huge fan of. I seen her perform live one night in DC in Washington. She began to freestyle about somebody fighting in the audience, and no one was paying her no mind 'cos they was paying attention to the fight. I was like: "Man, people don't know that this girl is really dope." And I said that whenever I decided to do an album, it wouldn't be complete without Da Brat because I was a huge fan of hers.'

One of Dupri's most important recent hip hop productions was Jay-Z's 'Money Ain't A Thang', nominated for a 1999 Grammy for best rap performance by a duo or group.

'Again, we did that song in two hours. I don't like to sit there and think about a song. If it's meant to go, it's meant to go. It's like you're pushing something through a hole. If you have to get somebody else to help you push it, it's not supposed to be there.'

In 1996, Dupri became the first producer to reach number one on Billboard's pop, R&B and rap charts with different singles. Two years later he finally released his own solo debut, *Life In 1472*, with guest appearances from Nas, Slick Rick and Jay-Z. Naturally, the hip hop press sought to compare it with the work of Puff Daddy in New York.

'I don't care about being compared to no producer that's been making a lot of moves, and Puff did a lot of things for New York, for R&B and for rap. He's done a lot culturally, just to make moves for blacks in general and businessmen. So people are going to compare us. I look up to Puff for doing what he does and continuing to do it, and I hope that he continues to do it, 'cos he motivated me to continue to do what I'm doing. I just wish people would compare me more to Quincy Jones as well as Puff Daddy. I feel until people start comparing me to Quincy I ain't doing enough of what I'm supposed to be doing.'

Dupri hopes he has helped make Atlanta an alternative home for hip hop.

'It started with Kriss Kross, Arrested Development, TLC and that was the first era of music. Then I brought Xscape and Da Brat. Each year I keep bringing out more and more people from Atlanta. All the things I do, whether they be artists from New York or LA or wherever, whatever I do, the Atlanta stamp is put on it.'

He believes that the reason major hip hop and R&B stars record in the area is because it gives them a chance to breathe outside of America's hothouse music industry cities.

'I think Atlanta is a place where you can keep a fresh mind, keep your soul pure, keep your mind free of law headaches or whatever. There's none of the congestion of the streets like in New York, and everybody fighting to go to the same places. Artists come out here and they see that, and it's like: "Wow! It ain't nothing like that where we at!" They can just relax a little bit more out here.'

For Da Brat, Atlanta is 'the new Motown'.

'All the hot labels are out here. You have LaFace, So So Def, and Bad Boy's trying to get a little spot out here. They are all moving, trying to get places out here. Yeah, I definitely think Atlanta's the new hot spot for the music industry.'

Several other groups have benefited from Atlanta's slower pace, notably LaFace's Goodie Mob and OutKast. The Goodie Mob observe the claustrophobic production values of Dr. Dre's N.W.A. work but combine these with cerebral lyrics about institutionalised racism and urban decay in the south. The biggest noise in Atlanta's underground is currently Massinfluence, featuring rappers Cognito, Audyssey and H20, keyboard player Venus Brown and DJ Abstract. In 1999 they released their debut album, *Live From Mitchell St*, which included the underground hit 'Clown Syndrome'. H20 describes the resurgent Atlanta scene.

'Everybody, when they think of Atlanta, the first thing that comes to their mind is Jermaine Dupri, then Goodie Mob and OutKast. Goodie Mob are definitely putting it down. Then there's the grass roots of it. This is a transient city, it's not everybody that's from Atlanta that is actually *from* Atlanta.'

H20 points to the Goodie Mob as the soul of the Atlanta scene.

'They created a sound, a form of hip hop for the south, and put an identity out for other kids to show that their stuff is really original. They're just creative kids, the whole camp is creative. And they give back and they show up at every hip hop function that they can. They're for real.'

Cognito describes Atlanta as neutral ground. He enjoys the familiarity and camaraderie and notes that the outlets for hip hop have grown quickly.

'Everybody seems to like everybody else. Everybody here is not from here, so when they get here they are more friendly. The weather's nice, the people here are nice, they got the southern hospitality. It's just a lot of space for people to breathe and go out, and everybody's not on top of each other. Atlanta is good neutral ground. It's in between the north, in between the west and east coast, and it's definitely not the mid west. I think the city's grown a lot from where it used to be. It went from one radio station playing all R&B and whatever number one hip hop record was considered rap at the time. That would be in rotation. Now you've got Hot 97 and radio station V103 playing all hip hop records. You might hear a lot of underground stuff. You've got the choice now and people are more open. Eight years ago you couldn't do it. Kriss Kross couldn't have happened, OutKast couldn't have happened, they didn't have the outlets. The labels out here wasn't open to hip hop. Before it was just bass music and R&B music.'

Despite the Atlanta family vibe, H20 has few kind words when asked about the influence of Jermaine Dupri.

'He's not even original. You can't influence nobody when your influences are showing, when you're reflecting someone else's image. You've got to reflect something natural to people.'

Cognito concurs.

'Jermaine Dupri is influenced by everybody else but he's got the money and he actually has the talent to do some original stuff. I'm not mad at his R&B stuff because that's where his creativity shines. But for him to start trying to rhyme and doing all this hip hop, I don't care if you was breaking with Whodini, or whatever. You're not breaking now, you're not doing anything for the culture now.'

## ► Missy Elliott – *Supa Dupa Fly*

In step with Lauryn Hill's rise have come breakthroughs for female MCs like Foxy Brown, Da Brat and Lil' Kim. For Virginian Missy 'Misdemeanor' Elliott, there is also a business agenda.

'I became involved in hip hop by getting a deal through DeVante Swing from Jodeci. When I first went to DeVante, I was singing more than rapping. I would do little eight-bar raps here and there. He was like: "You tight as a rapper." From that point on I just started turning the eight-bar raps into sixteen bars, then twenty-four bars, then a whole rap song. I began to want to rap more than sing. I just felt you had all these Patti LaBelles and Lalah Hathaways and different people that really sing. Maybe I should step back and just rap and sing a little bit here and there.'

Although there is now an established tradition of successful females in hip hop and rap, from Roxanne Shanté, Yo Yo, MC Lyte, Salt-N-Pepa and Monie Love onwards, most had little control over their business and management, with the notable exception of Queen Latifah. That was something Elliott intended to change.

'A lot of females just rap but they don't produce or write songs for other people or even write their own songs. If I could get my foot in the door, I wanted to write songs for different artists, I wanted to produce records. I wanted to have my own label, I wanted to get artists and sign them to my label. So far I've accomplished all of those things and there's still some more to go but those were my main goals. I think it made the other female rappers or singers say: "Hey, if she's doing it, maybe we could try." Because Lil' Kim, she has her production company now, Foxy has her production company now. So I think more women are starting to get involved in this industry and are not just the so-called artist.'

In an industry noted for its jealousy of success, Missy Elliott has maintained strong friendships with peers including Da Brat and Lil' Kim, plus R&B vocalist Aaliyah. They all appeared on her 1997 album *Supa Dupa Fly*, which rose to number three in the US pop charts on its way to platinum sales and a Grammy nomination. In 1998 Elliott enjoyed a huge hit appearing alongside Mel B of the Spice Girls with her song 'I Want You Back'. But it would not be wise to read too much into the sentimentality of the title.

'That was just a song that I put together actually, not an experience song. I think if you mess up I most definitely won't be asking to take you back!'

The lead-off single from Elliott's second album, *Da Real World*, somewhat controversially bore the title 'She's A Bitch'.

'I'm not calling myself bitch in a negative way. I'm a bitch of power and whatever I have to do to get what I want, if I have to be that bitch to get my label or be able to pick what I want to wear or get a movie deal, then that's what I'll be. But I'm not a negative bitch where I'm just saying I've got to have this, I've got to have that.'

# chapter fifteen

# back to the old school

➤ *Thugs 4 Life?*

Despite its grisly denouement, not every rap artist was ready to renounce the tenets of gangsta rap. For some, Tupac Shakur's 'Thug 4 Life' tattoo is a cultural artefact as powerful as the Dead Sea Scrolls. The most obvious example is DMX, the hugely successful and flamboyant Def Jam artist whose songs are littered with expletives, gallows humour and references to dogs and bitches (men and women in DMX's universe). Equally controversial are Queens duo Capone-N-Noreaga, who have helped foster gangsta rap's street-tough successor, 'Thug Rap'. Having hooked up with their impressively titled DJ Tragedy Khadafi, the duo made their debut in 1998 with *The War Report*, featuring production from Queensbridge godfather Marley Marl. Noreaga subsequently made his solo bow with 1998's gold-certified *N.O.R.E.* In his first interview since being released from prison, Capone (Kiam Holley) and colleague Noreaga (Victor Santiago) recite the duo's fundamental vision.

'We're like: "Fuck radio!" We need radio, but we're not going to aim for the radio. If the radio play our record, cool, but we're not sitting down in the studio making a record to go on the radio. We're going to come from our heart. We're not trying to fit the norm, we're trying to be as different as possible. It ain't nice in the 'hood so why we gonna make radio songs? That's what we're doing, we're keeping it original like hip hop started. Hip hop started from saying your feelings as opposed to saying what somebody thinks is your feelings. Think your own feelings with your inner self, as opposed to people telling you what to say, that's what we're trying to bring it to. We're trying to bring it to the essence of this motherfucker . . . I make music for niggers like me. I make the music for a motherfucker just like me.

I try to touch every area. I try to make shit for motherfuckers that don't even listen to rap — the computer kid, the teacher that's in the school teaching, try to touch her level. I might not reach 'em, but that's what I try to do.'

Gangsta rap has bequeathed its advocacy of heightened realism and moral indifference to a natural successor. Controversy sells far too well for the medium to disappear, and while America retains a black underclass, thug rap will continue to strut its bad attitude all over the Billboard charts.

## ➤ The Good Life Café

Though the end of the millennium saw hardcore rappers like Noreaga, DMX, Master P and Jay-Z dominate the Billboard charts, another back to basics movement gained parallel momentum. The 'new underground' scene can trace its roots to small clubs such as LA's Good Life Café, started by a middle-aged black woman, Bea Hall, in an effort to give local kids a place to congregate. Maintaining a strict no swearing, no drugs, no smoking policy, the Good Life Café nevertheless became the coolest hip hop joint in town — a new take on the coffee bar culture of the 50s that fostered the birth of counter-culture artists like Bob Dylan.

Medusa, an LA-based affiliate of Atlanta's Organized Noise collective, recalls how the Good Life's stringent door policies provided female MCs with a space to express themselves.

'It was a challenge for artists because you weren't allowed to use vulgarity or any profanity. All of the MCs that were relying on that in their rhymes had to come with some depth to get away from that. And it provided an arena where women felt comfortable to express themselves in poetry, in rhyme form and dance form, since Bea Hall was running it. You didn't feel all the testosterone running around and everyone wanting to be rough and rugged. It was very cultural, the vibe was nice.'

Among the influential groups to grow out of the Good Life Café, actually a wholefood store with a small performance area, were Delicious Vinyl's Pharcyde — 'An irreverent, self-deprecating kind of thing that really wasn't the rage of the day,' according to label boss Mike Ross. The single 'Ya Mama', drawn from 1992 debut *Bizarre Ride II The Pharcyde*, was an almost perfect recreation of 'dozens' insult battles. Another important group were the Freestyle Fellowship, five young men from South Central, each well versed in hip hop traditions, and capable of astonishing, extended freestyle exchanges. Despite a major label berth at Island Records in 1993, the timing was simply wrong for the Freestyle Fellowship. But others, notably the Jurassic 5 and Black Eyed Peas, ran with the Good Life influence.

## ➤ *Jurassic 5 – Concrete Schoolyard*

The fast-rising Jurassic 5, a multi-racial six-piece from Los Angeles comprising DJs Cut Chemist and Nu-Mark, plus MCs Akil, Zaakir, Marc 7even and Chali 2na, are the most prominent current graduates of Good Life.

'Groups like us, and every group that went to the Good Life every Thursday, you were hustling every week to come up with a hot song so you could show it off. I thought that made west coast hip hop the most productive it's ever been in history.'

Competition at the Good Life was consistently hot, and MCs would be dragged off the mic by opportunists keen to test their mettle. According to Jurassic 5, the ban on cursing instilled a sense of creative adventure in the participants. The venue also offered an outlet for those who felt no kinship with gangsta rap.

'If you weren't a gangsta rapper, you couldn't get a deal. That gave birth to places like the Good Life, for the MCs who wasn't gangsters at heart and who were talking about what they knew and what they felt.'

Afrika Baby Bambaataa of the Jungle Brothers welcomes the return of old school hip hop values that Jurassic 5 enshrined.

'People want the craft back and they want to see something original. The old school flavour embodies the true spirit of hip hop, the party, the fun, the lyrics about parties, fun intertwined with whoever you are and what you want to talk about. If you put out a new group that respects traditional hip hop values like Jurassic 5 and you tell the public what it is and they go experience it, it doesn't stop at just Jurassic 5. There's twenty years of traditional hip hop artists that are still alive and willing to get on stage and rock the crowds the way Jurassic 5 does it.'

Jurassic 5 wanted to pursue subject matter that was uplifting and educative.

'All of the MCs have kids. It's like watching a child listen to a radio and hear a song that they play seven or eight times a day, and watching that child learn that song. That's incredible, but it's a double-edged sword. All those lyrics that he learned, do they help? Are they intellectual? Are they something that you're cool with if your kid repeated them? I'm saying that if we have that power to affect children and people like that, I would love it to be in a positive manner, something that can help people intellectually, spiritually, physically or whatever.'

To Jurassic 5, gangsta rap was simply:

'Negative and very exploitative of violence and drugs. We were just talking about bringing it back to where rap started in schoolyards and playgrounds where kids are shooting basketball and playing the dozens and bragging on each other's mammas and stuff like that, where it was all fun.'

Jurassic 5 typify the groundswell of west coast groups who wanted their music to be considered part of the hip hop culture rather than simply rap.

'What I think makes hip hop so special is that there is a dance side to it, there is a visual artistic life, there is the MC, there is a DJ, there is a beat box. It's all these things incorporated into one cycle, and that's what makes hip hop unique. Basically there was a period when all the five elements spread out. They went and did their own thing. Graffiti wasn't necessarily so seated with hip hop. Breaking was, but it was kinda off to the left. Everything kinda branched out, but now they're slowly coming back and they're getting stronger.'

The staple inspiration for Jurassic 5's sound, according to Nu-Mark, is his archive of classic vinyl.

'About a month ago I was studying Main Source's album, so I go into the past. Then there's soul records which just blow me back every time I listen to 'em. So I feed off of old records as well as old hip hop records, and that keeps me going.'

To him, record knowledge as well as turntable technique remain the acid test of a DJ.

'I think the whole key is to become well rounded. A lot of DJs can rip it up on the turntables and do a lot of good tricks, stuff like that. The DJ improves when he spends time finding the dopest old records, the rarest records, then incorporates 'em with their technical skills.'

He is particularly galled at the image of sampling DJs as talentless thieves. For Nu-Mark, if he employs a sample, it is every bit as fastidious a process as a musician might endure.

'I grab a bass drum from one record or a snare drum from another record and a high hat from another record. Put that down, listen to the beat for about four hours straight to make sure it's even a good percussion centre. Find a loop or a piece of a loop, chop that up. It's like cooking, you're just adding a bunch of ingredients, messing stuff up, trying it. At the end of the day you might take three days to make one track and just throw it out and erase the disc. It's frustrating because there's a lot more to it than just sampling somebody else's work. You gotta find the break before anybody else does, you gotta bring it back, you gotta flip it differently, you gotta make it funky – that's probably rule number one – and then you gotta add a lot of flavour to it. I would never condone stealing somebody else's art, but I don't consider it stealing.'

Other keepers of the DJ flame include the Beat Junkies, a group of LA DJs who eat, drink and sleep DJ skills, and are also associated with the Fat Beats chain of vinyl specialists. The collective includes Melo-D, DJ Rhettmatic and Babu, who is also known for his work with LA's Dilated Peoples. The Beat Junkies are at the forefront of a renaissance in the fortunes of the DJ, for so long humbled in the hip hop hierarchy by the advent of the rapper.

'I think DJing has advanced a lot more in the last couple of years. Like everything else artistically, it will reach a plateau for a while, a peak, and be at the same level. And if no one comes along to create something new or something that hasn't been done before, it stays at that level. But there has been a lot of guys over the last three or four years that have a done a lot of new things on the turntables musically, production wise, including a lot of different kinds of music. I think it has helped it advance even more.'

## ➤ Dilated Peoples – The Main Event

Dilated Peoples are typical of the LA underground in that they consider themselves B-boys, first and foremost. Their breakthrough came in 1998 with a track called 'Work The Angles', one of the biggest underground hits of the 90s. MC Irascience takes up their story.

'Evidence [fellow Dilated Peoples MC and producer] and myself started as graffiti artists. I was involved with poetry and different things like that. I was in church where the music was always around, music in general. I enjoy using poetry to rock over the beats that I enjoy listening to, that was the bonus. A little later I met Evidence and we hooked up in '91 or '92, and started making demos together. That snowballed and we went through some different things. Then we found Babu and that clicked really positively and we have been blazing ever since.'

According to Evidence, the Dilated Peoples form part of a movement attempting to break the mould of west coast hip hop.

'It's breaking a lot of barriers. I think its definitely been an evolution of hip hop with Dilated and Jurassic 5 and whoever else. All these people are breaking the stereotype of what a west coast sound should or shouldn't be.'

## ➤ *Black Eyed Peas – Behind The Front*

The Black Eyed Peas made a huge impression with their 1998 *Behind The Front* debut, a collection of organic, sampled melodies, live instruments and fully-realised freestyle raps. 'Karma' was one of the more intelligent additions to the debate over the Biggie/Tupac slayings with its refrain of 'Ain't no running from karma' welded to the chorus of Blondie's 'One Way Or Another'. Breakthrough single 'Fallin' Up' cleverly defended their stance against gangsta rap materialism, rivalry and jingoism, as Will-I-Am relates.

'"Falling Up" is about the frustration of what the whole hip hop thing was going through. At that point the east coast/west coast rivalry was in full blossom. We were just trying to showcase how we're not about east coast or west coast, we're just about universal music. It's the reason why we didn't relate to gangsta hip hop. I live in a ghetto, I'm from the ghetto, I still live in the projects. But talking about it and always having to prove to somebody that's where I'm from to get respect is not what I'm about. I'm about trying to find a better way out. I don't want my mum to live there any more. Just the other day I was chillin' in the house and there was a shooting. My mum said: "Duck!" The sad thing was we were all laughing while we were on the floor. And to see my mum laughing and my sister laughing, because of a shooting right in front of my window, if you're sitting back and thinking about it – damn that. This is sad.'

Though groups like the Black Eyed Peas are closest to the original model of hip hop advocated by Afrika Bambaataa, the prevailing appetite for hardcore rap ensured some critics differentiated them from the pack with the unwieldy sobriquet of 'alternative rap'.

'I would say that we're progressive hip hop. You have your hardcore stuff, your love stuff for girls, your club stuff, and then you've got your progressive stuff where you try to progress to give hip hop a future. 'Cos once you saturate the market with gangsta or club rap, you have to start all over again. Groups like Lauryn Hill, us, the Roots, are giving hip hop a new thing for record companies to exploit. That's just the reality of it, 'cos the audiences got tired of that gangsta stuff. So we have to stay progressive and think of new ways of making hip hop fresh again. Recycle the stale air and make it fresh.'

For Black Eyed Peas, respecting hip hop's traditions is incompatible with the lifestyles of some of those who profited from the music. That's why they're happy to be called an underground hip hop group.

'Kinda like blues artists. Blues is not what it used to be, but it's still there. People that love blues, blues musicians, artists and fanatics, still appreciate it, and they love it for what it is. That's why we're underground. After the day's over and the stock market is closed, and the guys in the suits and ties with their bullet-proof windows in their cars, have gone to their mansions – we're still the creators, and we're still the fans.'

## ▶ *The Roots – Philadelphia Funky*

Fellow travellers with the Black Eyed Peas in combining live instrumentation with scratching and sampling, Philadelphia's Roots have perfected a similar old school mix of hip hop, though there is a higher quotient of jazz and occasionally even drum 'n' bass underneath the rapid-fire lyrics. MCs Black Thought and Malik B serve as additional instrumentalists as much as anything else in this heady mix. After a series of well regarded recordings beginning with 1993 'demo' album *Organix*, 1999's *Things Fall Apart* significantly enhanced their mainstream profile.

'Hip hop to me is just a way of life, it's a culture. The culture is comprised of so many different elements, so many things that are changeable, and other things that are just unspoken, things that are just felt. It's a very kinetic culture.'

Though they grew up in the shadow of Schoolly D, the Roots were never attracted to the premise of gangsta rap. According to Black Thought, they just address the same situations in a different way.

'I don't really rap about no sweet stuff! I won't be rapping about shopping, what I got, this and that. It'll be about different ways to imagine destroying MCs, physically or poetically. I think it's all in the way that you phrase what it is you have to say. If you just blandly say: "I walked down the block, pulled out my gun, pop, pop, pop, now you've got shot." You can talk about walking down the street and shooting somebody in a *poetic* manner, and in a different pattern that'll be catchy and people will be like: "Wow, yeah, lyrics!" It depends on how you phrase it.'

For the Roots, the distinction between underground hip hop and mainstream rap is as much as anything about quality control.

'I think we're underground in the quality of our music and our beats and our rhymes. We haven't really changed what we do in the studio, aiming for this and that commercial breakthrough, but at the same time our music is becoming more commercial. It's not like we're making more commercial music, but the music that we do make is becoming accepted on a wider scale.'

Their duet with Erykah Badu, 'You Got Me', is a typically earnest song about relationship issues.

'It's a narrative about the strains of maintaining a long distance relationship, as an artist, on the road, and the irony of it all. Because it's with someone that I met as an artist on the road. The music was written mostly by Scott Storch, and the chorus was written by Gerald Scott, both Philadelphia artists that we work alongside. So we had the foundation with them. I dealt with the music for a while, wrote the narrative, and we built up the track with our production squad, we all added on. In the end we got Erykah to sing the chorus, and that was just the icing on the cake.'

Another of the guest artists on *Things Fall Apart* (its title taken from Chinua Achebe's novel on the loss of traditional African culture during colonisation) was Mos Def, a contributor to the Lyricist Lounge, an east coast variant of LA's Good Life Café.

## ➤ *Lyricist Lounge – Kickin' It Freestyle*

According to its creators, the Lyricist Lounge grew out of the 'non-existence of any venue free of violence, where individuals could showcase their talent among their peers'. Founded in November 1991 by Anthony Marshall and Danny Castro, neither of whom were yet eighteen, it was originally based in a small Manhattan studio with a capacity of just twenty-six. However, the popularity of the freestyle open mic sessions grew rapidly. Music industry A&R men began to pencil the venue into their weekly itinerary.

In 1992 the Lyricist Lounge relocated to underground hip hop club The Muse. The attendance went up to 275. Its burgeoning popularity resulted in a nomadic existence thereafter, with host venues including the Village Gate, Supper Club, Marc Ballroom and various hotels. On 24 March 1993 the sessions were hosted by Doug E. Fresh and featured performances from Mobb Deep and a fourteen-year-old Foxy Brown, neither of whom were signed at that time. In May, Sean 'Puffy' Combs introduced Notorious B.I.G. (also then unsigned). Other notable hosts have included Guru (Gang Starr), KRS-1, Q-Tip (A Tribe Called Quest) and De La Soul. On 11 November 1995, at the New Yorker Hotel, the Lyricist Lounge hosted the twenty-first anniversary of the Universal Zulu Nation.

Danny Castro takes up the story.

'It started off in Lower East Side in Manhattan at this place, 45 Orchard Street, which was a small studio apartment. We just had three microphones, a cassette player and a 'jump' set and we used to invite people we knew to come down. I was going to school with a friend named Mike Thompson and we met his dad, Charles Thompson. He had a not-for-profit organisation called SBI – Sound Business Institute. He used to drill us on becoming entrepreneurs. He said he had this place that he used for rehearsal, because he played saxophone and he wasn't using it at the time. So we took advantage of the opportunity and invited some friends over. We did it once a week and in the beginning it was just a struggle to get people to come down.'

Anthony Marshall picks up the story.

'Lyricist Lounge overall is now more of a vibe. It's a brand name that we've created. It started as a open mic which went into a showcase which went into an album. It's not a club in New York, it's basically a name that we created and a vibe that we created and we take that vibe and move it around to different clubs and states.'

The Lyricist Lounge, according to Marshall, was at least partially a reaction against the bleakness and relentless predictability of gangsta rap.

'After a while it became annoying. God, what else can we talk about? We're in New York and we live in a messed up environment at times and yeah, there's a lot of shootings and different things that go on. But who wants to dwell on that? I don't want to keep talking about that. I don't support that. I'd rather support something positive, talk about something fine. I like to dance and I like clothes or whatever. That was enjoyable and was more what kids was rhyming about. Skills in general became an issue.'

Mos Def started out rhyming at the age of nine as a member of Urban Thermo Dynamics, who also featured his brother and adopted sister. He had recently appeared on albums by De La Soul and the Bush Babees. Together with Talib Kweli he released 1998's highly politicised *Black Star* album, described by the *San Francisco Bay Examiner* as 'this year's most intelligent new album . . . a stark contrast to a rap music era of lowest common denominator themes and issues'. As the duo state on that album's 'Hater Players' – 'Every day somebody asks me where all the real MCs is at. They're underground.' Mos Def, one of the beneficiaries of the Lyricist Lounge academy, recalls his first exposure to the club.

'One day somebody came and said a freestyle thing was going on in Chinatown. It was indoors, which was a novel idea. It was about forty MCs in a circle. People were bringing their beats and DATs and whatever. People was just rhyming. So that was my first exposure to Lyricist Lounge. It was a bunch of young kids that loved hip hop. It was a way for people in the street to become aware about some really talented artists. And for a lot of artists, including myself, a chance to sharpen their performance skills, which is something that you can't really be taught.'

For Mos Def, the Lyricist Lounge helped re-establish hip hop as a community-based art form.

'It's not this distant academic type of relationship that someone may be able to have with jazz. You can learn about jazz or learn about blues from a very historic sort of scholarly level, dealing with the people in that community at your will when you want to. It's not like that, hip hop, you gotta get into it.'

## ➤ *Rawkus Entertainment – State Of The Independent*

The Black Star album and 'Body Rock', Mos Def's collaboration with Q-Tip of A Tribe Called Quest, were both released on Rawkus Entertainment. Rawkus is one of several independents to have benefited from the new spirit of independence in the hip hop underground, alongside Hydra, Relativity and Payday. Jarett Myers of Rawkus takes up the story.

'Rawkus is something I started with my best friend, Brian [Brater]. It started out of our bedroom. It started off as just a place for artists who didn't feel they fit into anywhere else, as far as major labels and stuff, putting out joints, 12-inches. It's grown into something we're pretty proud of.'

The label started in 1995, with Jarret helping out with local MCs' demo tapes. The label began to take shape after he hooked up with the local branch of the Fat Beats vinyl emporium.

'We cemented a relationship with Fat Beats, which at the time was just a tiny little store. The first 12-inch, at the beginning of '96, no one would buy. We just couldn't do anything with it, there was no community there for it. Then two years later I finally sold through my first pressing of that record. So it took some time to develop a community of stores and consumers to vie for some of the stuff.'

Joe Levy at *Rolling Stone* talks of Rawkus as the new brand name for underground hip hop.

'They're smart. They understand that hip hop doesn't just flourish in the studio, it's gotta have a living, breathing life, and it's gotta come out of people's hearts. And they should sell as many goddamn records as they can make.'

Prince Paul welcomes Rawkus as an important new outlet for MCs who would otherwise have limited opportunities to record.

'Rawkus has definitely given an opportunity for kids who barely have a chance of putting out or financing records on their own, to at least get some distribution or exposure.'

Talk of underground hip hop, and Jarret balances a firm-minded idealism with a good sense of proportion and self-deprecating humour.

'We have our own support group. We have weekly meetings. We often come in and say: "I'm Jarret, I'm a recovering underground junkie . . ." I think of us as music fans, I think that's what our label is. We just wanna see people focus more on the music, and less on: "Did you hear so and so went platinum?" That doesn't mean that he's dope. Or: "So and so has this kind of car with a television in the backseat or a Playstation." That doesn't mean he's dope, but people who rhyme about that sometimes *are* dope, and that's where it gets confusing.'

Though a flourishing independent, Rawkus drew investment from Rupert Murdoch's nephew, Gerald.

'The only justification that I can give is – this is my label, this is me and Brian's label, period. I needed money at a certain time, I just weighed my options. I found them to be good people. They dug my business plan, and they're going to work something out that allows me to have a label. And I got some money when it was time for me to expand. I didn't really see it as any big deal. But I guess outside of America, people see it in different ways.'

To some, Murdoch's money would disqualify Rawkus from their status as underground figureheads, but it is a truism that there is little genuine independence in hip hop. The small print on any of the renowned 'personality labels' – Puff Daddy's Bad Boy, Master P's No Limit, Jermaine Dupri's So So Def or Russell Simmons' Def Jam – reveals they are all under-written by the same handful of dominant conglomerates (Sony, BMG, Seagram, EMI, Time Warner) which control rock and pop.

► *From Underground to Overground*

One of the acts who have worked with Rawkus are the fiercely inde-pendent Company Flow, comprising MCs El-Producto, Bigg Jus and DJ 'Space Ghost' Mr Len. El-Producto takes up their story.

'We're a bunch of cats who grew up and really, really idolised hip hop culture and everything involved in it. We're just expressing ourselves, trying to do our thing artistically. Also we're a group of cats who decided a long time ago that we would take control of our business and our future. We've done everything independently, we own our own label [Official – through Rawkus]. We own our own masters and we're just trying to take care of ourselves and to make good music, some hardcore, real hip hop. Nothing watery, nothing too danceable.'

To El-Producto, the underground route is the essential training ground for hip hop of any long-term worth.

'Every cat who ever came out with an album who made any noise or who changed the way people thought about the art form started underground. There are a lot of cats who just don't pay any dues and don't struggle before they get on. A lot of people just get signed: "Here, here's a bunch of money. By the way, you're going to do this and this and this." The underground scene is cats who have been struggling and cats who have been making music regardless of whether or not they were making money off of it. People are a little more creative, a little more expressive, because when you're doing it for years and you're not getting paid off of it, who do you have to please?'

Good Vibe are an LA collective doing something similar to Rawkus on the west coast, working with artists including Medusa, Pyro and Spontaneous. Matt Kahane and Chris Nagy put the label together while studying in Berkeley to 'get beautiful music that existed in our immediate area out to the masses'.

'In the beginning it was probably like Too $hort did back in the days, like Wu-Tang did. It was out of the trunk of the car, just get your hustle on, on the avenue selling tapes for five bucks.'

They relay their modest mission statement.

'Our vision is that with nothing but revolutionary artists and revolutionary business tactics we will first revolutionise the music industry and then revolutionise the world. Music and art in its purest form affects people in the deepest way. The artists that we are working with are people that care about art, music, the world. All we are trying to do is put those Good Vibes out there that major record labels have been ignoring.'

Good Vibe are not merely interested in releasing music, but conquering the business world too. To them, a considered financial strategy allied to good records, artwork and marketing allows them to retain their independence.

'It's a Good Vibe entertainment collective, that's the umbrella. A lot of our artists are involved on the business side as well. Pyro may be putting out records, but he's also at Harvard and he's getting his masters degree, figuring out how he is going to do strategic planning for us down the road.'

Canibus achieved one of the biggest underground breakthroughs of 1998 with '2nd Round K.O.', his debut album entering the US charts at number two. Such a sales profile effectively removes him from the underground pantheon, where he emerged as one of the ultimate 'battle' DJs. His experiences as support act on the Fugees' tour, however, are illustrative of the difficulties of underground artists making the transition to the mainstream.

'I been in front of crowds that don't want to hear no real deep, crazy underground shit. They want to hear something simple, something nasty, something talking about chicks, talk about what we make groupies do, talk just dumb shit. That's what some people want to hear. Some people want to hear you get on a mic and just straight shit on another MC or shit on somebody . . . You never see me out there just profusely talking about jewellery or chicks. There's other people out there to do that. I'd rather talk about things that are stimulating.'

## ➤ Eminem – Twenty-First Century MC

The biggest new artist in hip hop in 1999 might prove to be Eminem, whose career is linked directly to some of the underground institutions discussed in this chapter. The most gifted white MC since 3rd Bass's MC Serch, he appeared on a Lyricist Lounge showcase and released his *Slim Shady* EP through underground vinyl specialists Fat Beats. He has also recorded for Rawkus (as part of the 'Five Star Generals' project) and appeared on a Good Vibe compilation album. From Detroit via Kansas City, Eminem (so named from his initials Marshall Mathers) famously described himself as 'trailer trash' and saluted the *Jerry Springer Show* for being an accurate portrayal of American lives.

'I did live in a lot of trailer parks. Me and my mother would stay with other relatives and stuff, we never really had a place of our own. I went to a few different schools, everybody was into breaking and everything like that. That's my earliest memories of hip hop. When I was about eleven we moved to Detroit and when I came to Detroit, hip hop was huge – the Beastie Boys, Run-D.M.C., LL Cool J. Everybody was walking through the halls in school singing "fight for your right to party". Everybody loved rap and from there I just grew up on it. I think I fourteen when I wrote my first rhyme and it was just like LL Cool J. As I started getting older I started learning how to put words together, I started getting good at it.'

Although he dropped out of education, he would visit local high school lunch rooms and challenge other hip hop enthusiasts to freestyle throwdowns, trying to win money. At this stage, he was relatively unconscious of his skin colour.

'I never really cared. I never gave a fuck what colour I was. I don't think that was even crossing my mind back then, it was just fun to do it. I didn't wake up every day and look in the mirror: "Wow! I'm white!" It's not something I choose to dwell on.'

However, it came back to haunt him after releasing *Infinite* to an indifferent Detroit audience.

'For that time period, it was '95 or '96, the album was dope. The album got stepped on and I got a lot of criticism from it: "You're trying to sound like Nas! You're trying to sound like AZ! You're white, you shouldn't rap, you should go into rock 'n' roll." Just a lot of criticism, just a lot of bullshit that I was hearing.'

Eminem found himself working minimum wage jobs to make money, while devising his 'Slim Shady' persona.

'I was sweeping floors and cleaning toilets, cooking pizzas, flipping burgers, stuff like that. In my spare time I would write rhymes at work. I would write rhymes everywhere I went. I was always writing, still am always writing.'

In late 1997 he travelled to the Rap Olympics, an event organised by Rap Coalition founder Wendy Day and sponsored by *Rap Sheet*, where he battled some eighty MCs in the freestyle open.

'I took second place to a hometown favourite or something. It was bullshit. Everybody knew I got robbed there, but through that I learned. I used to take battling so serious, especially then. I was ready to kill somebody if I lost, I was ready to kill myself if I lost. I took it very, very serious.'

The convention did serve a purpose. Among those attending were Interscope employees, who passed a copy of his *Slim Shady* EP to president Jimmy Iovine. Dr. Dre was looking for acts for his new Aftermath label, and Eminem was recruited to write rhymes for Snoop Doggy Dogg on Dre's *Chronic 2000* project. The EP also impressed Danny Castro at Lyricist Lounge, who promptly booked him for a show.

'I paid my dues through the underground, that's where everything started from. That's where it all evolved from, just me having the *Slim Shady* EP, getting it on Unsigned Hype (the *Source*'s column highlighting new MCs), doing shows around New York. We got a little distribution deal through Fat Beats and was selling 100 or 200 pieces of vinyl and cassettes and CDs a week. An underground following has to be there, you've got to start off there or you don't you have nothing to fall back on.'

In April 1999 Eminem's debut album entered the US national charts at number two and within a month had achieved gold certification.

# postscript: from sugarhill to lauryn hill

At the 1999 Grammy Awards Lauryn Hill, a genre-defying artist but one essentially rooted in hip hop culture, was nominated for an unprecedented ten Grammys, winning five. But hers was more than a simple numerical feat. Hip hop artists were finally being judged in pop categories rather than marginalised in genre-specific ones. Hip hop was finally acknowledged as being part of the mainstream of popular American music. Hill also appeared on the cover of *Time* magazine under the by-line 'Hip Hop Nation'. As Chuck Phillips notes, Lauryn Hill's success serves as a valediction for the music.

'It took a long time. The record companies were so reluctant, they thought it was a fad. Just six years ago people thought it was going to go away. These guys are finally accepting it, whether they like it or don't.'

Geoff Mayfield supervises Billboard's chart coverage, and has watched hip hop defy obituary writers for two decades.

'I was a youngster when rock 'n' roll started but for years after it got off the ground older folks would cringe and say it's gonna fade, it will die. The same thing has happened with rap music. Not too many years ago it was not uncommon for me to get a phone call from a newspaper reporter covering music doing their year-end article about what the next year's trend is going to be. Almost every year I could count on at least one or two of these scribes calling me saying: "What about rap, is it gonna finally fade away next year?" It never did.'

Two decades have passed since the Sugarhill Gang released 'Rapper's Delight', and it is at least twenty-five years since hip hop began to take shape in Kool Herc's Sedgewick Towers housing block. That represents an eternity in an art form as instantaneous and fickle as popular music. Few would have credited hip hop with longevity, fewer still predicted its eventual popularity. Yet over the last quarter of the twentieth century, it has evolved with disorientating speed, redefining not only itself but the popular culture surrounding it.

Hip hop has become a global currency for social critique and epicurean expression, from champion German breakdancer Storm to South Africa's Prophets Of Da City – who celebrated the fall of apartheid with an unequivocal 'Excellent, finally a black president'. In the process, hip hop has proved itself better able to shape the zeitgeist and respond to cultural and philosophical change than any other strain of contemporary music. The aptitude of artists such as Black Eyed Peas, Mos Def and Jurassic 5 constitutes a promise of continued growth. The return to old school values by hip hop's next generation completes a cyclical odyssey that has enriched and informed, agitated and, most of all, entertained, as Joe Levy of *Rolling Stone* confirms.

'It's probably the dominant form in popular culture – the most creative, the most interesting, the most inventive. This is the most creative music we have right now and it's shown itself to be the most renewable. As long as there's music out there people can make hip hop from it. That appears to be one of the reasons why the music is so damn successful and so sustainable.'

It is little wonder that hip hop's foremost advocates and guardians, like Chuck D, are so fiercely protective of it.

'I'm always ready to fight the status quo, because this hip hop thing, I like to protect it like a Persian rug – it's strong but delicate. A lot of people step on it, but we're going to make sure they take their shoes off. You can rest assured of that. When Chuck D walks in the office of a head executive who's making his money off of rap music, my job is to make them tremble in fear, until they respect it.'

The felling of Tupac and Biggie in the mid-90s led observers to question hip hop's viability, only for a succession of artists to ensure it rebounded with ever greater force. The breakthrough of the Wu-Tang Clan, Missy Elliott, Lauryn Hill, Eminem and many others has brought hip hop to a commercial plateau beyond the most hysterical dreams of its progenitors. Such facts are easily substantiated by a perusal of charts and graphs. But hip hop's attainment in setting a benchmark for artistry and innovation is less readily acknowledged. Many rap records are undeniably offensive, worthless or mired in redundant cliché – but that is true of many other music genres. It should not obscure the fact that hip hop remains the most fertile, ambitious, irreverent culture in popular music.

# interviewees

**Afrika Baby Bambaataa** – Jungle Brothers MC and founder of the Native Tongues

**Afrika Bambaataa** – original Bronx DJ, Zulu Nation founder and 'Planet Rock' author

**Beat Junkies** – LA-based DJ collective of vinyl addicts

**Big Bank Hank** – the Sugarhill Gang's MC and bouncer-made-good

**Black Eyed Peas** – offbeat LA group applying old school values and using real instruments

**Bobbito 'The Barber'** – DJ, promoter, manager, record shop owner and former Def Jam intern

**Canibus** – next generation MC extolling the virtues of old school battle raps

**Capone-N-Noreaga** – New York-based 'thug rappers'

**Castro, Danny & Marshall, Anthony** – founders of the nomadic Lyricist Lounge

**Chuck D** – Public Enemy's spokesperson and political activist

**Company Flow** – torchbearers of New York's new underground scene

**Cool Lady Blue** – ex-pat English promoter at the Negril and Roxy

**Crazy Legs** – single-handedly rejuvenated 80s breakdancing as president of Rock Steady Crew

**Da Brat** – from So So Def stable in Atlanta, the first platinum-selling female MC

**Demme, Ted** – co-founder and producer of *Yo! MTV Raps*, currently a film director

**Dilated Peoples** – key participants in back-to-basics LA hip hop revival

**Disco Twins** – inimitable, excessively loud, DJ team from Queens

**DMC** – Darryl McDaniels, MC who took hip hop back to the streets with new school pioneers Run-D.M.C.

**Duke Bootee** – (Ed Fletcher) author of 'The Message' and Sugarhill's in-house writer

**Dupri, Jermaine** – producer, remixer and artist, head of Atlanta's So So Def Records

**Eminem** – widely heralded new MC currently tearing up the Billboard charts

**Fab Five Freddy** – hip hop renaissance man, graffiti artist, label owner, video director and raconteur

**Fine, Mike** – co-inventor of SoundScan's chart monitoring system

**George, Nelson** – author of *The Death Of Rhythm & Blues* and *Hip Hop America*, now a film director

**Gordon, Alan** – editor of *Rap Pages*

**Grandmaster Caz** – old school hip hop DJ and MC, a member of the Cold Crush Brothers

**Grandmaster Flash** – the consummate, highly-skilled technician of the wheels of steel

**Grandwizard Theodore** – a Grandmaster Flash acolyte and inventor of the scratch mix

**Holman, Michael** – promoter in Bronx hip hop's early days, also manager of the New York City Breakers

**Ice Cube** – once of N.W.A., a solo artist routinely identified as rap's supreme lyricist

**Ice-T** – the west coast's original gangsta rapper, and venomous wit to boot

**Isaacson, Rich** – one of the co-founders of Loud Records, home to the Wu-Tang Clan

**Jazzy Jay** – hip hop musician, Zulu Nation DJ, car mechanic to Rick Rubin and anecdotal treasure trove

**Johnny J** – producer to Tupac Shakur, among others

**Jorge 'Fabel' Pabón** – old school B-boy and breakdancing authority

**Jurassic 5** – LA advocates of old school values, arguably the best new hip hop vibe in town

**Kahane, Matt & Chris Nagy** – heads of LA's underground label Good Vibe

**Kid Freeze** – famed breakdancer (when his old pa lets him . . .) & CEO of Dynamic Rockers

**Kid Ice – aka Chris WongWon** – a member of the infamous 2 Live Crew

**Kool DJ Herc** – old school DJ and founding father of hip hop

**Le Blanc, Keith** – the hard-hitting 'white boy' drummer at Sugarhill Records, later of Tackhead, etc

**Levy, Joe** – *Rolling Stone* music editor, formerly respected critic of the

*Village Voice*

**Lynch, Monica** – president of Tommy Boy Records

**Massinfluence** – Atlanta's underground hip hop purists

**Mayfield, Geoff** – director of chart coverage at *Billboard* magazine

**MC Hammer** – the biggest selling rapper of all time

**MC Ren** – original member of N.W.A. and now solo artist

**Medusa** – graduate of the LA's Good Life Cafe, but affiliated to Atlanta's Good Vibe collective

**Melle Mel** – the most explosive old school hip hop MC of them all, leader of the Furious Five

**Missy 'Misdemeanor' Elliott** – business-savvy Virginian producer, singer, MC and songwriter

**Monie Love** – member of the Native Tongues collective, token Brit and now a DJ on Hot FM

**Mos Def** – hard-rhyming underground MC and part-time actor, also half of the Black Star project

**Myers, Jarret** – co-owner and founder of Rawkus Entertainment

**Nate Dogg** – angelic singer with a thuggish demeanour, kennel-mate to Snoop Dogg

**Phillips, Chuck** – renowned *LA Times* music writer

**Posdnous** – De La Soul's spokesperson and key Native Tongues alumnus

**Prince Paul** – hip hop auteur, a member of Stetsasonic and the Gravediggaz and producer of De La Soul

**Pryce, George** – damage control expert at Death Row Records

**Rev. Calvin Butts** – ordained opponent of gangsta rap

**Rivera, Lance 'Un'** – CEO of Untertainment and close friend of Biggie Smalls

**Robinson, Bobby** – 60s R&B veteran and proprietor of Enjoy Records, first home to Grandmaster Flash

**Rodney C** – celebrated old school MC, formerly of the Funky Four (Plus One) & Double Trouble

**Roots** – Philadelphia's critically-revered take on late-90s hip hop

**Ross, Mike** – co-founder and owner of LA's Delicious Vinyl

**Rubin, Rick** – the man who discovered LL Cool J, the Beastie Boys, Public Enemy . . .

**Rza** – playmaker and producer behind the Wu-Tang phenomenon

**Shocklee, Hank** – alongside Chuck D, the cornerstone of Public Enemy's Bomb Squad production team

**Silverman, Tom** – founder and CEO of the enduring Tommy Boy imprint

**Simmons, Russell** – Run-D.M.C. manager, Def Jam CEO and rap's first empire-builder

**The 45 King** – DJ, producer, vinyl trainspotter and master sampler

**Thompson, Jack** – right-wing Christian attorney who took a legal big stick to 2 Live Crew

**Tone Loc** – high-living party animal who sang pop-rap breakthrough 'Wild Thing'

**Tucker, C. Delores** – civil rights veteran who tried to gag gangsta rap

**Vanilla Ice** – the first popular white rapper and 'most despised man in hip hop'

**Warwick, Dionne** – R&B singer of 'Walk On By' fame and opponent of gangsta rap

**Wimbish, Doug** – bass player behind many of Sugarhill's hits, currently working with Herb Alpert

**Young MC** – solo artist and co-author of Tone Loc's pop-rap hits

# glossary

**Afrocentric** – the propagation and celebration of African culture

**B-boy** – originally a 'break boy', relating to the dance style which accompanies hip hop music, but also used to describe someone immersed in hip hop culture

**B-boying** – the dancing which accompanies hip hop music, often featuring a number of athletic twists, spins, locks and turns

**bass music** – a form of party music popular in Miami, characterised by deep bass beats and accelerated rhythmic tempos

**beats** – the music's rhythmic backbone, derived from drumbeats

**biting** – the copying of style or technique in any element of hip hop

**Bloods** – one of the dominant LA gangs, distinguished by their preference for red

**blunt** – cannabis packed into a hollow cigar

**breakbeat** – the climatic instrumental 'break' section of a record, often extended by hip hop DJs.

**breakdancing/breaking** – see B-boying

**chill** – to calm down/relax

**crib** – the subject's home

**Crips** – the other dominant LA gang, known for their use of the colour blue

**cut-out** – a discounted record

**def** – a hip hop superlative meaning especially good, now somewhat dated

**diss** – to 'disrespect', a put-down or insult

**DJ** – disc jockey, the cornerstone of hip hop's early growth

**dope** – a superlative expressing approval

**electro** – marriage of hip hop and electronica pioneered by Afrika Bambaataa

**flow** – style in which an MC both constructs rhymes and delivers them

**fly** – attractive and/or revered

**flyer** – a piece of paper or poster announcing forthcoming events

**freestyle** – improvised rapping, often without music

**gangbangers/gangbanging** – members of a gang/engaged in gang activity

**gangsta** – a form of rap relating tales of criminal activity

**g-funk** – Dr. Dre's blueprint of gangsta rap lyrics and 70s funk grooves

**gold record** – an album selling 500,000 copies or more (in America)

**graffiti** – the visual stamp of hip hop, employing aggrandising themes and vibrant colours, often sprayed illicitly in urban areas

**griot** – a West African religious storyteller

**hardcore** – a rough-edged variant of rap, often focusing on sex/crime narratives or harsh aspects of life in urban environments

**heads** – generic term for people, sometimes denoting kudos ('real hip hop heads')

**hip hop** – the culture embracing rapping/MCing, DJing, graffiti and break-dancing

**homeboy/homey** – a neighbourhood friend

**'hood** – an abbreviation for neighbourhood

**juice** – power, often electrical. Also sometimes used to signify 'respect' (see 'props')

**MC** – the master of ceremonies, later rapper (also referred to as emcee)

**MCing** – see rapping

**mic** – abbreviation for microphone

**mix tapes** – audio documents of hip hop parties, or selections from a DJ. Mix tapes have become a vehicle for underground DJs to display their skills and often use exclusive tracks

**new school** – a somewhat confused term, initially invoked to describe Run-D.M.C.'s breakthrough in the mid-80s, but occasionally applied to anything contemporaneous

**old school** – a term denoting the subject's early involvement in hip hop (generally considered to be from the mid-70s to the mid-80s)

**phat/phattest** – superlative, often related to 'beats', indicating good or excellent

**platinum record** – an album shipping one million copies or more to retail (in the US)

**props** – the 'proper respect' due to someone

**rap** – term often used interchangeably with hip hop, but which strictly denotes only one aspect of the music, the MC's delivery of rhymes

**rapper** – alternative description of an MC

**rapping** – lyrics/rhymes spoken rather than sung over music

**sampling** – the duplication of 'found sound', be it from records or other media

**scratching** – a way of manipulating a record back and forth to produce sound, pioneered by Grandwizard Theodore and popularised by Grandmaster Flash

**swingbeat** – a hybrid of hip hop and R&B pioneered by producer Teddy Riley

**tag** – street name of a graffiti artist

**wack** – very bad, terrible

# index

### The cover-mounted CD accompanying this book contains the following tracks:

**Afrika Bambaataa & Soul Sonic Force – 'Planet Rock' (1982)**
The defining track for the downtown New York scene as hip hop migrated from the Bonx to mainstream New York society and began to attract its current worldwide audience. The most sampled record in hip hop, 'Planet Rock' also launched electro, an electronic derivative of hip hop and funk, through its marriage of kraftwerk, 'found sound' and hip hop percussion.

**De La Soul – 'Me, Myself And I' (1989)**
The cornerstone single of De la Soul's massively successful *3 Feet High And Rising* album, 'Me, Myself And I' spent 17 weeks on Billboard's singles chart in 1989. Widely credited with expanding rap's subject matter and audience, 'Me, Myself And I' also earned a 1990 Grammy nomination for best rap performance.

**Wu-Tang Clan & Onyx – 'The Worst' (1998)**
A collaboration between Staten island's burgeoning hip hop collective, Wu-Tang Clan and Onyx, the definitive powerhouse New York hardcore rap group of the early 90s. This track featured on the Miramax film *Ride* and was also included on Onyx's 1998 Tommy Boy album *Shut 'Em Down*.

**The double CD to accompany the Channel 4 series 'The Hip Hop Years', including tracks from the programme, will be available autumn 1999.**